Between Sessions
Beyond t

edited by Joan Raphael-Leff

CPS Psychoanalytic Publications
University of Essex, Colchester, UK
2002

Dedicated to the Journey
– on and off the couch

First published 2002
University of Essex,
Colchester

ISBN 1-904059-09-0

1.   Psychoanalysis, Psychoanalytic Psychotherapy
2.   Parent-Infant Psychotherapy
3.   Organizational studies
4.   Trauma & political violence
5.   Ethics & professional conduct

A catalogue record for this book is available from the British Library

Library of Congress Cataloguing-in-Publication Data available

Printed and bound in Great Britain
By Biddles Ltd, Guilford & King's Lynn

Mind the Gap / Marion Milner*

("What is mind? No matter?"
What is matter? Never mind.") Who said this?

"Mind the gap!" shouts the mechanical voice at the Embankment
Tube station
"Mind the gap!"
I do, I did, I never have fallen between the platform and the train
I don't mind, it doesn't matter
Or does it?

I do mind the gap between the rich and the poor.
And I do mind the gap between what I can dream of for the earth
And what we are doing to it.
Destroying the living matter on which we depend for life-
Like the Amazon Forests

And I mind that I did not think
It mattered that I did not mind
When we came to the
End of the matter
So that there were
No more gaps
To mind
Body and Mind, two sides of the same join you said?

I minded when I did not mind
That the matter did not matter any more
But I do know that it's
Out of the gaps
That new things grow.

*   A tribute on her 80th birthday to British Psychoanalyst Pearl King
from Psychoanalyst Marion Milner then in her 95th year
[reproduced here by kind permission of Margaret Walters on behalf of the estate]

A Reminder to the Binder/ Donald W. Winnicott*

Binder, who serenely bindest
    Kanthack volumes year by year,
Is it true thou never findest
    Muddy evidence of tear-

Dropt by dresser, blankly staring,
    Jaws agape, brain out of use,
Deaf to stertorous voice of W____g,
    Deaf to W____g's grand abuse?

Can it be thou carest never
    In thy work to realise
What the sweat, the hard endeavour,
    What the weary long-drawn sighs-

Clerks and dressers, grimly grinding,
    Have expended to prepare
Records worthy of thy binding?
    Can it be thou dost not care?

Binder, year by year who bindest
    Reams of closely written sheets,
Do not think that what thou findest
    Is the sum, there's more than meets-

The eye: sheets burnt, sheets torn in pieces,
    Lunch denied to inner man-
Binder, where thy binding ceases
    There the dresser's toil began.

*Unpublished poem by Winnicott from his medical school days, found among his papers by his biographer Brett Kahr, whose book *D.W. Winnicott: A Biographical Portrait* received the Gradiva Award for Biography. [The poem appeared in the in-house medical students' St.Bartholomews Hospital Journal, Vol.8, p.107, 1921. W____g is probably 'Wearing', a teacher, and the hint of in-jokes is tantalising]

...The poem seems apt as prologue, illustrating playful application of creative talents, one theme of this book. And it serves as a reminder to our own binder and readers of the effort and worthiness of the many 'closely written sheets' bound between the covers of this book.

CONTENTS:

THE INFANT & THE BABY WITHIN:

Part II: BEYOND THE COUCH

Applications of Psychoanalytic Understanding in Society

ORGANIZATIONS:

Part III: BETWEEN SESSIONS

vi

Part IV: THE EMBODIED THERAPIST

EPILOGUE(S)

ILLUSTRATIONS:

CONTRIBUTORS:

Alcira Mariam Alizade M.D., psychiatrist and training analyst of the Argentine Psychoanalytic Association. Current chair of COWAP, the IPA Committee on Women & Psychoanalysis. Author of: *Feminine Sensuality* (Karnac Books 1992); *Near death: Clinical psychoanalytical studies* (Amorrortu, Buenos Aires,1995); *Time for women* (Letra Viva, Buenos Aires, 1996); *The Lone Woman* (Lumen, Buenos Aires, 1999); *Positivity in Psychoanalysis* (Lumen, Buenos Aires 2002)

Barbie Antonis born Cape Town, South Africa, came to London aged 12 with her family. Studied Psychology and Biochemistry at University; did research in Child Development and taught at Cambridge University before training as psychoanalytic psychotherapist with BAP, and then as a Psychoanalyst. Now works as Consultant Adult Psychotherapist in NHS Parkside Clinic, London and in private practice. Two grown-up children.

Jean Arundale Ph.D. is a Full Member and Training Therapist of the British Association of Psychotherapists where she teaches clinical and theoretical seminars. She came from a background in philosophy and psychology. Editor of the *British Journal of Psychotherapy.*

Christine Anzieu-Premmereur, adult/child psychiatrist and psychoanalyst, trained at the Paris Institute. Was in charge of a department at the *Alfred Binet Center,* a psychoanalytic child guidance center, offering psychotherapy to babies and parents. Now in private practice in New York. Teaches child psychoanalysis at NYU & Columbia Universities. Authored a book on the role of play in child psychotherapy.

Ron Baker M.R.C.Psych., Training and Supervising Psychoanalyst, British Psychoanalytical Society. Honorary Member, Danish Psychoanalytical Society; Author, Psychoanalytical papers on Humour, Theory of Clinical Technique, Selection of Control Cases, Cinema etc.

Tessa Baradon, trained at the Anna Freud Centre, where she established and directs its Parent and Infant Project, which provides training to psychoanalytical and other professionals in the UK and abroad. Was responsible for planning and provision of services for parents/infants in local authority Social Services Departments and the National Health Service. Recent publications address issues of technique and processes of change in parent-infant psychotherapy.

Juma Basak, Member, Indian Psychoanalytical Society (Calcutta); and of the International Psychoanalytical Association; Psychoanalytic Consultant in High School, Calcutta; paper, 'Psychoanalysis: Method and Training - Difficult Moments' , for IPSO, 2001, Nice; Assistant Editor, *'Samiksa'*, Journal of the Indian Psychoanalytical Society.

Moty Benyakar
Member of Psychoanalytic Society, Argentina and Israel Psychoanalytic Society. Psychoanalyst. Elected President of the Section of Stress and Trauma of the World Psychiatric Association. Professor in Faculty of Medicine, Tel-Aviv University, and Buenos Aires. International Coordinator IBIS (International Bioethic Information System).

Astrid Berg is a psychiatrist, child psychiatrist and Jungian analyst in private practice. Founding member and current President of the Southern African Association of Jungian Analysts, represents it on the executive committee of the International Association for Analytical Psychology. Founder, University of Cape Town Parent-Infant Mental Health Service in 1995. Senior consultant in the Department of Psychiatry, UCT.

Ruth Berkowitz is a Full Member of the British Association of Psychotherapists where she trained in both adult and adolescent psycho-analytic psychotherapy. She is currently Chair of the Psychoanalytic Psychotherapy Training Committee. She is Principal Adult Psycho-therapist at the Portman Clinic, London and in private practice.

David M. Black is a founding Member of the Foundation for Psychotherapy and Counselling. He qualified as a psychoanalyst with the British Psycho-Analytical Society, 1991, and is now in private practice in London. Author of *A Place for Exploration*, the official history of the Westminster Pastoral Foundation, and papers on psychoanalysis and its relation to science and the religions.

Emanuel Berman is a training analyst at the Israel Psychoanalytic Institute, and a professor at the University of Haifa and at New York University. In addition to numerous papers in journals, he edited *Essential Papers on Literature and Psychoanalysis* (1993), and wrote *Impossible Training: A Relational Psychoanalytic View of Clinical Training and Supervision* (forthcoming).

Gudrun Bodin, Ph.D. is president of the Danish Psychoanalytical Society and psychoanalyst in full time private practice.

Abraham H. Brafman M.D. is a psychoanalyst of adults and children and he worked in the NHS as a Consultant Child and Adolescent

Psychiatrist. He now works as an Honorary Senior Lecturer at the University College Hospital Department of Psychotherapy, besides running seminars for training organizations. In addition to papers on infant observation, work with adolescents and other subjects, he has also written a book *Untying the Knot* on work with children and parents.

William Brough, M.D. middle child of a north country mining family, left school at 14, as his mother was dying of cancer. As a Conscientious Objector during World War II, he served with the International Red Cross, in charge aged 22 of the Ambulance Service of the Chinese Fifth Army in Burma, and later, as a Company Commander, parachuted in the jungles in Burma; decorated a number of times. He qualified medically in Newcastle-upon-Tyne, was a Physician at the Mayo Clinic, USA; returning to London for Psychoanalytic training, he then practised in the North-East of England, in Newcastle and then Middlesbrough.

Susan Budd, member of the British Psychoanalytical Society, now Works in Oxford. She was previously a sociologist and historian, and General Editor of the New Library of Psychoanalysis. Author of several books, most recently a volume edited with Ursula Sharma *The Healing Bond: therapeutic responsibility in patient-healer encounters*, and many articles, most recently 'No Sex Please, we're British: sexuality in English and French Psychoanalysis', and 'Insiders and Outsiders: the legacy of Charles Rycroft'.

Don Campbell is a training analyst (for children, adolescents and adults). He is president of the British Psycho-analytical Society and psychoanalyst in private practice and also works at the Portman Clinic in London. He has published on such subjects as suicide, violence, child sexual abuse and adolescence.

Jorge Canestri, M.D. psychiatrist, psychoanalyst. Training/supervising analyst for Associazione Italiana di Psicoanalisi (A.I.Psi) and Asociación Psicoanalítica Argentina. European Co-Chair, Ethics Committee (IPA), Chair,Working Party on Theoretical Issues of the E.P.F., Chair, 42nd Congress of the International Psychoanalytic Association (IPA) in Nice (2001). Member, Conceptual and Empirical Research Committee (IPA). Has published numerous psychoanalytical papers in books and reviews.

Patrick Casement, formerly a social worker, trained with the British Association of Psychotherapists, and later the Institute of Psychoanalysis in London where he is now a training and supervising analyst. Author of *On Learning from the Patient* (1985), Tavistock Publications, and *Further Learning from the Patient* (1990), Routledge, (combined as

Learning from the Patient (1990), Guilford Publications). His third book, *Learning from our Mistakes*, is currently in press.

Marcia Cavell is Visiting Professor, in the Department of Philosophy, University of California, Berkeley. Having completed work as a research candidate at the Columbia Psychoanalytic Institute for Training & Research in New York City in the 70's, she is currently in full training at the San Francisco Psychoanalytic Institute. Author of numerous articles, published both in philosophy and psychoanalytic journals, and a book, *The Psychoanalytic Mind: From Freud to Philosophy* (Harvard UP, 1993)

Lynn Champion from East Africa had a Kleinian Analysis in London, and trained at the BAP. Later worked with refuges in Macedonia with Medact/Unicef, with Health Workers in Rwanda with *Medicine san Frontiers*, and then taught Freud and Baby Observation at Essex University. As a child therapist specialized in uncontrollable, angry children, ran suicide and children's groups. Now living in British Colombia or sailing, is writing a book about Asperger's syndrome.

Nancy J. Chodorow, PhD is Professor of Sociology and Clinical Professor of Psychology at the University of California, Berkeley, faculty member of the San Francisco Psychoanalytic Institute, and a psychoanalyst in private practice. Her books include *The Reproduction of Mothering, Feminism and Psychoanalytic Theory, Femininities, Masculinities, Sexualities*, and *The Power of Feelings*.

Jeni Couzyn trained at the Guild of Psychotherapists, London. Publications include eight books of poems, recently *In the Skin House* (Bloodaxe). Editor of three anthologies, among them *Contemporary Women Poets*, (Bloodaxe). In recent years founded and is Artistic Director to The Bethesda Arts Centre, in the semi-desert of the Great Karoo in her native South Africa. She has one daughter, and lives in London where she works as a psychotherapist in private practice.

 M. Fakhry Davids is a member of the British Psycho-Analytical Society and the Tavistock Society of Psychotherapists.He is Honorary Consultant Psychologist at the London Clinic of Psychoanalysis, and is a founder member and Chair of the South African Psychoanalysis Trust, London. He has a long standing clinical and research interest in the psychology of racism, on which he has lectured widely.

Jean Dix a counselling psychologist working full time in the NHS for a specialist psychotherapy service in Middlesbrough, UK. Currently in my second year of training as a psychoanalytic psychotherapist with North of England Association for Training in Psychoanalytic Psychotherapy (NEATPP).

Takeo Doi, M.D. Member, Japanese Psychiatric Association and Japan Psychoanalytic Society. Was Professor of University of Tokyo School of Medicine and the International Christian University; Director, National Institute of Mental Health, Japan; Now Consultant in Psychiatry, at St. Luke's International Hospital where he began in 1956 as Psychiatrist-in Chief. Publications in English: *The Anatomy of Dependence*, 1973. *The Anatomy of Self: the Individual vs. Society*, 1986, both Kodansha International. *The Psychological World of Natsume Soseki*, Harvard UP, 1976.

Ofra Eshel is a Training and Supervising Analyst in the Israel Psychoanalytic Society; co-founder, coordinator, lecturer and supervisor at the Program of Psychoanalytic Psychotherapy for Advanced Psychotherapists, the Israel Institute of Psychoanalysis. She teaches on the Program of Psychotherapy, Tel Aviv University, Faculty of Medicine, and is also Book Review Editor of *Sihot - Dialogue*, Israel Journal of Psychotherapy.

Karl Figlio is a psychoanalytic psychotherapist. He is Director and Reader at the Centre for Psychoanalytic Studies, University of Essex, and Associate Member, London Centre for Psychotherapy. Author of various professional papers and a book, *Psychoanalysis, Science and Masculinity,* Whurr publishers, 2000.

Angelo Fioritti 43, psychiatrist, lives in Bologna, Italy, where he was born. His professional interests are mainly in the field of social psychiatry; in particular he has researched and published on the issues of assertive outreach, dual diagnosis, violence and aggression, and organisation of services. After practising for about 15 years in Bologna he has recently taken over the responsibility for the Mental Health and Drug Abuse Programs in nearby Rimini.

Peter Fonagy, PhD is Freud Memorial Professor of Psychoanalysis and Director of the Sub-Department of Clinical Health Psychology at University College London. He is Director of the Child and Family Centre at the Menninger Foundation, Kansas. He is also Director of Research at the Anna Freud Centre, London. He is a clinical psychologist and a training and supervising analyst in the British Psycho-Analytical Society in child and adult analysis.

Penelope (Pip) Garvey is a member of the British Psycho-analytical Society; she originally trained as a Clinical Psychologist. She has chaired several committees concerned with the issue of confidentiality. Currently Chair of the steering committee of the International Psychoanalytical Association funded research study on confidentiality being carried out by the British Institute of International and Comparative Law.

Abigail Golomb is a psychiatrist and child psychiatrist, and training analyst in the Israeli Psychoanalytic Society. She is the director of Infant Psychiatry and the Forensic Assessment Unit for Children and Families at the Tel Aviv Mental Health Center. She is a member of the EPF Trauma Group and the IPA Group on Terror.

Tirril Harris trained with the British Association of Psychotherapists. In part-time private practice, and in social psychiatry research with Professor George Brown at the Socio-Medical Research Centre (formerly at Bedford College, now at St Thomas' Hospital, Kings College London). Training and supervising psychotherapist for the London Centre for Psychotherapy and a founder member of the International Attachment Network.

Jeremy Holmes is a psychiatrist/analytic psychotherapist working in the NHS in the West of England. Currently he is Chair of the psychotherapy faculty of the College of Psychiatrists and author of many articles, chapters and books on attachment theory and psychotherapy (most recently *Narcissism*, Icon Books 2001, *The Search for the Secure Base: Attachment Theory and Psychotherapy*, Taylor and Francis 2001, and *Psychotherapy Integration*, OUP, 2002). Plans to retire soon to spend more time with his patients.

Earl Hopper is a psychoanalyst, group analyst and organisational consultant in private practice in London, where he is an Honorary Tutor at the Tavistock Tavistock & Portman NHS Trust. He is also on the Faculty of the Post-Doctoral Program in Group Psychotherapy of Adelphi University in the United States. He is a Past-President of the International Association of Group Psychotherapy, and a Past-Chairman of the Group of Independent Psychoanalysts of the British Psycho-analytical Society.

Natalia Indrasari, Psychology graduate from University of Indonesia, Jakarta; MA in Psychoanalytic studies, University of Essex, UK, and currently taking a Master of Science degree in Counseling Psychology at Chaminade University of Honolulu, Hawaii, USA.

Judith Issroff South African-born and medically qualified, completed professional training in London at Tavistock School of Family

Psychiatry and Community Mental Health and the British Psychoanalytical Society (in adult & child psychoanalysis). She is a consultant child, adolescent and family psychiatrist, currently working in Coventry CAMHS NHS. Also qualified in group analysis, Group Relations Training and conflict mediation. She has published professionally and her poems appeared in British, South African, Israeli, New Zealand and American anthologies.

Brett Kahr, is Senior Lecturer in Psychotherapy, School of Psychotherapy and Counselling, Regent's College, London, and Winnicott Clinic Senior Research Fellow. Author of *D.W. Winnicott: A Biographical Portrait* (Gradiva Award for Biography, 1997); Exhibitionism, Icon Books; Editor *Forensic Psychotherapy and Psychopathology: Winnicottian Perspectives.* For five years, Course Tutor in Mental Handicap, Child & Family Department, Tavistock Clinic. He is also a professional songwriter - C.D. 'Dangerous Cabaret: The Music & Lyrics of Brett Kahr' (Dress Circle label)

Olya Khaleelee began her career as a social scientist in the field of organisational behaviour research, later moving into consultancy. She now works as a corporate psychologist, organisational consultant and psychotherapist in private practice. She combines a psychoanalytic approach with systems thinking, thereby creating a bridge between the consulting room and the world of business and the public sector.

Sudhir Kakar is a psychoanalyst in New Delhi who has been a visiting professor at Universities of Vienna, Melbourne, McGill, Chicago and Harvard. His most recent books are the novels *Ascetic of Desire* (1998) and *Ecstasy* (2002) as also a new translation (with Wendy Doniger) of *The Kamasutra* for Oxford World Classics Series.

Alan Kindler is in full time private psychoanalytic practice in Toronto. He is a member of the International Council for Psychoanalytic Self Psychology and Director of the Institute for the Advancement of Self Psychology in Toronto. He is a training analyst with the Toronto Institute of Psychoanalysis and on the faculty of the Toronto Institute for Contemporary Psychoanalysis. He is an Assistant Professor of Psychiatry at the University of Toronto and a staff psychiatrist St. Michael's Hospital.

Ilany Kogan, Training Analyst, Israel Psychoanalytic Society. Books include *The Cry of Mute Children – A Psychoanalytic Perspective of the Second Generation of the Holocaust* (Free Association Books, 1995) based on 15 years extensive work with Holocaust survivors' offspring. [published in German (Fischer Verlag, 1998); Romanian (Editura Trei,

2001); French (Delachaux et Niestle, 2001)]. Member, Advisory Board of the Fritz Bauer Institut for Holocaust Studies, Frankfurt. Member, Steering Committee of the Trauma Network, Hamburg.

Gregorio Kohon is a training analyst of the British Psycho-Analytical Society. Authored *No Lost Certainties to be Recovered* (1999), and edited *The British School of Psychoanalysis - The Independent Tradition* (1986), and *The Dead Mother - The Work of André Green* (1999). Born in Buenos Aires he published three books of poetry (in Spanish), and contributed to numerous anthologies of Latin American literature. The manuscript of his novel *Red Parrot/Wooden Leg* was finalist in the 2001 Fernando Lara Fiction Prize, Editorial Planeta (Barcelona).

Valli Shaio Kohon is a child psychotherapist, trained at the Tavistock Clinic, London and a psychoanalyst in private practice with both adults and children. She also works at the Anna Freud Centre as a toddler group leader.

Elliott Jaques is Research Professor in Management Science at George Washington University. He took his MD at Johns Hopkins Medical School, and PhD in Social Relations at Harvard. Qualified with Melanie Klein at the British Psychoanalytical Society in 1951, and was its Scientific Secretary for some years. Author of the mid-life crisis, and 22 books including *Human Capability* (1994), *Requisite Organization* (1996), and *The Life and Behavior of Living Organisms* (spring 2001).

Bella Jozef Emeritus Professor of the Federal University of Rio de Janeiro. Winner of several prestigious international prizes, amongst which the Academic Palms (France), Order of Sun (Peru), Order of May (Argentina), Book Prize (OEA), Brazilian Academy of Writers and was a the Woman of the Year of the National Council of Women in Brazil. She teaches regularly in Spain, France, London, Colombia, Argentina, Mexico and was Visiting Professor of Hebrew University in Jerusalem. She has written 12 books, amongst which *History of Hispano-American Literature; The Mask and the Enigma; The Space Recovered,* and hundreds of papers.

Moisés Lemlij, M.D., is a Training and Supervising Analyst, Member of the Peruvian Psychoanalytic Society, Director of the Interdisciplinary Seminar on Andean Studies (SIDEA) and Associate Member of the British Psycho-Analytical Society. Twice Vice President of the International Psychoanalytic Association, he is currently its Treasurer. He has edited more than thirty psychoanalytic and interdisciplinary books, and is co-author of *Entre el mito y la historia* (Between Myth and History) and *El umbral de los dioses* (The Threshold of the Gods).

Vivienne Lewin is a Psychoanalytic Psychotherapist in private practice. She is a Full Member, and Training Therapist and Supervisor of the London Centre for Psychotherapy. She is currently working on a book about psychotherapy with twins.

Ivan Lust, M.D. is a child- and adult psychiatrist, and training analyst of the Hungarian Psychoanalytical Society. In addition to clinical work with adults and adolescents and teaching psychoanalysis at a university postdoctoral program he is a member of the Theoretical Working Party of the European Psychoanalytical Federation

Jehane Markham. Poet. Born 1949. Recent work includes The Birth of Pleasure (1997) a verse play based on the myth of Cupid and Psyche. 20 POEMS Rough Winds Productions (1999) and My Mother Myself (2000) an audio tape of the poet and her mother, Olive Dehn, reading from their work.

Elizabeth Lloyd Mayer Associate Clinical Professor in the Psychology Department, University of California at Berkeley and Psychiatry Department, University of California Medical Center, San Francisco; Training and Supervising Psychoanalyst at the San Francisco Psycho-analytic Institute; Fellow of the International Consciousness Research Laboratories at Princeton; private practice in Berkeley, California. Her book on anomalous experience and unconscious mental processing will be released in 2003.

Joyce McDougall - Graduate of Otago University, New Zealand trained at the Hampstead Child Training Centre, London. In 1954 moved to Paris, where she trained and is now Supervising and Training Analyst to the Paris Psychoanalytic Society. Author of numerous articles and books including: *Plea for a Measure of Abnormality; Theatres of the Mind: illusion and truth on the psychoanalytic stage. Theatres of the Body: a psychoanalytic view of psychosomatic phenomena* and *The Many Faces of Eros: a psychoanalytic exploration of human sexuality* translated into Spanish, German, Swedish, Italian, Danish, Portuguese, Hebrew, Japanese, Greek and Finnish.

Jan McGregor Hepburn is a psychoanalytic psychotherapist in private practice in Northumberland. A full member of the LCP, she qualified in 1984 before moving to the North East of England in 1988. In 1990 she became involved in setting up a local psychotherapy training, NEATPP, to BCP standards. Jan is a training therapist and supervisor, and became Course Director in 2001

Marion Milner (1900-1998) was a distinguished British psychoanalyst. A prolific writer and painter she belonged to the Bloomsbury Group (introduced by her Nobel-prize winning brother). Her writing includes many articles and books, *including A Life of One's Own; Experience in Leisure; On Not Being Able to Paint* (under the name of Joanna Fields)*; Hands of the Living God.* At 87 she published an autobiography and when she died was completing *Bothered by Alligators* based on diaries about the childhood of her only son.

Pirkko Niemelä, Psychoanalyst, is Professor of Psychology at the Department of Psychology at the University of Turku, Finland teaching developmental psychology and psychotherapy and doing research on the development as a mother, early interaction, etc. Developing new kinds of psychotherapy programs, e.g. presently a program in mother-baby interaction therapy.

Johan Norman M.D., is a child and adolescent psychoanalyst and training analyst/supervisor in the Swedish Psychoanalytical Society; Member of the ACP. Worked in Infant-Parent Unit in Stockholm 1995-98. President of the Swedish Psychoanalytical Society 1989-93, Convenor, European Standing Conference on Child and Adolescent Psychoanalysis 1989-93. Chair, IPA Committee on Child & Adolescent Psychoanalysis (COCAP) 1998-2001, and now Consultant to it.

Malkah Notman Training and Supervising Psychoanalyst at the Boston Psychoanalytic Institute. Clinical Professor of Psychiatry at Harvard Medical School at Cambridge Hospital. Graduate of the University of Chicago, and Boston University School of Medicine. Psychiatry residency at Boston State hospital and Beth Israel Hospital in Boston and on the staff and faculty of Harvard Medical School, and Tufts University Medical School where she was Professor of Psychiatry. In practice of psychoanalysis and psychiatry.

Jack Novick, Ph.D, child, adolescent and adult psychoanalyst. Trained at New York University, Anna Freud Centre, and British Psycho-Analytic Society. Now training/supervising analyst of New York Freudian Society. Chair Child and Adolescent Psychoanalysis Committee of Michigan Psychoanalytic Institute. Formerly Chief Psychologist, Youth Services, University of Michigan Psychiatry Dept. Currently Clinical Associate Professor at its Medical School; Family Consultant/ Co-chair of Research at Allen Creek Preschool and in private practice. Co-author with Kerry Kelly Novick of *Fearful Symmetry: The Development and Treatment of Sadomasochism.*

Siobhán O'Connor is an Associate Member of the British Psycho-analytical Society. She works in Northern Ireland as a Consultant Psychiatrist/Psychotherapist. For the past five years she has had responsibility for a Psychiatric Intensive Care Unit and a Continuing Care Ward for the severely mentally ill.

Susie Orbach co-founded the Women's Therapy Centre in London and the Women's Therapy Centre Institute in New York. Visiting Professor at London School of Economics. Her recent books include *The Impossibility of Sex,* imagined stories about therapy told from the therapist's perspective, *Towards Emotional Literacy* and *On Eating.* Advisory Board member, International Association for Relational Psychoanalysis and Psychotherapy.

Marianne Parsons Child and Adolescent Psychotherapist and Child and Adult Psychoanalyst. Trained at the Anna Freud Centre and the British Psycho-Analytical Society. Was Head of the Clinical Training at the Anna Freud Centre and Editor of the *Journal of Child Psychotherapy.* Now in private practice, and at the Portman Clinic where she is Course Director of their Diploma in Forensic Psychotherapeutic Studies.

Martha Papadakis Psychoanalyst, Member of British Psychoanalytical Society. Born in Australia and trained in psychology and social work in inner London before having a family and starting the training. Private practice for more than 20 years as well as teaching, running groups.

Renos K. Papadopoulos, PhD, is professor at the University of Essex, consultant clinical psychologist at the Tavistock Clinic, training and supervising Jungian psychoanalyst, and systemic family psychotherapist. As consultant to the UN and other organisations, he has worked with refugees and other survivors of political violence in several countries.

Rosine Jozef Perelberg Training Analyst/Supervisor, British Psycho-Analytical Society. PhD 1981 in Social Anthropology, London School of Economics. An Associate Editor New Library of Psychoanalysis 1989-1999; on Editorial Board International Journal of Psychoanalysis. Honorary Senior Lecturer in Psychoanalytic Theory, University College, London. Co-edited Books: *Gender and Power in Families* (1990), *Female Experience* (1997). Edited: *Psychoanalytic Understanding of Violence and Suicide* (1998) and *Dreaming and Thinking* (2000).

Sheena Polett, is an Associate Member of the British Psychoanalytical Society and a Consultant Psychotherapist in Cheshire, UK where she has developed a service comprising two psychotherapy teams: one serves individual adults, the other provides rapid access to psychotherapeutic help for couples and families, especially when children are very young.

Saul Pena Pioner of Psychoanalysis in Perú; Honorary President of the Peruvian Psychoanalytical Society; Past President of the Latin American Psychoanalytical Federation; Founder Member of the Royal College of Psychiatrists, UK; Training analyst, supervisor and professor of the Institute of Psychoanalysis, Lima Peru

Joan Raphael-Leff, Psychoanalyst & Social Psychologist. Professor of Psychoanalysis, University of Essex. Chair, IPA's COWAP, 1998-2001. 70+ publications, mostly on gender/generativity, and 9 books, including: *Psychological Processes of Childbearing; Pregnancy - the inside story; Spilt Milk - perinatal loss & breakdown; Ethics of Psychoanalysis; Parent-Infant Psychodynamics - wild things, mirrors and ghosts* and *Female Experience* (co-edited with Rosine Jozef Perelberg).

Celia Read, [the cover artist] is a full member of the London Centre of Psychotherapy and has been in private practice as a psychoanalytic therapist since qualifying at the LCP in 1981. She completed training in the fine arts in 1991 and since then divides her working day between consulting room and studio. She is represented by The Cadogan Contemporary Gallery, London, SW3 www.artcad.co.uk.

Jim Rose, member of the British Psychoanalytic Society, and its Honorary Treasurer 1997-9. He works in private practice and has published professionally in IJPA. In addition, he specialises in working with adolescents/ young adults at the Brandon Centre for Counselling & Psychotherapy for Young People in Kentish Town, London.

Ismond Rosen, Training Analyst of the British Psychoanalytic Society, was awarded the first posthumous Fellowship, Royal College of Psychiatrists. Writings include many papers, a book *Sexual Deviation* (OUP, 1963), an unpublished autobiography and *Stories on Sculpture.* He left 400 works of art, some in permanent exhibitions, in the Vatican, Kirstenbosch, SA, Heilleiger Kreuze Kirche, Berlin, and RSM, London.

Eyad El Sarraj, a Palestinian Psychiatrist (born Beersheba 1944; exiled to Gaza, 1948) trained in Medicine in Alexandria, Egypt, and Psychiatry in London. Founder and Director General of the Gaza Community Mental Health Programme, and Secretary General of the Palestinian Independent Commission for Citizen's Rights. Winner of the Physicians for Human Rights Award in 1997 and the Martin Ennals Award for human rights' defenders in 1998. He publishes extensively on issues of peace, civil society, psycho-politics and as human right's activist has suffered hardships from both Israeli and Palestinian Authorities.

Michael Sebek, Ph.D., CSc. Born 1946 is a training and supervising analyst of the Czech Psychoanalytical (Provisional) Society The I.P.A, Associate Secretary for Europe President of the Czech Psychoanalytical (Provisional) Society. Associate Professor of Medical Psychology and Medical Ethics, Charles University, The 2nd Medical Faculty, Prague

Ellen A Sparer Ph.D., is a member of the Paris Psychoanalytical Society, where she did her psychoanalytic training. She is also a licensed clinical psychologist in the state of California. She works in Paris, primarily in private practice and part time for the Jean Favreau Center, the outpatient clinic of the Paris Psychoanalytical Society.

Luis Rodriguez de la Sierra y Escobar, Training Analyst of the British Psycho-analytical Society, is also a Child psychoanalyst, a psychiatrist and a Group psychotherapist.& nbsp;He has published papers on Drug addiction, Adolescence and Child Analysis. He presently works at The Anna Freud Centre, The London Clinic of Psycho-Analysis and University College Hospital. Dept.of Psychological Medicine.

Valerie Sinason is a poet, child psychotherapist and adult psychoanalyst. Currently Director of the Clinic for Dissociative Studies and Consultant Research Psychotherapist at St Georges Hospital Medical School Psychiatry of Disability Dept. She is President of the Institute for Psychotherapy and Disability and has published 12 books and over 60 papers on abuse and disability. Latest edited book is *Attachment, Trauma and Multiplicity, Working with Dissociative Identity Disorder* (Routledge, 2002)

Sharon Stekelman qualified in medicine in the 60's and worked in general medicine for five years before undertaking psychoanalytic training. Became a full member of the British Psycho-analytical Society in the '80's. Until 1991 she worked in various NHS settings including in-patient and Child Guidance centres and now works privately. One of several areas of interest is the relationship of psyche and soma.

Harold Stewart is a Training Analyst and Supervisor of the British Psycho-analytical Society; Consultant Psychotherapist (retired) Adult Dept. Tavistock Clinic. Author of *'Psychic Experience and Problems of Tecnique'* (Routledge, 1992), *Michael Balint: Object Relations Pure and Applied* (Routledge) and other papers.

Judith Szekacs, Ph.D. a Hungarian psychoanalyst living and working in London, is member of both Societies. Founding member of the Sandor Ferenczi Society, Budapest. In 1992 founded IMAGO East-West, later the Multilingual Psychotherapy Centre (MLPC) in London where what has been lost and found while changing countries, cultures and languages can be explored and old-and-new territories discovered.

Helen Taylor Robinson Member British Psychoanalytic Society, Course Coordinator Interdisciplinary Studies for University College London Msc in Theoretical Psychoanalytic Studies, and Editor for the Winnicott Trust. Special interest in teaching and writing on the relationship of the Arts, particularly Literature, to Psychoanalysis.

Alex Tarnopolsky, MD was born in Argentina, trained in the British Psychoanalytic Society and lived in London for over 20 years. He now lives in Toronto where he is a Training Analyst in the Canadian Psycho-analytic Society and Professor of Psychiatry, University of Toronto.

Carol Topolski trained as a psychoanalytic psychotherapist with the BAP. For a dozen years, she was a senior film censor for the British Board of Film Classification, alongside her practice, having come from a professional background in prisons, probation and Women's Refuges.

Frances Thomson-Salo trained with the British Psychoanalytical Society as an adult and child Psychoanalyst, is now a Training and Supervising Analyst of the Australian Psychoanalytical Society. She is a Senior Lecturer on the University of Melbourne Grad. Dip/Masters in Infant Mental Health. Published on work with infants and children, including editing *Childhood depression: Why is it hard to understand?* Royal Children's Hospital, Melbourne, 2000.

Judith Trowell, Consultant Child & Adolescent Psychiatrist, Psychoanalyst and Child Analyst has books and chapters in *'Child Welfare and the Law', 'The Emotional Needs of Young Children and Their Families'.* Co-editor of *'The Importance of Fathers'.* Also works with child protection and child welfare court cases offering assessments, court work and treatment in addition to training and research.

Elizabeth Tuters worked as a social worker in Toronto and at the Tavistock, UK in the 70's, then trained as a psychoanalytic child therapist in Toronto, and an adult psychoanalyst in Montreal. Was a fellow of Zero to Three, Washington. Team Leader in the Infant Program at the Hincks Dellcrest Center, Toronto. On Board of Directors of the Toronto Child Psychoanalytic Program, and World Association of Infant Mental Health

Isaac Tylim, Psy.D. IPA, Training Analyst, Fellow, Faculty and Supervisor at the Institute for Psychoanalytic training and Research (IPTAR), Faculty and Supervisor at New York University Postdoctoral Program on Psychoanalysis and Psychotherapy. Assistant Professor of Psychiatry, Downstate Medical Center; Secretary, IPA UN Committee.

Sverre Varvin, MD Training analyst in the Norwegian Psychoanalytic society. President from 1994-98. Vice president of International Psychoanalytic Association (from2001-) Senior consultant psychiatrist at the psychosocial Center for refugees, University of Oslo

Ivan Ward is the Director of Education at the Freud Museum. He is editor of the *'Ideas in Psychoanalysis'* series published by Icon Books, of which his book *'Phobia'* is a part, and author of *'Introducing Psychoanalysis',* Icon (2000).

Hisako Watanabe, paediatrician and child psychiatrist, is Assistant Professor, Department of Paediatrics, School of Medicine, Keio University. Director of the Infant Child and Adolescent Mental Health Unit, Keio University Hospital, Tokyo. Regional Vice-President of the World Association for Infant Mental Health. Applies a combination of concepts from infant psychiatry and Japanese AMAE, a culturally rooted intersubjective mode of intimate interpersonal relationships.

Estela V. Welldon MD DSc (HON) FRC.Psych is an Honorary Consultant Psychiatrist at the Tavistock Portman NHS Trust, Founder and President for Life of the International Association for Forensic Psychotherapy; works in private practice as a psychotherapist and organisational consultant. She is author of books and other publications dealing with perversion and criminality.

John Woods, Member of the British Association of Psychotherapists, the Association of Child Psychotherapists, and the Institute of Group Analysis. He works independently and at the specialist Portman Clinic in North London. His play 'End of the Abuse' was performed in a London fringe theatre. Currently completing a handbook on therapeutic work with adolescent abusers and a play about ethical problems of psychotherapists.

Harriet Kimble Wrye Training and Supervising Psychoanalyst, Los Angeles Institute & Society for Psychoanalytic Studies (LAISPS); Advisory Board, International Assoc. for Relational Psychoanalysis & Psychotherapy (IARPP); Editorial Board, Gender & Sexuality. Over 25 published articles on psychoanalysis and film; Co-author: *The Narration of Desire: Erotic Transferences & Countertransferences* (AP, 1994).

Between Sessions and Beyond the Couch

PREFACE:

This is an extraordinary book. Rare in *composition* – with over 90 contributions, including poems and works of art, from psychodynamic clinicians originating in a variety of trainings, and working in different countries around the globe. It is unusual in *style* – since each contributor chose to examine for this publication a topic close to her or his heart – these offerings are passionate and informal, yet invariably lucid, in accessible verse, prose or art form. As to the *contents* – this lively focus not only discloses personal issues usually left obscure, but brings into the foreground aspects that tend to remain behind the scenes, namely, *the therapist as embodied and worldly.*

While there has been a shift in current psychoanalytic writing towards acknowledging the analyst as a subjective, responsive presence in the consulting room, it rarely addresses the psychosomatic toll of *being* one. Similarly, while recent papers tend to unfurl hidden layers of countertransference within the clinical situation itself, we do not often hear what happens between sessions, or about work in the absence of clients, or what happens when both therapist and patient are thrust into unusual circumstances, such as violent or traumatising situations.

So, with inevitable overlap, this book covers various dimensions of engagement with our 'impossible profession' as Freud called it. It is a multicultural, multifaceted acknowledgement of our own particular occupational hazards and rewards, roughly divided into four sections – **Behind the Couch; Beyond the Couch; Between Sessions** and **The Embodied Therapist**. The first two deal respectively with clinical issues within the consulting room and interdisciplinary applications of psychoanalytic understanding beyond the couch. Written contributions for these sections were solicited by personal invitation or through newsletters of various training institutes. The book is also based on questionnaires and personal interviews with many IPA analysts, and psychoanalytic psychotherapists in the UK and abroad over the past six years. Utilising this pooled experience, the last two sections of the book focus on the variety of ways we find to sustain ourselves within the spatial skin we share with our patients, and how we choose to replenish ourselves between sessions.

The response has been overwhelming and due to lack of space I have had to close the contents list despite some other fine contributions. However, these wait in the wings for volume two and I hereby invite further contributions from readers, based on your own clinical and/or extra-mural experience, which you feel may be of interest to colleagues in the psychoanalytic community. [jraphael_leff@compuserve.com]

Interconnectedness:

> *'... something that often overwhelms us*
> *- memory   a recollection that*
> *whatever we're striving for now*
> *was once closer and truer*
> *and that its union with us*
> *was incredibly tender...*
> *After the first home*
> *the second seems hybrid*
> *and windy...*
> *...for womb is everything'*
> [R.M.Rilke, <u>Duino Elegies</u>, pp.74-5, 8th elegy,
> p.37, transl. D.Young, New York:Norton,1978]

Psychoanalytic therapists of any school (whether Ego or Self-Psychology, Drive or Relational) share three fundamental taproots: existence of the *unconscious* as ineffable contradictory, unknowable yet persuasive forces. *Resistance* to an incipient desire to make meaning and to discover the repressed/dissociated/unformulated unknown; and *transference* of (often unprocessed) emotional experiences across frontiers, from past to present, psyche to soma and between self-and-other.

A further common denominator across the very different approaches and topics of the contributions to this book, is a tacit clinical aim of providing patients with a metaphorical *'home'* in therapy. One in which ephemeral wisps of memories and desires alluded to by Rilke above, may indeed be recaptured, emotionally relived and processed. Foreclosure is avoided by sustained evenly suspended attention – the analyst's counterpart to the patient's freely-associative narrative – turning one's 'own unconscious like a receptive organ towards the transmitting unconscious of the patient' (Freud, 1912, SE12:115) and inner self, thus opening oneself up to the confluence of intersubjectivity.

This book addresses what so often remains unquestioned in the process – *the <u>effects</u> on therapists of the recurrent experience of offering hospitality to uncensored otherness within one's internal 'home'.* Stretching our reflective frame of mind to host our unconscious registrations and to envelope the patients in our care, we each invoke a contained but permeable space in which exquisitely responsive and vulnerable, we are open to admission of the primitive and unexpected from <u>without</u> and <u>within</u>. That this is also a *portable space*, is evidenced by those chapters dealing with issues far beyond the consulting room.

Like our very first home – the metabolising womb – therapeutic engagement tries to offer a place of safety in which growth and striving can occur. Nourishing and dispersing waste products and toxins, at times at the expense of the therapist's own constitution. Like intrauterine occupancy, the 'second' home of the consulting room is also a *temporary state* – a twosomeness whose ultimate function, from the very moment of first encounter, is to expel the patient at term into separate existence. Our therapeutic task is thus also midwifery – fostering development without inducing premature labour; tolerating the necessary pain without springing into action; attenuating anxiety without dismissing it or defending ourselves against its messages. In short, pacing ourselves to the creative process and awaiting rather than hastening the myriad mini 'births'.

From work with expectant and new parents, I recognise the crucial importance of *self-replenishment* for the nurturer while hosting physical or emotional 'symbiotic' states. As therapists we not only provide nutrients and containment, we *absorb* – taking in raw, painful or hurtful emotions, often with no further outlet but to listen, collect and hold these until they can be processed for and by the patient. The very receptivity we offer to whatever the patient cares to bring, takes a heavy toll of the therapist whose susceptible, fallible and corporeal presence underpins, realises yet disavows transferential guises of ascribed familial properties.

While introspective and countertransferential processes undoubtedly demand an emotional tax, endurance of the torsion thus generated also stimulates *reflection* and *curiosity*. And, as the papers in this book attest, breeds an extraordinary blend of creative elaboration and range of problem solving. These writings are responses to puzzles which have arisen from the analytic encounter – incidents on and off the couch, sociopolitical and ethical demands, extra-curricular interests or and transitions between consulting room and other spaces.

1. Behind the couch:

The 35 contributions in the first section of the book address intriguing issues that arise within the intimacy of the clinical situation or at its limits, relating to facets of interaction with the patient, present or absent. They also deal with aspects of frame and setting of treatment, both on and off the couch, with adults, children or parents and babies. In common, these papers illustrate the frustrations and disappointments as well as rewards of the embodied, gendered therapeutic situation Likewise the analytic paradox that to listen sensitively we need to be uniquely 'porous' – alerted to the patient's unconscious and open to deciphering its derivatives. Simultaneously, we remain receptive to mental registrations of otherness and emotional ripples on unguarded frontiers within ourselves. Reflecting on these fragments of preconscious dreamlike imagery and ideational representations to convert them into verbal formulations and trial interpretations, necessitates a cognitive gear-switch while yet remaining impressionable and attentive to anxieties. These writings constitute the creative harvest of both mindful engagement (or disengagement) and retrospective mulling over.

II. Beyond the Couch

In some cases the psychoanalytic 'tent' can be stretched to encompass events far beyond the consulting room. Part II raises organizational and sociopolitical issues ranging from the managerial to disasters, war and terrorism. The first and last sections of this collection of 27, depict clinicians expanding their psychoanalytic understanding and skills to social and academic arenas, and likewise, importing understanding from other spheres into the psychoanalytic. The middle section focuses on therapists who bravely extend their efforts to work with and within areas of violence and political persecution. As these writing illustrate so candidly, the impact of trauma on thinking and symbolisation affects not only victims and survivors, but those striving to help them. Some of these papers have been written under conditions of great stress and danger, and delivery of one paper was prevented by grievous strife.

III. Between Sessions

In this penultimate part, the 35 contributions engage with a variety of topics relating to professional conduct and ethical issues, some grave, others more lighthearted and experimental. The last two subsections actualise 'dreamings' – applying what has been gleaned from the couch to creative endeavours and worldy adventures. These writings share a lively approach to pursuing and juicing life's fruits.

IV. The Embodied Therapist

The concluding part returns us to the issue of the physical toll of our sedentary profession and psychosomatic effects of constant absorption and processing of our own pain and that of others. I used that metaphor of pregnancy above advisedly – there is an aspect of two-bodied bi-directional interchange in the consulting room, and reluctance to explore it may be detrimental to both clinical practice and our own self-knowledge. Bringing in practical issues of prevention and maintenance, of self preservation and sustenance, this section explores replenishment, reminding us to provide comforts for ourselves that we are prone to neglect in caring for others. I trust it will be useful and stimulate readers to share their own observations for a future publication.

A final note: rather than adopt a consistent house-style, out of respect for the multicultural nature of the contributions, contrary to usual editorial practice I have preserved each author's idiom and regional spelling.

JRL June 2002

PART 1: BEHIND THE COUCH
ON THE COUCH:

Last session   Jehane Markham

Lying on the Corbusier chaise-longue for the last time,
watching the clouds bump along
and you behind me in your chair,
your words still in the air.
An intimacy gained closer than
any lover or friend,
all the gaps that we've peered through-
but never got to the end.
Goodbye is a lumpy, sparkling thing,
hanging above us in the sky.
The small room floats us away
down a river of talk
and all that we don't say.

1

What's inside Pandora's box   Ellen A Sparer *(Paris)*

> *'It has been said that the English and Americans*
> *have everything in common except the language.*
> *The same could be said of the analyst and the analysand;*
> *The language is apparently the one existing means of communication*
> [W.R. Bion, *Caesura 1977*]

> *To speak analytically is to release the language from mourning.*
> [A. Green, *Le Langage en Psychanalyse, 1984*]

Although the unconscious is not structured like a language, it does have a language of its own. Interpreting the play between the conscious and unconscious languages of the protagonists in the analytic setting is the psychoanalyst's delicate and complex task. Might we not say that an interpretation is an invitation for the unconscious to express, in its own language, the subject's instinctual movements towards and desire for the object? For certain patients, it is the language of the interpretive work in the analytic setting, which facilitates instinctual binding.

Having lived now for many years in a country and a language other than that of my birth and youth, I have not only become attentive, as are all analysts, to the significance of the instincts as well as the conscious and unconscious fantasies as they appear and develop during the course of an analysis, but also to the particular sense attributed to the use of the language. Thus, it was with an intrigued ear that I took in Achilles' initial remark: "I don't know if I should be here or if I should see a sexologist", he softly uttered. "I am twenty-three years old and I have never had an orgasm…uh, well except at night, you know what I mean, out of my control…" As I listened to him stumble and search for words, I found myself wondering aloud why he hadn't sought an analyst who spoke his mother tongue, Greek. He had come to Paris six months earlier for his studies, but I needn't worry, he assured me, he would rapidly master French. He liked my accented French and wondered where I was from. "I've never been attracted to Greeks. No Greek lover, no Greek analyst," he declared. It would take time before I fully grasped the significance for him of having a space that I could not penetrate, his private 'Greek space', around which we would painstakingly weave a psychic tapestry, despite his Achilles' heel.

And Achilles heel he had. Born nine years after his sister, his haemophilia had not been diagnosed until the age of two or three following repeated and inexplicable difficulties healing from scratches or apparently innocuous wounds. He had grown up in a 'cocoon'; covered by

2

his 'colourless' mother, and 'invincible' father. Would I be able to pull him out of the Styx, and despite his vulnerability let him sail on his own? Could there be enough movement within the analytic setting so that he could let go of Thetis' invisible, 'colourless' hold on his heel; would he be able to leave with a representation of me in my absence?

I would remain an invisible object for a long time; my 'subaltern' place identical to that of his colourless mother. His mother would fly to Paris at his whim, and take care of everything for him. He exalted at her lack of French. "She could never talk to you", he crowed! "Only I speak French. It is a barrier between her and me!" As the weeks went by, I was to learn that Achilles' Greek was a 'dead' language. The dialect of his home region was close to ancient Greek and he had developed a personal language that was unbeatable, "invincible", he said. Forbidden group games and most sports as a child, he had become an outstanding student, and spoke a Greek that would 'kill' me if he spoke it to me. In fact would have killed a Greek-speaking analyst. Had I a 'Greek mummy' before me, preserved, embalmed, in mortal danger if separated from his mummy?

Achilles spoke frequently about his 'goddess', a dazzling and flamboyant female vocalist, whose posters and photos were plastered all over his apartment. A friend had told him he would never succeed at masturbating unless he got rid of the goddess who took up all his space, but he sighed and said, "I took down her pictures, but I feel void, empty, emptied without her all around me." He put them back up. Surrounded by his flamboyant goddess, and held by his colourless mother, Achilles came regularly to his sessions. When he left my office, however, I disappeared, completely; he had virtually no psychic capacity to represent my absence, and my 'rule' that he had to pay for missed sessions provoked scathing comments about my god, money. He was looking for my Achilles heel, in order to poison me and thus mortally infect the therapy. But as long as he could not kill the therapy or me with his arrow, he could perhaps survive.

Towards the end of the first year, pointing to a box in my office he said, "Do you know about Pandora's box? Only hope remains". The following week, feeling very melancholy at his mother's immanent departure, (who was returning to Greece at his father's request), he had the idea that he was losing his hair. He fantasized drowning himself in the bathtub. Thinking that his mother would be very sad if he committed suicide, he sat in his tub and for the first time in his life, succeeded in masturbating until ejaculation. And wept. After his mother's departure, he succeeded a second and yet a third time! And wept.

3

At twenty-four he discovered that his mother could leave him to join his father (Braunschweig & Fain), without his having to fear castration or drown in sorrow. His body had become a world with access to autoerotic pleasure. While he wept, recognizing in her absence, that they were two, not one and she that she had left him to be with his father, he could find pleasure in his own body. "Why did I cry?" he asked me. The embalming fluid had made way for real tears.

'It is probable that thinking was originally unconscious, in so far as it went beyond mere ideational presentations and was directed to the relations between impressions of objects and did not acquire further qualities perceptible to consciousness until it became connected with verbal residues'(Freud, 1911:221). His mother's absence, evoking the primal scene, in conjunction with a barrier represented by the French language for Achilles, provided a caesura between himself and his mother. The reality principle could supersede the pleasure principle. These 'impressions of objects' could now be translated, via French, into words. French taking on the function of transforming primary into secondary processes, having the 'quality perceptible to consciousness' and translating into words, Achilles' attachment to the object which had always satisfied his desires. No longer a mummy, he wept finding himself in a body other than that of his mother's, wherein his sexual instincts were now able to bring him autoerotic satisfaction. French had become the emblem representing the difference between himself, his sister and his parents. Confronted with the psychic absence of an established difference between the sexes as well as between generations, the analytic work in French created a barrier, and thus a beginning differentiation between his/his mother's bodies. A body of his own(McDougall). The French language has helped the analytic setting to take on a function of a non-murderous thirdness (Green). His Greek, ancient and dead, preserved him from his own destructiveness, but made him a kind of Greek mummy wherein it was impossible for Eros to bind with the destructive instincts.
Three years later, at his last session before the summer holiday he asked, "Will you be here when I return in September? Like Penelope." "Yes", I answered, "Like Penelope I will be here when you return".

References

Braunschweig D., et Fain M. (1975), La nuit, le jour. Essai psychanalytique sur le fonctionnement mental. *Le Fil Rouge*, Paris PUF
Freud, S(1911) *Formulations on the Two Principles of Mental Functioning* SE.12
Green, A.(2000) *André Green at the Squiggle Foundation*. Ed. Jan Abram, Karnac Books
McDougall, Joyce (1989). One Body for Two. *Theaters of the Body*. Norton

My favorite Zen anecdote
Ivan Lust *(Budapest)*

Freedom is a very important issue in Western philosophy as well as in psychoanalysis. Following my interest in Eastern thought I have gradually discovered some important similarities between psychoanalytic and Buddhist attitudes, both emphasizing freedom's inner aspect, the freedom of the mind.

First, I would like to recall a short episode of a long psychoanalytic psychotherapy. My patient at the time, a young man, was having great difficulties in living up to his job's requirements, and he was hardly able to get any of his school-work done. His relationships were characterized by the double bind emotions of desperate clinging and yet hopeless isolation. This duality manifested itself by his stubbornly insisting on the continuation of the treatment, and yet, regularly being late and not being able to surrender himself to his emotions, and thoughts during therapy. The sessions were spent on his endless expositions. Usually, I was unable to focus my attention on him. It was almost like being in hypnosis: first I felt very sleepy, then my forehead and eyelids started to turn numb, and heavy. At this point, the patient usually interrupted his loud ruminations, and made a remark concerning my slackening of attention. As it turned out later, he had a similar experience, while listening to what I had to say. He did not hear, or understand anything of what I said. After a while, we started discussing these episodes of losing connection. Slowly, it became obvious, that at such occasions I went through what he used to experience while listening to others, especially to his mother. If, during those times, I managed to stay alert, and started talking, then the situation was reversed. My patient withdrew the projective identification, and in turn, he was the one, who lost contact with me.

By being a depressed, low energy therapist, who was unable to focus his attention on him, I embodied an abandoned little boy, who was unable to maintain his security by clinging onto his mother's gaze. At the same time, this state prevented the patient from clinging onto, and getting reinforcement from my gaze, and attention. Thus, my patient created a 'bad-mother object' out of me, who was unable to ensure the child's refueling by joint attunement. In the absence of normal attunement, my patient was forced to pay close attention to every bat of my eyelid, so he would not be left alone, once again. As soon as we started discussing these mutual experiences, I became able to pay attention to him more frequently, and in a better way.

Once when he arrives very late for the session, we start making fun of the reasons why he has been late. "You cannot put this on my account" –

5

he says laughing. There is a small pause in the conversation, and he begins ruminating about something. Once again, I need to force myself to pay attention. "Back to the good old ways" – I think to myself. He suddenly gets stuck, and looks at me with a confused, upset expression on his face. "I lost track"-- he says. "You may continue anywhere" — says I – "this is a moment of freedom". He contradicts me: "It cannot be a moment of freedom, because I am not able to continue what I have meant to say"— he says. "Well, it's true, if you look backwards, where you came from. But if you look forward, looking at the many different possibilities for continuation..." – I say. He agrees, and laughs with relief. From this point on, he really lets it go, and talks about how difficult it is for him to stop any activity once he has started. He brings examples from work. If he is not able to resolve something, he keeps persisting compulsively. He is not able to switch gears. Hours and days pass this way. He tells me, that it is like trying to pick up a coin from the smooth floor with bare hands. The only thing that would help is a sharp object. "With teeth and nails" – I say. Based on this – this time truly free associating – he recalls a story, when he was buying a present for someone, with his mother, and sister. He considers the amount of money to be spent too much, and explains this to them, in an objective manner. His mother is taken aback, but she cannot find anything to counter his argument. When they part, she says to him: "Anyway, you are going to get a hair cut, aren't you?" The patient gets really angry. "You could have told your mother: 'Let my hair go'..." — I tell him. He recalls similar stories, with increasing rage, and fantasizes about punching with fist into his mother's face.

Losing track was a critical point in the conversation quoted above. For me, it meant a release from constraints, the possibility of opening up. For my patient, the free space opening between the lost track and the many possible new roads to take was a threat. The patient's returning problem – and that of our mutual history – is losing track, as well as a sudden disruption of inter-subjectivity. His associations suggest furious clinging. The coin, he was unable to rub up from the floor, illustrates how difficult it is for us to create this open space.

During the sessions, time after time, I find myself on my patients' crowded inner stages. Once, and again, I am put into the role of the evil pursuer, an abandoned or tortured child, or perhaps, a sexual seducer. I am often just a voice, an unfinished movement, a mouth full of teeth, a painful touch, a protectively, or threateningly erect figure. My freedom is lost, and regained, minute after minute. After my patients have left, I might as well feel free. But there is a great mess left after them – inside me. While I am trying to rearrange what's left in me after the sessions,

6

things that tightly fill up my inner space, the sessions are continuing inside me. The Zen anecdote reminds me of this.

"How can we gain absolution?" – asked a monk from the master.
"Has anyone tied you down?" – asked the Zen-master laughing.

The monk hopes that the Zen-master's great wisdom will help him to get loosen his bonds. His answer points to the fact, that when the monk is expecting absolution from him, he, himself creates a situation of subjugation and hopelessness. The humor implied in he concretization of the problem, however, means, that in the here and now, when the question is posed, they – the master and the monk – are the only people present. Hence, the monk has no reason to bare his old bonds. At this moment, he might as well be free. The monk recreates the life-history of the tied person at each moment, when he does not make the best of this freedom.

After my patients have left, I let the ties left from the sessions get loose. I start watching the pictures, conversation-fragments, emotions swirling in my mind with a cheerful indifference. I am not trying to follow up on them, to integrate them into a coherent whole, or even to forget them. I just let them come up, and disappear. After a while, different pictures, and fantasies appear. The inner objects, and fragments left from the sessions are slowly being replaced by those of my own inner world. The space becomes more airy. I am back in the present again. The evening may start. I am free for the day.

A female patient and her baby   Martha Papadakis *(London)*

The following work was literally being done in the presence of the baby, when she was around 8 months of age. Mother had been bringing her since shortly after her birth. There was the privilege of witnessing the unfolding relationship between my patient and her daughter during the first year of life, rather like the experience of a baby observation, but there were real technical problems of conducting an ongoing psychoanalytic encounter which predated the birth of this first child. This has been most a interesting problem to work out together. In the material the conflict in my patient, also linked to her return to part time work and therefore some greater degree of separation from her infant, unfolds on two fronts: her communications in the transference within the sessions and the baby's behaviour who through out our meetings had important matters of her own to communicate, primarily of course to her mother. It is inevitable that this must also imply, on another level and as a consequence of the importance of the bond between mother and infant as the foundation for all other relationships, the unconscious communication of certain aspects of the patient to her analyst in the maternal transference.

A fortnight before the end of the term the patient reported a dream:

> *She is staying in a hotel and comes to a window with a beautiful view of lakes and trees. She wants to show her companions, but they are ensconced with a man discussing nests and are not interested in what she wants to show them at all.*

Her associations concern the lucky family of her cousin, who have, like her, just had their first baby. They are prosperous and have no money problems. Her cousin's labour was easy and this woman has help in her large house to assist her in the early emotionally demanding months after the birth. Turning to her own lot my patient thinks the view looks miserable; she recalls how difficult was her own delivery, and now having to prepare to return to work in a few months time, albeit after a year's leave, and the impossibility of finding anyone suitable to look after her baby despite the fact she has not yet started looking for such a person. All this makes the whole plan look insuperable. It seems that she is looking at everything in the worst possible light, even though she thinks at the same time of how much she loves the father of her child and would in no way exchange the happiness she has with him for the materially rich life of her cousin. This comment I felt came from a genuine contact with her feelings for her husband and the goodness of the marriage. She had no associations to the men and the talk of nests, other than the connection of chicks to nests.   Though in the dream she is having a 'beautiful view' of sexuality - the lakes and trees and the fertility of that garden - her love for her husband and the baby they have made together - this aspect is not recognized as herself, and instead has become the cousin of her associations, whose lot is coveted under the heading of an 'easy' life, when her own, by comparison, is seen as so hard. I think further away in the background this must be linked to her view of her own fertile, creative mother with her babies, perceived as something effortless. While interpretation brought this split more into the open a lot of work was needed to integrate these two seemingly completely separate parts of her which did not recognize each other. Perhaps the men and their nest talk, anticipating the man 'taking most of the day to handover' in the next dream, may concern her fear of her over involvement with her infant, and her need for a man (father, husband and analyst) to help her free herself to work as an adult, not instead of, but in addition to her newly discovered and all consuming functioning as a mother, to the benefit of both herself and her child. So, with this background in mind I will turn to the next session.

On this day the baby comes in a pram, rather than in mother's arms as usual. As the vehicle is wheeled in to the consulting room there is an impression of a bright wakeful, pair of eyes peeping out from under the bonnet of the pusher. In this way her Mother's hope that she might prolong her baby's nap which began on the journey to the session, so my patient might be able to lie down again on the couch are in vain. This has proved increasingly problematic in recent months. We are becoming accustomed increasingly to a situation of her sitting on the couch attending to the baby who is more and more active and insistent on contact and interaction with both adults, while we attend to the patient as best we can. Now, from a faint outline an object relation is beginning to emerge that is more clearly identifiable; in which there is a pushed out and disconsolate older sibling, faced with a mother overly preoccupied with the new baby and a father absent. Who between us was going to be thrust into these respective roles contributed to an ongoing tension in the sessions.

The patient begins by reporting a situation in her department at work. A struggle is going on, she thinks, to make her responsible for arrangements that the staff are competent to continue to carry out, as they have during her maternity leave. She is worried that everyone, having managed her absence and acquitted themselves without problems, will take her return as an opportunity to throw up their hands as though they cannot do it, like Mr J. who wants to talk over every little thing with her, when she has not got the time, nor is it, in her opinion, her job. She thinks democracy is best, but still a head, a prime minister, is also necessary for a government to function. She compares this with a kind of dependency model where certain things happen when 'mummy' comes back after a separation. Everyone stops doing what they were able to before and turns instead into grizzling babies.

Here the patient, I think, refers to a perspective on regression that is destructive to ego functioning and development. The greater equality of adult and peer relationships more characteristic of siblings, where everyone at best pulls their weight, collapses in an orgy of dependence on the mother. On the return of the absent object the most infantile forces are unleashed, as though in the midst of this free expression everything will find its right level, but in fact this leads to anarchy. Such an idea was contained in the cathartic method that Freud eventually found so limited, and abandoned for the more complex structural model of intra psychic conflicts and their resolution through repression, as well as expression.

To return to the session, the patient then reports the following dream:
She needs someone for long mornings, but a man says it has got to be a fulltime person, but she cannot afford that, nor the time to hand over which is taking just about the whole day. There is no solution and she is dismayed. Meanwhile as she is talking the baby who has emptied the waste paper basket, spits out a nut she found in it and becomes restive, pulling plants and papers off a low table. She holds her little arms aloft and cries out. Her mother picks her up. We have come to understand that this is a summons to her mother to raise her up to stand on the high back of the couch. Then holding onto the bookshelf, and situated between her mother and the analyst thus, she looks down at us and from one to the other and a smile of great pleasure suffuses her tiny face, as if to say, "Look at me! See I am in my Special, Favourite place! "

Here we are, held in this triangular configuration, a sort of Oscars' situation - 'and the winner is...' the baby! Held up by her mother's hands on this minuscule stage she is the little star and we are the audience. In the course of her travels around the room she has discovered 'the navel of the world', and situated herself at the epicentre. The primal scene has sustained a total reversal, with the couple being the witness to the baby doing the performance.

Time is short, the session is flying by in the midst of all this activity. What to attend to? And how to put it together in a way that is true and meaningfully illuminates what is happening. I interpret she is telling me she is suspicious of and then rejects regression as the principle of mature relations, which in fact involves work for all parties. If 'handing over' means all of herself to this Mummy-Baby position, then it entails abnegating herself as a 'fulltime person' who has different departments internally as well as externally, but with 'head' in charge. A model that is both flexible and structured. If something called 'the baby' is running the institution nothing can work properly. This 'baby' tells her she cant afford the reality, particularly of time, to confront conflicts and discover in turn the solutions this can give rise to, which involves work together, for all

10

the parties involved. She is becoming more aware of the importance of other relationships than the baby to help her to do this (husband and analyst) both to manage her infant, internally and in her baby, and all the other aspects of her life as well. I also say to her that I think in my presence she is working this out with her own child, and that she feels the need of my actual presence while she is doing this work (something I will come back to). I have the impression she is paying attention to what I am saying and that she feels what I have said meets a need in her, in that she becomes calmer in herself, and more reflective.

What I did not say, there was not time, and anyway these are rather my reflections particularly regarding the concrete nature of this working out, concerned the following. This infant, I thought, was learning with her mother how to be part of the world, not forever and always the centre of it. A very idealized and probably self- idealized place is associated with being at the centre, or being The centre and for a time in the course of development this must be so. I thought we found ourselves both observing and participating in the shift of axis from this centre to a more moderate place. I think this mother was depending on me to articulate these conflicts for her, while they were happening and she felt overwhelmed by them. The same process was happening to the consulting room. It was becoming increasingly a playground, with a couch for a climbing frame and an office table for a gym, inexorably this decreed the movement, as we watched, of the analytic process to the periphery of this same room, shattering into the scattered contents of the waste paper basket, that was then shoved in the mouth, as babies do. Without time and thought it was impossible for analyst and patient to make the necessary transformation properly. We found ourselves in a position where what we were trying to work out together - to arrest fragmentation and bring the different psychic parts together - was what we found ourselves literally in the middle of; the fragmented bits and pieces of the analysis

The baby had to come down off that stage and let her mother have her couch back for her analysis, and her analyst recover her analysand on the couch, to fulfil her function as the Analyst. This is commensurate with letting the parents be the couple again, repossessing themselves of their privacy and their sexuality once more, and this is part of what my patient is working out with her infant and with me. This mother is working out how to be able to be more separate from her baby, not ensconced in the nest on top of her baby or her baby on top of her. This means facing that, as a mother, she also wants to work and has areas of her life that function away from her baby that existed before she was born and which need to be recovered again within another and completely new perspective. She is beginning to discover through her own experience that 'the beautiful view' seen through the window, of sexuality and its procreativity in the lucky cousin of her associations, is in fact the new and beautiful world she is finding and starting to put together in herself.

11

Twins in Psychoanalytic Work   Vivienne Lewin *(London)*

Working psychoanalytically with twins presents a particular challenge to the analyst that often goes unrecognised. Analysis of the twin in the transference is vital for satisfactory resolution of the work.

Development of identity

For all infants emotional growth involves a relationship with the parents, who provide a developmental framework within which the baby can grow towards an individual identity. The infant-mother relationship is usually the primary bond and one where intimacy exists within an inherently unequal situation. Alongside this relationship, the parents are a mature couple. The recognition by the child that the parents work closely together in a productive relationship, and also have separate interests that they follow individually, and that the parental relationship excludes the child in particular aspects, is an important concept in the child's growth towards maturity.

There is a tendency for twins to regard themselves as a couple, and to turn to each other for help in processing emotional issues, rather than to the parents. Twins are not, however, an adequate developmental unit in the same way that the mother-infant couple, and the generative parental couple, are. While they offer special support and closeness to one another, the twins are both immature, and unable to function in a mature capacity to each other. Each twin has a unique relationship with the parents and it is necessary for the parents to intervene in the twinship to enable each twin to develop a secure sense of individual personal identity. The failure of parental intervention, whether from a lack of available parenting or the twins turning away from the parents, leaves the twins no alternative but to use each other as developmental objects. Separateness is then viewed as a threat to the twinship. In this situation, the painful losses engendered by growth and the recognition of difference are avoided. The end result is a state of arrested emotional development and they remain bound to each other in a relationship of shared identity.

The dynamic aspects of twinship

Twinning i.e. seeing the other as like self, in either singletons or actual twins is a mechanism that has several functions. Twinning may be used in any relationship to try to gain a better understanding of oneself by trying to find the self in the other, a mirroring, a seeking out of sameness. In this situation, known or unknown aspects of the self are projected into the other with the hope for better understanding of self. Twinning may also be used to avoid knowing aspects of the self that are felt to be unwanted, by splitting them off, projecting them into the other, and disowning them, in an attempt to be rid of them. It is as if the two become opposite halves of one unit.

Twins, whether mono- or di-zygotic, have a built-in mirror image. The other twin is ever-present as an available object for twinning processes. As a result of their immaturity and inability to process projections in the way the parents can, difference and separateness are not adequately established. The bond between the two may be intensified and may become so close as to exclude all others, most notably the parental contact necessary for development. The twins then become enmeshed in the twin relationship, with a consequent confusion/fusion of identities. The enmeshed twinship may be used as a defence against the recognition of the need for the development of separateness and a personal identity for each twin. The twins function as a pair united against the world, as two halves of one.

The intervention, with the loving understanding of a mature maternal object, in the twin relationship, can ameliorate the inherent rivalry between the twins, the intensity of the aggressive, sometimes violent feelings, and their dependence on each other. However, in the situation when the twin is the primary object, the twins remain in a state of constant rivalry, a destructive stalemate, with repetitive situations of victory for one, and vanquished for the other.

The twin in the transference

The twinship, whether enmeshed or more separate, is reflected in psychoanalytic work. At various times the analyst is perceived primarily as a twin, rather than as a parental figure. The perceived twinship with the analyst (the twin in the transference) may be used by the patient to try and establish sameness, in order to avoid an understanding of the self in relation to the other. The transference twin is a refuge from the unpalatable truth of difference and separateness. The creation of an imagined identical twin in the analyst with a view to maintaining sameness, perpetuates the idea that the patient has omnipotent control of the analyst. The pain of emotional growth and development towards maturity is then avoided. The denial of difference and separateness, particularly of generational difference, is a central aspect of the work.

The transference twin created by the patient is a complex organisation that requires careful and detailed analysis. While it involves similar processes to ordinary twinning, the existence of an actual twin with whom the patient has a significant relationship creates an additional dimension to the transference twin. Without such analysis fundamental aspects of the

13

personality will remain unknown, and the twin will continue within the limiting twinship, blocking movement towards separateness. When the twin in the transference is not analysed, there is a lack of resolution and an unsuccessful ending of treatment. The resistance of twins to coming into treatment is a reflection of the fear of separation and disruption of the twinship.

When a twin dies in infancy, the surviving twin is too young to mourn adequately the loss of its womb companion, and it will be much affected by both this loss and the complex feelings created by the situation in which the parents have both lost and gained a child. The surviving twin creates a phantasied twin that is totally within its control, in denial of its loss. This phantasied-dead-twin is used in the analytic work to maintain a barrier between the analyst and the patient. The twin/ phantasied-dead-twin couple is regarded as the essential pair from which the analyst is excluded. Analysis of the phantasied-dead-twin in the transference is subject to particular resistance. Relinquishing the phantasied-dead-twin involves recognition of the loss of and mourning for the twin in a situation inherently fraught with guilt.

Transference relationships

Is 'Narcissistic' Pejorative?   Takeo Doi *(Tokyo)*

I wonder if Freud knew that the term 'narcissism' he coined for the putative state where all currents of love originate would be used pejoratively. I think he must have been aware of the pejorative overtone of the term since in his scheme of things the origin is by nature primitive, undeveloped. Interestingly, he used the term narcissistic neurosis for the psychotic state. Also, he argued that the tenacity of one's ideal is narcissistic. Furthermore, Freud justified his postulate of narcissism as follows: 'The primary narcissism of children which we have assumed and which forms one of the postulates of our theories of the libido, is less easy to grasp by direct observation than to confirm by inference from elsewhere. If we look at the attitude of affectionate parents toward their children, we have to recognize that it is a revival and reproduction of their own narcissism, which they have long since abandoned.'(Freud, 1914, p.91) There is another statement of his to the same effect:'This situation is that of loving oneself, which we regard as the characteristic feature of narcissism. Then, according as the object or the subject is replaced by an extraneous one, what results is the active aim of loving or the passive one of being loved, the latter remaining near to narcissism.'(p.133)   Thus, whether to love others or to be loved by others, it can't escape being an expression of self-love. One may say indeed that Freud had no high opinion of humanity.

It was only Michael Balint who took issue with Freud on the question of narcissism, since he was of the opinion that narcissism may ensue only as a secondary state following the break of one's initial object relation. I think this is a plausible hypothesis, but curiously, no other analyst seems to have agreed with him on this point. For instance, Heinz Kohut, whose theory deviated considerably from Freudian orthodoxy, resembling that of Balint in some important respect, still lets his edifice squarely rest upon the Freudian concept of narcissism.   And I should say that precisely because narcissism is the sole motive, the word love is not even mentioned in Kohut's theory. As a matter of fact, in such case, there should be no genuine love either. For one would love the other or love to be loved by him or her only for the sake of self-love. Surely narcissism should prevail!

I have been in agreement with Balint's position on narcissism since I discovered that *amae*, an everyday Japanese word, should correspond to what he described as passive object love or primary love. I have written about the subject extensively both in Japanese and English.   I corresponded with Balint on this matter and even met him once to discuss it. But here is the rub. Don't think that *amae* always refers to a pristine

15

state of being loved. On the contrary it is quite customary nowadays that one means self-indulgence by *amae*. To attribute *amae* to someone therefore can be pejorative more often than not. Thus the offended party may go great length to deny it. It is apparent that *amae* here is equated with being narcissistic.

What does all this mean? Have Japanese people as a whole been under the influence of Freud all these years? Never! By no means! Because the usage of *amae* in the sense of self-indulgence can be traced far back in history, though it seems to have increased in the 20th century. It was after all a sign of the *Zeitgeist* which extolled independence even at the expense of indispensable dependence, leading to the emphasis of all-important self-love. In this regard one may then wonder if Freud himself also was not under the influence of the same *Zeitgeist* when he invented the concept of narcissism. Wasn't it more likely so than otherwise?

References:

Doi, T.(1989) The concept of *amae* and its psychoanalytic implications.
    International Review of Psychoanalysis, 16:349-354
Doi, T. (1992) On the concept of *amae*. *Infant Mental Health Journal*,
    13/1:7-11
Freud, S. (1914) *On Narcissism: an introduction*, SE 14

MRS ABC*   William Brough *(Teesside, UK)*

Mrs ABC was 48, but looked more like 84, when I met her almost two years ago. She was the picture of misery – grim, gaunt and worn. She had been in and out of psychiatric hospital many times over the past ten years, with 'severe depression'. This included cutting herself and overdosing with whatever came to hand, reinforced with excessive amounts of alcohol.   She'd had most treatments known to modern psychiatry - except psychotherapy. And so she came to us.

Mrs ABC declared that her experience of this world was that the sooner she departed from it, the better. It had now reached the stage of not being worth the effort to stay alive. Her recent attempt to end her life had almost succeeded, and she regretted to find, on recovering consciousness, that she was still alive. Yet she had once had a good job - owned a house, and at one stage had probably been quite a presentable and attractive woman. Mrs ABC had been married in her thirties to a Mr ABC. After six weeks, he left her for a woman whom he had not even met at the time of the marriage. The essentials of the history are that from the age of 5 to 13, she had been sexually abused by 3 uncles, whom I have called X,Y and Z. Uncle Z, was her mother's brother, the other two were 'honorary' uncles, who were married with children, while Uncle Z was single and childless.   They were all friends and neighbours of her parents, and had a babysitting function for them.   I do not know whether, at this early stage, when she was very young, she had ever wondered if this curious sexual activity was associated with babysitting, or whether it was something which happened to everybody. Nor do I know whether she was ever involved with more than one of these men at the same time, or if it had ever been a group or a gang activity - or even if the involvement of any of them had been known to the others. It was presented to me as if it were three separate arrangements. I had no reason to suppose that it was not penetrative, genital intercourse at some time.

At her menarche, when there was now a possibility of pregnancy, one of these uncles dropped out, but the other two continued. I am not know how long it continued into adult life, but one thing was sure - her parents did not know what was going on. They must never know about it. The knowledge would kill her mother, if she knew that her own brother was treating her daughter, his niece, in this way. Furthermore, she was sure that her father would kill the uncles, all of them, and so end up in prison. I suspected that the two wives of uncles X and Y not only knew but colluded. The two uncles, X and Y, were now dead, while Uncle Z was still alive. These uncles were all of my vintage, which meant that there was a clear route for the transference that might gather around a therapist of my age. In recent years she had lived with her frail mother, who needed her care. When Uncle Z also became frail, her mother and he decided to

17

join households - without the consultation and agreement of Mrs ABC. This, unsurprisingly, led to an increase of her hospital admissions. Furthermore, she was so committed to the protection of her mother, that she allowed her mother to extract a 'death bed promise' from her, that after the mother died, my patient would stay on as housekeeper for Uncle Z and continue to care for him. This amounted to a returning of Mrs ABC to the earlier setting of childhood. Thus she was 'caught' in the same way, as she had been long ago. Uncle Z seems to have seen this as an opportunity to "try it on again", as he had done when she was a child, this time in the middle of the night in an otherwise empty house. Following further overdoses, she was admitted to hospital. This time only for a brief period because the ward was to be closed for repairs. She knew this in advance, but when the time came nevertheless, for her to be discharged, she was distressed and protested vigorously. This made it possible for her to remain in hospital, while attending her psychotherapy.

What I was able to offer to Mrs ABC were fortnightly visits of an hour. There was a lot of talking to do and some painful re-living of her past. She was certain there was *Nothing* and *Nobody* who could help her. The enormity and the extent of her problems and the utter impossibility of changing anything, in this " -- -- world", was beyond human capacity. The message I received was that the countdown had already begun. This time she really was going to succeed in killing herself. She bombarded me with her anger from the word go. She did not want to live in this awful world. In the telling of it, she was pouring her pain and misery into me. This was the grief that had lain embedded in her since early childhood. This is what we call 'containing'. The cutting and the overdosing and drunken bouts eventually began to abate somewhat, because there was now a different or additional vehicle for the evacuation of the misery, the pain and the despair that she had carried inside her for so long.

However, the major issue remained. The attacks on herself, although less, were still continuing. In any of them, she could end up dead. It became clear to me that she had taken over the abusing role from these uncles and was continuing to do this to herself. Formerly she had been the victim and others were the attackers, but now, although she remained the victim, she had taken over the role of being the punisher. I wondered aloud to her whether she felt there was something that she had done for which she felt she ought to be punished.

Central to it all, was the fact that I was of the same vintage as the uncle trio, and proposing to spend an hour a fortnight alone with her in my room. She needed to feel secure with me, yet, as before, this situation held the potential of exploitation. As well as all this, it was likely that she had some anxiety that I might press her to discover whether she had had any gratification, or satisfaction, or pleasure, or even curiosity, about the sexual activities in which she had participated. Whatever she had felt about this at the time, not only did she now regard them as wrong, but she felt she ought to have stopped these activities at the time.

I chose to deal with this in two ways. If there was something she ever wanted to tell me about, I told her she could do so when she was good and ready - and I was prepared to wait. The other way was to point out that during much of the time of the activity, she had been young, if not very young. Then, she had the resources, the strength, the appearance, the courage of a child, but she had been confronted with the task of an adult. The others involved, while they had the appearance and age of adults, were in fact, immature and fell short of being grown-up. So if there was something that she and they did not get right at the time, we need not be too puzzled about it. While there was nothing to applaud about the uncle trio, or anybody else on the scene, I also let her know that I did feel a twinge of pity and sorrow for them. But to whitewash them, or to let them off, was the last thing I wanted to do. They could have done with help themselves, because I could see that they must have missed out on some of their own growth and development in childhood.

At first, Mrs ABC was not clear what bearing her past experiences had on her present predicament, or what she wanted to do about it, or what she wanted me to do about it. There had been, and still was, a mixture of anger, hate, shame, disgust, wishes for punishment and revenge, to lash out and disgrace those involved - although most of them were now dead.

I am going to take an aside to tell you something about my early days in China, during World War Two. Every possession left unguarded was stolen. The rationale was that if the owner did not value and regard as precious what they had, then others, who wanted these things more, were justified in taking over possession. Something similar seems to have happened for my uncared for little girl who had grown up to be my Mrs ABC. My guess was that the adults in her life had not been cherished or properly cared for themselves. So not having learned to value themselves, had found it difficult to value her. Her task now, was to recover the ability to value and care for herself.

There was a particularly bleak point in the treatment, about this time, when a profoundly depressed woman friend of my patient killed herself. This was a great loss to Mrs ABC who had shown considerable kindness and compassion for this similarly afflicted friend. She became very suicidal and I thought I had taken on more than I could manage and would lose her, despite the support I was having from my colleagues. I eventually pointed out that while she could show considerable kindness and caring to others, all she was showing to herself so far, was anger, hate and defeat. I told her that she knew something about *giving* kindness, but not about how to *receive* it. Once, when her uncle Z was 'trying it on', after her mother had died, I was able to point out another piece of the problem to her.

19

That is, that she was continuing to act as if she was still the little girl that she had been, and not the grown woman that she now was. This led to the understanding that "the uncle nonsense of the night" would go on for just as long as she allowed. Until she told him plainly and clearly to stop it! Eventually, she stopped her uncle by use of an indelicate expression, which I had heard formerly in time of war. She told him to "piss off" - and so he did. One of the things within her new-found power, was that she might now stop punishing herself. She had suffered more than enough for whatever she had done intentionally or unintentionally. I let her know that in my opinion, any time now would be right for her to stop attacking herself – and replace this with a little cherishing..She began to have something to smile about. Her weight increased from 6 stone to 7½ stone and it showed on her face and that of her junior nurse escort.

Mrs ABC now had a new problem to cope with, she had to make a financial decision. If she stayed where she was as her uncle's housekeeper, she would almost certainly inherit his house - to which in a sense she was entitled - for her cooking and cleaning care of him in recent years. But to benefit financially, or in any other way from Uncle Z's estate was difficult. The idea of taking money from someone who had sexually abused her, was not straight forward. There was something about it which was akin to being a prostitute - though we were both at pains not to use that word. Then I discovered something which she and I already knew, but had lost from the front of our minds. It was that she herself had a house, a derelict, almost abandoned house. This was not far away and was in much need of redecoration. Until now, it had just been left there and was rotting away. Now we could see that this unoccupied house represented something of Mrs ABC herself. That is, her own unused, abandoned self. This derelict house needed fixing up, just as she had needed fixing up herself. So she contacted a younger sister, whom she found had also been molested by the same Uncle Z, but who, unlike my patient, had dealt with the uncle very promptly in the appropriate manner at the time - and had lived to tell the tale. This sister was very good at wallpapering and painting. She was delighted to make contact at last through the blanket of despair that had separated the two sisters through those lost and precious years. So it was not only the house that was being recovered, but the two sisters and their relationship. The sister was delighted with my patient and her achievement. These two got their acts together. Thus the physical act of restoring and mending the house was part of the equation of her repairing and restoring her own life and her existence. We decided to delay the ending of our sessions until her own house was ready and she was well into it. Then she could let me go with the knowledge that she had been able to face something that she had hitherto felt was unfaceable.

* [Edited by Dr Mary B Heller from a longer paper presented at the APP/Specialist Psychotherapy Service, Middlesbrough, Teeside 20.3.99]

Pets Behind the Couch   Tirril Harris *(London)*

When I was training I remember a fellow trainee responding to our tutor's earnest discussion of analytic sibling rivalry with a quip that he was less worried about sharing the couch with his psychotherapist's other patients than with the dogs. I remember how shocked I felt. In those days we were concerned never to depart from blank screen emulation. In those days too toilet training was a key focus of our preoccupations and projections concerning pets invariably involved transgressions against the canons of cleanliness. For me Robin's canine joke summoned fantasies of rubber gloves and buckets, with the hapless analyst forced to pretend that nothing had happened. Confident that I myself could only work correctly if I saw my first training patient outside my home, I was content with the surges of criticism I felt towards Robin's psychotherapist.

After qualification I learnt that Robin's training therapist had been none other than my mother. Thus the offending curs had been none other than Good Old Gobbo and Piccola Pixie. My view of Robin's predicament then underwent some revision. I confess that this was not due to any loyalty on my part towards my mother who had been named as the sinful practitioner, but more to the identification of Robin's analytic siblings. I found myself incredulous that he could not have relished, even if only in fantasy, the possibility of spending his analytic hours romping with Gobbo and Pixie on the overample couch she had installed. True the shrill cacophony of their terrier barking was earsplitting, but they were such good friends.

But the change in my outlook cannot be attributed entirely to the revelation of the dogs' identities. More important was the sea change that had come over the world of psychoanalytic psychotherapy and its practice since the late 1960s when I began training. And this itself is not independent of societal change as a whole since the Second World War. Something was mollifying the rigidity of the rules by which we lived and worked, rules which fed the shame which required therapy to be unravelled, and this meant the rigidity of the psychoanalytic frame could also soften. So long as it didn't happen too frequently things could now be allowed to go bump behind the couch and patients' responses to these bumps utilised as material for exploration of projection and even transference. I was thus now relaxed enough to work at home, to recognise that the weeds in my front garden allowed a way in to the negative transference I could never have benefited from in the Clinic premises in Fitzjohns Avenue and that the sticking front door could turn the housewife's disgrace into a therapeutic key, unlocking a flood of fantasies concerning rejection and exclusion. Nevertheless my first experience of a pet overstepping the traditional psychoanalytic boundaries was therapeutically unproductive, succeeding only in leaving me shaky. As a young woman, Christine, who was happily working towards termination mused yet again on her new found calm when visiting her mother, I suddenly saw, almost on the ceiling, staring fixedly straight down at the couch, Ellie the tabby, perched on top of the tall book shelves, a Carollian Cheshire Cat but decidedly without the grin. There was something uncharacteristically sinister about the intensity of her stare and I could feel waves of paranoia engulf me. Surely she could not have leapt up there on her own? Would it not be better to warn Christine to forestall a similar panic when she finally noticed her, as she inevitably must lying at the angle she was? But she didn't, and as she pondered further about Mother I realised that Ellie was in no mood to move, her eyes were now drooping, her fearsome stare well screened. Today I might quiz myself about projective identification: was my paranoia something to do with Christine's feelings about her mother? Was Ellie's final somnolence something to do with my feelings about Christine's mother? But at the time I just whistled inwardly with relief.

Today Ellie is no more, but two border collies have become my therapeutic aides. Their barks are deeper than were those of my mother's terriers, and they have what I turn to an advantage in being mother and son, though one is black and one is red, both with a white shirtfront. Partly because I am old, and partly because I have become more and more convinced of the important truths conveyed in Attachment Theory, I find their presence at my front door affords me many opportunities to use them to help people remember and make links. But in contrast to the way pets are often imported by parents to encourage responsibility in their offspring through adoption of disciplining and nurturing roles, the issues which arise in my consulting room are practically never those of toilet training or cleanliness, of inferior animals interfering by transgressing strict rules. They may be issues of fear, as with Peter whose intellectual dedication to the psychotherapy process made him ask if he ought to practice confronting the dogs with a pat each time he arrived. (I let him decide and he managed not to feel a failure on the occasions when he subsequently forgot to follow his own prescription). More usually the issues involve reflections on dependence, separation, loyalty and responsiveness. For example only this week the dogs have featured in two sessions. First Penny told me as she rose to leave that she thought she was coming to be able to "love your dogs", only seen by her briefly on arrival. I had responded with some anodyne smile knowing we were already over time, but next session she conveyed that she had expected me to find greater significance in her pronouncement. I was gratified that she was able to tell me what I was supposed to have interpreted. (She had much earlier told me that her father used to take her to the park without saying a word, and she felt this silence showed he did not love her, commenting that it was as if he was just taking a dog for a walk. I had responded that I found myself wondering what else he had done that made her so sure he didn't love her when after all many people who walked dogs did indeed really love them. She had murmured that she supposed that could be true, after which she stopped in her tracks, and then really began to question her interpretations of his relationship with her).

The following day Eric told me that the dogs' barks on his arrival had reminded him how he had read this week that any boy who pines for a dog is a boy deprived of affection and didn't I remember how he had spent his childhood longing for a dog in the family? As an adult Eric had briefly owned a dog, but had had to give him up when he separated from a partner. Once encouraged he was able to move on to talk about the responsiveness of this pet, the way he had validated Eric's identity by his style of greeting him, and how he, Eric, had felt less self-centred because he was able to empathise with his dog.

So perhaps where this is really leading is that we need to think more about pets *during* sessions, not just between sessions. By working with fantasies and memories of pets we can facilitate reflective emotions concerning intimacy with patients who would be unable to explore so freely if constrained to focus only on human relationships. Evidence on imprinting, bonding and grooming among other species suggests that we might learn much about psychological development by taking a more ethological perspective. However bringing the idea of pets from between to within sessions is not the same as bringing actual pets from behind the couch to sit upon it. I am lucky to have a separate entrance for my consulting room. The dogs are seen to belong in the main house. They are not even behind the couch, let alone on it in the way Robin was implying. One of my patients left a former therapist because her request that the cat not be present during her sessions was responded to merely with interpretation not with agreement. Whether or not we are back here to the theme of analytic siblings, it is a reminder that, vital as it is to be flexible, there is still an important need for some kind of boundaries, and an even more important need to understand what it is that the boundaries protect.

OFF THE COUCH:

Falling Apart on the Analyst's Couch*
[to the tune of 'Raindrops on roses and Whiskers on kittens']

1. Infant observation, unconscious allusion,
   Kleinian theories, my head's in confusion,
   Paranoid, schizoid, depressive or worse,
   Psychotic states are the analyst's curse.

2. Ego defenses, there's such a profusion,
   Splitting, projection, denial, delusion,
   Good breast and bad breast, a part object state,
        A harsh superego proclaiming my fate.

Chorus
     No more partings. No more endings.
     I just want to stay
     Forever reclined on my analyst's couch,
     and then I will feel...okay

3. What are you feeling? and What are you dreaming?
   What are your thoughts? Are you plotting and scheming?
   Nothing is private.. so just spill the beans,
   Nothing you say's ever quite what it seems.

4. Jealousy, rivalry, envy and hatred,
   Where is the love in which I was created,
   Oedipal fantasies filling my head,
   I'm going to stay on my therapists bed!

Chorus   No more partings etc.

5. Maternal reverie, holding containing,
   Fears and projections are waxing and waning,
   Interpretations are challenging me,
   Towards Reparation and Depressive P!

Chorus   No more partings etc.

Jean Dix *(Middlesbrough, UK)*
* Poem written in the car on the way home from therapy.*

24

Concluding Remarks

Joyce McDougall *(Paris)*

One of the recurring incidents in my practice that has surprised me is the kind of spontaneous intervention I sometimes make to an analysand as he or she is leaving my office, along with the consequences that such remarks may induce.

The first incident that comes to mind is that of Raven, a ;;dance therapist of 25 who came to analysis because of serious depression and outbursts of panic anxiety that frequently interfered with her professional work. During one particularly trying session on a Friday night she berated me throughout for, among other angry recriminations, not enabling her to find a lover, for not allowing her to earn enough money to buy a studio apartment, for having analysed and eventually taken away an old symptom which had always exercised a calming effect, of fine cutting and blood letting on her own body. As she was leaving my consulting-room she said, "Well this weekend I shall commit suicide; there's nothing left for me to live for so I'm going to put an end to my life." Having heard this threat on other occasions I called out after her retreating back, "If you do that I'll never speak to you again!" At her Monday session she said she laughed all weekend over my absurd statement and then added "Perhaps for the first time I believed that you really care for me."

I once quoted (McDougall, 1982) an analysand called Isaac who came to analysis because of overwhelming panic anxiety following a wasp-sting when he was 40. As our analytic voyage proceeded his unmanageable psychic suffering gave way to the creation of a number of phobias, including that of entering crowded spaces. We were able to reconstruct, among others, archaic fears of a smothering engulfing mother and the phantasy of the female sex as an endless chasm. At one such session Isaac recounted a terrifying experience while shopping in a supermarket. As he was preparing to leave he said, "when I came in I thought you looked attractive in that pink suit but I was terrified to look at you" then on leaving he looked me straight in the eye and said, "I have no difficulty in looking at you as I go out" to which I replied "It's a relief to get out of the supermarket?" And we both laughed.

As I noted in the original vignette I sometimes detect a couter-transference tendency to making seductive remarks to analysands who have had seductive mothers and even though it is tempting to lay the blame on the analysand's discourse which is frequently geared to arousing such reactions this nevertheless does not exempt me from having to elaborate the reason for which I would allow myself to react in this way.

One final vignette comes to mind: this is a 'joke' recounted by one of my analysands who is in the process of terminating a long psychoanalytic

25

voyage (and which gave rise to some interesting associations on his part and various interventions on mine). The vignette went like this:

"Hey Dr. McDougall did you hear about the gay analyst on the very last day of his psychoanalytic treatment? He says to his analyst 'As you know this is our very last day. I feel I have accomplished so much in these six years with you: I now fully accept my homosexual orientation, I have successfully terminated my doctorate - and I even have a stable partner. So I make one last request. Just as we say goodbye, there where we usually shake hands at the door, may I give you a kiss? The analyst announces that this is out of the question, that analysts do not permit their patients to kiss them. Well then, says the analysand, would you permit me to give you a parting kiss? No way! replies the analyst; analysts do not allow their analysands to kiss them. The patient persists - but look, I am filled with gratitude and I would like a last act of sympathy between us - to which the analyst replies 'Now that's enough! As a matter of fact I shouldn't even being lying on the couch with you at this moment!'."

On this humorous note I too shall bring to a close my free associations around the theme of concluding remarks.

Reference

McDougall, J. (1982) *Theatres of the Mind: Illusion and truth on the psychoanalytic stage.* New York, Basic Books, 1985.

Salutary Tale   *Harold Stewart (London)*

I had recently qualified as a psychoanalyst and was practising in the Harley Street area. My patient, a young woman who had been diagnosed as a severe borderline schizophrenic was in the third year of her analysis. She had recently been toying with the idea of not leaving at the end of her session and I had been offering her interpretations of why she might be having these feelings, transference interpretations of both the here-and-now and of the past there-and-then.

However her desire not to leave grew stronger and she began to prolong the end of sessions by not getting off the couch after I had indicated it was time to leave. I continued to interpret as well as I could until at the end of a session she said that she was not going to leave no matter what I said and that I couldn't stop her from staying unless I removed her physically. This I had no intention of doing and so I said that I would have her removed if she refused to go. She asked how and I said I would call in the police. She then said that I wouldn't, so I went to the telephone in the room, dialled 999 and spoke to the police, who said they would be along as soon as possible. Luckily this was a session followed by a break and so no patients were waiting, and she probably knew it.

I then went back to my chair and waited. She now said that I had only pretended to call the police and I answered that we would see. Shortly afterwards my receptionist let me know that a plain-clothes policeman had arrived and I asked her to send him up to my room.
As he walked in through the door my patient got off the couch, gathered her coat, and left.

She started the next session by saying that she was very glad that I had really sent for the police because it meant to her that if I said something like that, I meant it. In this way she said I was so unlike her parents who were always threatening but in fact did nothing.

One moral of this tale is that in such situations with such patients, interpretations may not be enough to deal with them and something else, some action or direct straight talking, is necessary. The analyst has to show his mettle as being more that a skilled interpreter.

The second moral came when I chatted with the police sergeant after the patient had left. I apologised for having to call him out in this way, but he replied: "Don't concern yourself about it, sir. We're up and down Harley Street every day taking patients out of the doctors' consulting rooms".

Invisible Stress

David M. Black *(London)*

Everyone enters the oddly constructed architecture of psychoanalysis by one narrow doorway or another. For myself, I entered it by way of something called 'pastoral counselling', then by psychotherapy, and only gradually discovered, to some extent, the layout of the whole large building.

This story belongs to some of my earliest experiences in the counselling ante-chamber. I couldn't at first see counselling as 'work'. There was nothing I could imagine more interesting than sitting with another person and hearing how their life felt to them: how could this be 'work'? and why did people say it was tiring, even stressful?

Then one day I was asked to see a tall, quite attractive, pale young woman. She sat in front of me, gripped me with her gaze, and began to tell me of her troubles with eating. She was in the habit of eating very little, apparently, but then, every now and again, she would let go and eat a huge amount - of what, I forget - and after that she would tickle the back of her throat and throw up. I had never heard of bulimia, and was politely intrigued to hear of these curious preoccupations.

But then something began to happen which first worried me slightly, and then, as the minutes passed, made me acutely anxious. I started to feel sick. There was no overt reason for it. I didn't find what she was telling me disgusting; I didn't even find it particularly 'serious', as I might think now that I was hearing about 'serious pathology'. I noticed, of course, that what I was feeling seemed to parallel something in what she was telling me, but I couldn't see any connecting link. All that was happening was - she was talking, I was listening.

My feeling grew worse and worse, and finally there was nothing for it: I had to excuse myself, went to the toilet, and was violently sick. I returned to the room and with immaculate puppylike professionalism made no reference to what had occurred. Neither did she, though I thought she looked at me strangely. She never came back, after that first meeting. I hope she went elsewhere, and found someone with more experience to help her with her (serious) problem. But the episode has stayed in my mind, over nearly thirty years, as my first introduction to the invisible stresses of the 'talking cure', the invisible, unconscious, finally un-understandable communications which we are continually having to field and cope with - hopefully by some more mental form of digestive process than was available to me at that time. And these stresses and communications remain demanding and mysterious, to body and psyche, even though as time goes on we attempt to enlarge our therapeutic imagination and also learn something invaluable called theory which - almost equally mysteriously - does indeed make a difference.

Between Patients

Patrick Casement *(London)*

Introduction

In this short statement I have chosen to consider three different situations when no patient is present, to reflect upon how I happen to use those times.

The gap between sessions

The most common time between patients is that built into any analytic schedule, the time between sessions. I used to think that this was mainly for writing notes, and for a while I conscientiously did just that in the time after each 50 minute session. But when my schedule became more filled up I began to find that this practice did not help as much as I had imagined. There were several problems with it.

One problem arose directly from my too regularly writing notes between sessions, in that I was then not as fresh for the next patient as I would wish. It only gradually dawned on me that I actually needed to use that time to 'lie fallow' rather than have even those minutes filled with further attention to clinical detail. I also came to realize that notes made later had a quite different quality. My memory had by then become more processed and these later notes often turned out to be of more clinical use than the more nearly verbatim detail I had sometimes recorded immediately after sessions.

I also began to find that when I relied less on notes my clinical memory became more readily available to me, and it also had more dynamic relevance to the session in process than would have been the case with detail(s) carried over from a written record. In addition, I came to see what Bion was getting at when he advocated that we should enter each session 'without memory, desire or understanding' (Bion, 1967).

So, my note-taking is now much less frequent, and this is seldom how I use my time between sessions except for the occasional noting down of a few key words upon which I may later fill out my recollection of a session. For the greater part during this time I now attend to whatever can best help to clear my mental tapes, as it were, before starting with the next patient.

Waiting for a patient to arrive

I will not pretend that what I shall now describe is always how I spend the time waiting for a patient, but it is certainly how I intend to spend it at times of stress in my clinical work.

When a patient is late, unless I have allowed something to divert my attention, I would always register this, though not necessarily to comment on it when I see the patient. I keep it in mind and wonder about it. But when this lateness is uncharacteristic of the patient I listen more specifically for what could be communicated by it.

One particular example comes to mind, when a once-a-week patient had not turned up, and she had never before been anything but exactly on time or early. By 5 minutes into the session I was beginning to feel anxious. My mind then went back to a year before when this patient had been referred to me from a Psychiatric Hospital. She had been discharged after a suicide attempt. I now recalled that she had been more depressed in the previous week than at any time since she had started working with me.

By 10 minutes into the session I was beginning to sense that there could be something seriously wrong. I wondered about 'phoning my patient's flat, where she lived on her own. Of course she might be on her way, perhaps delayed by public transport, so it would then not matter if I 'phoned as no one would answer. However, if she *was* still in her flat she might feel intruded upon by my ringing her there. I felt in a dilemma. But I decided it was better to ring than to risk an actual suicide.

When I rang, the 'phone was continually engaged. I then asked the telephone exchange to check whether this was 'engaged speaking' or not. They reported that the 'phone was 'off the hook' and there was no-one speaking. I therefore asked the telephone engineers to connect me to the patient's 'phone (which in those days they were able to do), so that I could call out her name. After doing this for a while and getting no reply, I telephoned the GP to say that I considered there to be a risk of suicide here. He immediately went round to the patient's address, and after getting help to gain entry he found the patient unconscious after a serious overdose. In this instance, listening to my patient's absence had clearly helped to save her life. So, there had been a very serious communication in her unusual absence, and my 'starting the session without the patient' had helped me to pick this up.

Since then, when a patient has not come, I have often sat in my otherwise empty consulting room noticing whatever comes to mind, whether in thoughts or feelings or in images, in relation to that absence. And it has been surprising how often this has helped to alert my listening to some unspoken communication(s) from a patient.

Cancelled sessions

A supervisee once left me a message saying: "As my patient has cancelled all 3 sessions since my last supervision I am ringing to say that I am cancelling my supervision." My reply to this was: "In my way of thinking, patients can't cancel sessions. They can only choose not to attend, but the session still exists. We therefore should not agree with a patient's idea that a session has been cancelled even if that is what they have communicated. So, if your patient has missed 3 sessions we have a lot to think about at your usual supervision time."

The point of this vignette is to invite some thought into how we spend time that is freed up by patients who announce that they are not coming to a session.

My own practice is to observe all sessions as still existing whether or not a patient is going to attend. I also make it my practice to plug in my consulting room telephone, in case patients chooses to ring during their time. After all, they are still paying for this. Just occasionally, a patient *has* telephoned during that time. And when that has happened I have always been glad that I had continued to regard the session as still there for the patient.

A prolonged absence

I had one patient who came from a background in which she had been placed for adoption. Her reading of this had been that her mother hadn't wanted her.

In the course of quite a long analysis (5 times pw) this patient went abroad during my summer break. At the end of this she wrote saying she had got into some important experiences where she had been on holiday, and she felt it was important for her to remain there for another month. Would I please keep her times for her and she promised she would pay for those sessions when she got back. Her fee then was only a token fee, so I was not going to be seriously disadvantaged by having to wait to be paid. I wrote back agreeing to keep her times.

At the end of that month I received another letter from this patient saying she had decided to stay away for longer still, so would I please extend the same arrangement? She would let me know when she would be coming back.

Throughout this time I observed this patient's sessions. In particular I put my diary on the table that stands between the chairs where I would have been seeing her, as she was then still not using the couch. I also re-

31

connected the 'phone. So, even though I did not spend all of each session *actively* thinking of this patient, I always had her 'in mind' for each of these times.

After an absence of about 2½ months, and I had as usual just put my diary in place for this patient's session, I heard the door bell and opened it with the buzzer. And there she was. She hadn't let me know when she was coming back. Instead, she had come unannounced, expecting to find that I was either out or had someone else there in her place. The last thing she had expected was to find that my consulting room was set up ready for me to see *her,* if she came. She remarked on this and, in the discussion that followed, she learned that I had in fact kept each one of her sessions specifically for her throughout her absence. But, understandably, she had needed to test me out on this.

As this analysis continued it became apparent that, quite apart from any insight this patient may have gained during it, one of the most telling experiences for her had been that I had truly – and not just in words – kept her in mind during her absence. She could not remember having had that experience with anyone else before.

Concluding remarks

What I have tried to communicate in this brief statement is just something of the value to be found in keeping patients in mind, as well as re-finding our own minds in the time between sessions and between patients.

Reference

Bion, W R. (1967). Notes on memory and desire. *Psychoanalytic Forum* 2: 271-80.

Surviving the Empty Couch   M. Fakhry Davids *(London)*

I used to feel a slightly delinquent sense of pleasure when a patient cancelled a session – like a schoolchild secretly pleased that his teacher's illness would give them that treasured bonus of free time. I thought this feeling was gratitude mingled with guilt: there is always so much to do and here was the chance to catch up, but how could I not be actively engaged in the treatment when the patient was paying for it? Early on in my training I comforted myself with the thought that it would all get easier: perhaps I adhered to an overly strict work ethic – a manifestation perhaps of a harsh, as yet not-fully-analysed, superego? But things turned out to be more complicated.

On one or two occasions I tried to sit in the room without the patient, ostensibly to allow myself to have thoughts and feelings about the patient and the work. (There was a rumour doing the rounds then that Kleinians are perfectly capable of starting a session without the patient!) But this was mightily difficult, as one thing after another kept intruding into my mind and interfering with my concentration. Then it dawned on me that sitting dutifully in a room might well amount to denial of patient's absence – was I treating it as a mere technicality, and insisting that the work carries on all the same? Anyhow, my unconscious, it turned out, was not quite so cooperative, and I was to learn that though I could have access to thoughts and feelings pertaining to the patient, they would not necessarily occur to order within the allocated fifty minutes.

We discussed the problem in clinical seminars. One seminar leader had found something that worked with a patient who regularly missed sessions – he would deliberately not do anything else during the patient's time, but instead have a relaxing soak in the bath (he worked from home). There he would allow his mind to roam, and occasionally one or two insights pertaining to the treatment might present themselves. Of course, this was difficult if one did not work from home, when the temptation to take advantage of the patient's absence to get on with something else is very great indeed.

Why is the patient's absence so difficult to bear? I think it is because, in order to work well, we must have some narcissistic investment in our work. Patients sense this commitment from our palpable satisfaction, often subtly conveyed, when things go well. This is different from a transference (where the patient thinks we care because they project a caring internal object into us) for it presents an aspect of our real selves, which patients can put to use for their own purposes, knowing that they can touch us by doing so. Because of our personal investment we are deeply affected by disruptions to the work, and it is this that makes them

33

so hard to tolerate. I would like to describe two instances of this struggle, involving different work in the countertransference, as they arose in the treatment of a seriously disturbed man who had had a breakdown in his early twenties, and came into analysis in his late thirties.

Mr A was a highly intelligent and cultured professional whose previous psychotherapy left him with impressive insight into his psychopathology, but he came into analysis with its hold over him quite undiminished. He was my first patient of the day, and from the outset, was often quite late, or missed sessions altogether. This wore me down, and I would eventually find myself tarrying over coffee or in the shower, arriving at work at precisely the beginning of his session, leaving no time to unlock and prepare the place beforehand. Uncannily, that would turn out to be the one morning when he would be there waiting, sometimes in the pouring rain. Though he was invariably forgiving of my lateness – how could he complain given his appalling treatment of me? – it was of course a major setback, for how could he expect to develop trust in such an object, which he knew to be a central component of his psychopathology? Of course there was little point in protesting that I had been in good time on all the preceding days when he himself was absent or very late (which was actually true).

It was relatively easy to move beyond this phase once I recognised my own shame and guilt at failing to keep the setting secure, and also how much I hated him for messing me about. (Initially there had been polite telephone apologies, but these soon gave way to a situation where mostly I did not know whether, or when, he would come.) But I could also see my lateness as an attempt to project into him the experience of being kept waiting, and this made me curious as to why I should find that experience so intolerable. In order to get to this I would, of course, have to ensure that I wait for him. I bought a new alarm clock with a fail-proof snooze function that went off at five-minute intervals, and set it fifteen minutes earlier – at least now I could delay and still be on time! I was aware of resenting my patient for causing me so much trouble, but I stopped checking the answering machine last thing at night and first thing in the morning.

I had found a way to accept that I had to be there irrespective of whether he was, but being present in the sessions without him was not easy. At that time of morning the newsagents were still shut, and without a newspaper to read over a second cup of coffee I often found myself dozing off in my chair. Was I just overworked? Did he exert total control over my mind through his lateness and absences? Was my hatred and cruelty towards him so intense that I had to put my entire mind to sleep? Or was I simply wiping out the whole sorry experience, waking afresh, as

34

it were, for my second patient of the morning? Try as I might I could not answer these questions, and nothing would counter the impulse to doze off. However, I found that if I kept these questions in mind when I next saw the patient they could be incorporated into the work, thus bringing into play a countertransference component that was unavailable in the earlier phase.

Although his attendance was sporadic and unreliable, work incorporating the above countertransference manifestations was nonetheless sufficient to move things on, leading to a period of punctilious attendance lasting some sixteen months. This allowed deeper aspects of his pathology to be touched, bringing paranoid anxieties connected with separation directly to the fore. Towards the end of this period his dreams indicated a subtle moving on from his paranoid preoccupations. For example:

> *He seems to have been away from home and is struggling to find his way back. He stumbles into a garden, which turns out to be that of his parents' home. At the far end he can make out a gathering of people, like a garden party, with his parents as hosts. He wonders what he has been missing out on whilst away, but just then he encounters a bouncer with whom he deliberately picks a fight. He goads the bouncer so that the fight goes on and on, and though he's much the smaller of the two and gets hurt, he knows that in the end the bouncer will end up in trouble for attacking the host's son*

This was the first time in the analysis that the parents were represented as an ordinary (rather than grotesque and awful) couple, and the dream ushered in a renewed period of sustained absences from sessions, following much the same pattern as before.

The provocation in the dream was defensive against thinking, and it was clear that his absence from sessions was intended to provoke in quite the same way. But by now I had established a rhythm of being there well before the start of his sessions, and I found the period of dozing off had passed. The patient himself was also a little more considerate in that he informed me when he would not be coming (mostly through messages left in the middle of the night).

Being fully awake for these sessions I now became more ambitious – might I be able to put the time to constructive work? Routine work – reading circulars, magazines, newsletters, sometimes journal articles, administrative work, meddling with bits of computer programmes that I had not come to grips with etc – seemed possible, but truly creative work not. Whenever I wanted to work on a paper – either through preparatory reading, or actual writing and editing – I could make no headway. For

35

months and months I agonised over this, berating myself that I had not allowed myself to be properly helped by my own analysis, hence I could not now use the gift of prime early morning time constructively. I became more and more despondent. Eventually, one evening, an obvious observation occurred to me: that I felt guilty at how much time I 'waste' on mindless routine things. I could now see that the patient was using his absence to rid himself of unbearable guilt for the many years that he devoted to picking fights with his parents as a way of nursing a grievance against them. The dream brought him to the verge of insight into this: *what has he been missing out on while away?*, but this threatened him with unbearable guilt at the thought of all the wasted years. With the help of my own countertransference feeling of guilt, I could now see the wasted sessions as mindless repetition whose purpose was twofold: to pick little fights over missed sessions; and to re-enact the waste (by now wasting sessions), thus bypassing unbearable guilt.

In this brief contribution I have suggested that the patient's absence is an attack on our very real commitment to the analysis – a narcissistic blow that inevitably takes its toll. Insight into our vulnerability is an important first step in fortifying ourselves to ensure the survival of the setting. Once that has been achieved we are ready for the much more complex task of allowing ourselves countertransference responses and observing them. I hope I have showed that these are yielded up in their own form, at their own time, and in a process that can involve real, difficult and painful internal struggle on our part.

When Hope Goes Wrong   Susie Orbach *(London)*

*I'm introduced to a lively and engaging woman at a party. On hearing my
name, she says,"Oh, yes, I know you, you saw my friend Janine for
several years. I feel so sad about Janine" she says with a question in her
eyes.*
*"'I don't really understand why she can't get her life together. She's
lovely and pretty and very bright and, her family seem really good too"*

*I felt my body chill. I wondered what she knew. How good a friend was
she. How much had Janine shared with her about an ultimately
disappointing therapy.*

It is in the nature of our work to disappoint. The patient comes
expecting, if not **the** answer to their life, then answers for **a way to live
their life**. We offer them instead of answers, a relationship within which
they explore what impedes them and through that therapy relationship we
hope for the process of transformation. Of course, what we know and
what they may not know (when they enter therapy and analysis), is that
the things that perplex or impale them, the symptoms or traumas or
situations of pain from which they can neither engage or get beyond
invoke processes in the therapy that will end up helping them reposition
themselves vis a vis themselves. They will deconstruct aspects of their
defence structure and the shape of their inner object world so that they are
psychically equipped to handle what has been so difficult in new ways. In
this form of disappointment we suffer no pain, for we believe ourselves to
be providing something richer and more transformative.

But what about when we really disappoint the patient and ourselves?
What happens when we offer something less rather than something more.
What happens when what we offer appears as temptingly out of reach,
seductive, ungettable to? What happens when we come to a sense that the
therapeutic work is not only **not** productive but may be counter-
productive? And what are we as clinicians left with when we recommend
the ending of a therapy we feel is unhelpful.

It's easy enough to provide theoretical answers to a therapy that
doesn't work. We may see the difficulties of the patient as having
occurred so early and so consistently, the mismatching or the neglect
within the early parenting baby couple so extreme, or the inconsistency of
the parenting and the defences the patient has built up as so successful that
the patient's use of the therapy can only be limited. However, theorising
the reasons for therapeutic failure and working through the distress this
causes to a patient doesn't alleviate us of the terribly painful feelings

which can come up for us between sessions, outside sessions or when assessing new patients.

The relief a therapist can feel when such a therapy is terminated can, of course, be considerable. One no longer has to confront daily one's sense of failure, of not making the right kind of difference. One no longer has to confront daily the despair, the anger or the upset that occurs. One no longer has to confront daily, the piercing of personal grandiosity or guilt. But while being able to leave such feelings behind is welcome, there are a set of difficult and uneasy feelings we are vulnerable to when a therapy ends.

As I stood at this party thinking of a way to extricate myself from a conversation with Janine's friend, I was acutely in touch with great feelings of sadness about the experience with Janine. Why, I felt once again, was I not able to reach her? What were the clues I had missed in the first year or so that therapy might not turn out to be useful for her? How much did an unsuccessful therapy contribute to damaging her hope further?

In writing about Belle in *The Impossibility of Sex* I tried to explore the impact of therapeutic failure on an imaginary therapist[1]. Here I want to address the really quite different feelings that can exist for the therapist when the therapist precipitates an ending[2].

Perhaps what we have to take on and have to accept when we do this work is that when we fail (as we are bound to) and when we have gone beyond the blow to our sense of self, our narcissism and grandiosity, we've looked at how hard it is to be wrong, the taking responsibility for the therapy not working can leave us with a scar of shame and hurt. No amount of analysing it away takes away from the feelings.

My brief conversation with Janine's friend was uncomfortable because it dipped me into the shameful and perplexing feelings that I was left with. During the therapy with her friend, I had often felt great feelings of being iced out in the countertransference. There were plausible reasons to do

---

[1] The fact that I am writing again about this, tells me that how difficult this issue is to cope with if we don't resort to a strategy of blaming the patient for our inability to help them.

[2] This is different from when a patient initiates an ending or a therapist takes up the opportunity to make an ending when a patient is unsure on whether or not to continue or not or when a patient 'sacks' their therapist by not showing or with a Dear John letter.

38

with her very early history which made sense of this. She had been left at six weeks with strangers when her parents went travelling and throughout her childhood, her attachments were threatened in one way and another. She developed a way of being that appeared self sufficient but unlike many women whose defences against dependency[3] are extremely overdeveloped, she froze rather than being able to explore emotional contact when it was on offer.

The shame and the hurt I experienced in the countertransference are the uncomfortable feelings that were restimulated in me by Janine's comment about her friend. Of course I can explain the feelings by reference to my ex-patients mental state. She felt shame that she was insufficiently loveable not to be disregarded and left. She felt shame that her mother was unable to give her a sense that she was valued and wanted. She felt shame that she was unable to access a relationship with me that could do more than simply reiterate what she had always felt. And I of course felt shame that I was unable to reverse any of this, that I had re-enacted without then moving on to transforming this experience for her.

There are no consolations for experiences such as these. There is no way, I believe, to dismiss them or move beyond them. Such an experience doesn't seem to modify over time. That's not to say it is always with me, but when it is stimulated, the hurt, sadness and shame aroused seem just as acute.

Perhaps this is our cross to bear. This is the price of being a therapist who sees people in extreme difficulty, some of whom are able to use the therapy relationship and some who aren't. Often we have profoundly moving and gratifying experiences in our work. We feel privileged and lucky to have turned lives that have felt unliveable into lives that are generative and satisfying. But it ain't always so. If we don't blame the latter group for their failure, if we don't use the failure as either their responsibility or ours but we maintain it as just what happened, if we move into a kind of depressive position vis a vis our own disappointment, shame and hurt about the experience, then we are bound to be left with this rather undigestible sadness and we are going to be confronted by the sorrows that accompany 'failure' on the job.

---

[3] See *Understanding Women: A Feminist psychoanalytic Approach* Luise Eichenbaum and Susie Orbach 1982, Penguin, Harmondsworth.

Travelling patient, mobile therapist

Sudhir Kakar   *(New Delhi)*

In the last couple of decades, the faster pace of globalization in India (as also in other countries) has been accompanied by an increasing mobility among many professionals who move easily and frequently between different countries. These are not migrants but persons who are away from the home country on more or less temporary work assignments. They often return home on vacations. Some of these are patients I work with in psychoanalytic psychotherapy. And since I, too, am sometimes away from Delhi (where I practice) on visiting professorships in Europe and USA, my mobile patients and their non-sedentary therapist look back in wonderment at the times when the outer framework of psychotherapy was fixed and unchanging. Day after day, month after month, year after year, the patient came to the same place, at the same time and where even the breaks in treatment—the therapist's vacations—were completely predictable.

My dilemma, then, was to deal with situations where the therapeutic contact with a patient is intermittent but not broken. A couple of years back, one patient who was going away from Delhi asked, 'Why don't you try it? What do you have to lose?' With some trepidation, eyes lowered in embarrassment at the vision of psychoanalytic pioneers who not only saw their patients almost every day of the week but even took them along on their vacations, I agreed. And I have not regretted it.

I am talking here of continuing the psychotherapeutic contact over the Internet at pre-arranged times, twice or thrice a week. This is not therapy by e-mail but 'talk' through cyberspace even if the 'talk' is typed rather than spoken. At the moment, I have five patients of this kind; two in different parts of India, one in the USA, one in Malaysia and one in France. The therapy is not exclusively over the Internet but is interspersed with face to face sessions whenever their travels (and mine) bring us together for a while—which is at least two to three times a year over a week each time.

Before giving my preliminary reactions to this kind of therapeutic contact, let me briefly mention the mechanics of the sessions. The time and the day of the week for each session is predetermined. During the 'chat' (an unfortunate Internet term for talking on the web), whenever the patient expects a response from me, he/she types a question mark at the end of the sentence (otherwise we'd be interrupting each other all the time). The patient also regularly reports on the feelings he/she is experiencing. Any dream to be discussed is sent earlier by email and is before us on the screen as we try to make sense of it during the session.

In this short communication, I do not intend to enumerate all the shortcomings of this kind of psychotherapeutic encounter, as compared to the 'real stuff'. I was as dismissive of this enterprise when it was first suggested to me first, as I am sure, many of my colleagues continue to be even while they read these lines. It is not my intention to suggest that therapy of this kind can ever replace the intimacy of the personal encounter in the normal therapeutic setting. I only submit that when maintaining such a therapeutic contact becomes dictated by necessity, it can be a surprisingly satisfactory substitute for what cannot be really replaced. My observations on my experience with therapy using the Internet do not constitute its advocacy but are offered as helpful hints for colleagues who may be forced by circumstances to take the same route and continue a therapy 'by other means.'

I found that carrying on therapy through the Internet is at its most effective with patients who have been in normal psychotherapy for only a short time, that is, less than thirty to forty sessions. Generally, at the beginning, the patient's sensitivity to the physical presence of the therapist as also to the prosodic aspects of his words—tone, accent, pauses, silences, intonation, is not highly developed. This also holds true for the patient's sensitivity to the visual aspects of a face-to-face therapy, that is, to the therapist's involuntary gestures, facial mimicry, positions of body or the expression in his eyes. The patient's initial emphasis on words as a means of communication is well suited for the Internet therapy where words are the sole means of communication. I also found that some patients are able to manifest, recognize and articulate their erotic transference towards the therapist faster over the Internet, with its illusion of distance and hence safety, than in the much more intimate setting of normal psychotherapy. In fact, one of my patients who had begun to send and discuss erotic dreams involving me over the internet, temporarily stopped dreaming altogether when we met again for a couple of weeks of face to face sessions.

My second experience of this type of therapy is the fact that it forces the therapist to become more active, in the sense of having to give frequent interpretations. The maintenance of the therapeutic alliance over the Internet needs more words from the therapist. The therapist's typed 'hmm-m' after a patient's typed question mark expecting a response does not seem as appropriate as it does when the 'hmm-m' of acknowledgement is uttered from sitting on a chair behind the couch or in

41

front of the patient. And there is a limit to how many times the therapist can type 'Go on' in response to insistent question marks.

Perhaps a distinct advantage of the Internet session is that one is able to 'save' the session by a click of the mouse and have its word by word protocol available for leisurely perusal and study. This particular feature is a mixed blessing. On the one hand, besides being invaluable aide-de-memoirs, the session protocols can help improve the style of a therapist's interventions. They are like the video feedback people use to improve their public speaking skills, where they can immediately see the mistakes they have made and confront the bad habits they have acquired over the years in the use of language. On the other hand, the existence of such detailed protocols can lead to some loss of spontaneity on part of the therapist. As a document which at least in fantasy is potentially accessible to others (especially colleagues), the therapist may feel an unconscious demand to take more than the required care in formulating his interpretations over the Internet.

I hope that these introductory remarks have intrigued as many colleagues on the possibilities of using the Internet (when it becomes necessary to do so) as they have confirmed others in their conviction to never move away from the 'purity' of the traditional setting. To the former, I can only repeat the words of my patient, 'Why don't you try it? What do you have to lose?'

"Rubber Banded Together"
A countertransferential collusion or the need for accuracy in the assessment of a rubber fetishist patient?

Estela Welldon *(London)*

A number of years ago, thirty to be precise, I began to work at the Portman Clinic, a London-based outpatient facility for the psychotherapeutic treatment of social and sexual deviants. This followed a long period of working in therapeutic communities with patients with delinquent and criminal problems. The prevailing and most important working philosophy in these communities was the provision of democracy to the extent that both patients and staff appear to the outside people to be the same. This free expression of feelings including anger and irritation coupled with the fact that both staff and patients called each other by their first names, and all wore casual clothing. Hence, I was pleasantly surprised, in my new job, to find myself surrounded by well-dressed psychoanalysts, who were extremely polite, even addressing each other in most formal ways. This was a far cry from my previous jobs where much confusion and frequent embarrassment amongst visitors were the rule.

At the Portman I began to learn of the subtleties involving transferential and countertransferential processes which include the patients' need for control, their apparent jocular attitude which effectively covers distress and isolation; their attempts to seduce the therapist into collusion and unconscious participation in their delinquent behaviour.
I shall always be grateful to our senior colleagues, the 'oldies and goldies' who enabled their juniors to deal competently with those difficult predicaments. However, occasionally I was also glad to have evidence of their being able to make mistakes too! Shortly after my arrival at the Portman, and anxious to have as many difficult patients as possible, I was allocated a young, attractive, recently married man with a bizarre sexual perversion. This, he told me, involved the use of very complicated rubber gear all over his body, including head and limbs with the aim of producing an almost total sensory deprivation, at which point, uncertain at his own survival, he would reach orgasm. If anything went wrong he would face death. I met this therapeutic challenge with some fear and trepidation but also with wanting to know more. I was painfully aware that my knowledge of the subject was scarce and inadequate. In search for more information, I was daring and not very cautious. Hence, I decided on a Saturday morning while doing my weekly grocery shopping in Soho, to enter a so called 'sex shop' where I could learn more about the quality of my patient's desired rubber. To my bewilderment I found out that the rubber, till then, assumed by me to be of the kind used for underwater

43

sports; was actually quite different. It was as thin as a second skin to be used over the body. This new knowledge gave me an unexpected but immediate access to meanings and symbolisms to which I had been previously blind. Indeed, I became aware that my patient, despite his apparent success and well-being, was in need for a second skin to be used not only as a protection against all possibilities for pain but also as a container for much anguish and anxiety of paramount proportions. I was overjoyed that my new discovery would be used effectively in the service of a more thorough understanding of the real nature of his problems.

However, there were other unsuspected problems to be faced that Friday morning when presenting my patient in the clinical seminar to the rest of the staff. In doing so, I explained my sense of inadequacy in understanding my new patient's predicament. Furthermore, I added that my zeal in comprehending it all, had taking me to visit the sex shop. This was not kindly taken. Indeed, the opposite happened. Suddenly my seniors were up in arms alarmed at my alleged collusion and 'partnership' with my patient's perversion. I felt humiliated and misunderstood. I was immediately overtaken by speculative 'interpretations' from my older colleagues about my countertransference reaction in being 'seduced' by my patient. I was infuriated and found this very difficult to take.

I got a sudden inspiration and presented a challenge back to them. If any of them knew the exact nature of the rubber employed for this man's perversion, I would accept without hesitation their interpretations of my own 'acting out'. However, if nobody could offer an adequate description of the quality of the rubber, their 'judgement' of the situation had to be reviewed, since my 'detour' in Soho would be considered of a scientific nature and not an acting out. This was eventually accepted with some reluctance. To my relief and delight a description of the thick rubber used for underwater protection was offered. I was now able to explain what the rubber was really like and we all were able to participate in a rich exchange of ideas. Anyway, it was a narrow escape. So much for the rough learning of the implications of transference and counter transference in working with the perverse patient.

SEEING, SITTING & SETTING:

… I know that Prof. Dr. Sigmund Freud will open the door which faces me […] I was to greet the Old Man of the Sea, but no one had told me of the treasures he had salvaged from the sea-depth… He is the infinitely old symbol, weighing the soul, Psyche, in the Balance. Does the Soul, passing the portals of life, entering the House of Eternity, greet the Keeper of the Door? It seems so. I should have thought the Door-Keeper, at home beyond the threshold, might have greeted the shivering soul. Not so, the Professor. But waiting and finding that I would not or could not speak, he uttered. What he said – and I thought a little sadly – was, 'You are the only person who has ever come into this room and looked at the things in the room before looking at me.'   [HD *Tribute to Freud*, McGraw-Hill 1956, pp.96-8]*

The Master H.D.

He was very beautiful,
the old man…
"every gesture is wisdom"
he taught;
"nothing is lost,"
he said; [I]

I was angry with the old man
I wanted an answer
a neat answer,
when I argued and said, "well tell me,
you will soon be dead,
the secret lies with you,"
he said
"you are a poet"; [IV]

So I went forth
blinded a little with the sort of
terrible tears /that won't fall;
I said good-bye
and saw his old head
as he turned,
as he left the room
leaving me alone
with all his old trophies,
the marbles, the vases,
the stone Sphinx,
the old, old jars from Egypt;
He left me alone with these things
and his old back was bowed [IX]
[H.D. *Feminist Studies*, 1981 7:3]

The American poet Hilda Doolittle was analysed by Freud during the hazardous period of 1933-4. Forming a friendship that lasted until his death, she sent gardenias to welcome the safe arrival of his 'gods' in London. In 1944, H.D. published a 'Tribute to Freud'. Reviewing it Ernest Jones called her 'a poet of rare delicacy and distinction', saying: 'The book, with its appropriate title, is surely the most delightful and precious appreciation of Freud's personality that is ever likely to be written. Only a fine creative artist could have written it. It is like a lovely flower, and the crude pen of a scientist hesitates to profane it by attempting to describe it. I can only say that I envy anyone who has not yet read it, and that it will live as the most enchanting ornament of all the Freudian biographical literature'. [International Journal of Psycho-Analysis 38:126]

Freud and his Chair in Maresfield Gardens
[Freud Museum, London]

Freud's Chair   Ivan Ward *(London)*

As Educational Officer I am made aware of deep seated feelings and resistances aroused in visitors to Freud's house. Reactions to his curiously shaped desk chair are a case in point. The chair was probably given to him in 1930 by his eldest daughter Mathilde. Designed by Felix Augenfeld, a friend of Ernst Freud, it was apparently tailor-made to Freud's particular requirements. "She explained to me that S.F. had the habit of reading in a very peculiar and uncomfortable body position. He was leaning in this chair, in some sort of diagonal position, one of his legs slung over the arm of the chair, the book held high and his head unsupported. The rather bizarre form of the chair I designed is to be explained as an attempt to maintain this habitual posture and to make it more comfortable" (Augenfeld-Lobner 8. 2. 1974)

What is represented as the inevitable outcome of an explicit design brief and the solving of 'technical' problems, can be seen from another perspective as a veil which allows aspects of the unconscious to come into play. In short, Augenfeld's reasoning is a rationalisation which does not do justice to the almost tangible sense we have that the object embodies meaning...

To most people the chair looks like a person, and one can assume that to Freud and Augenfeld too this resemblance did not go unnoticed. What, then, is described as a 'bizarre' object, resembles the most common and familiar object in the life of a human being. But if it is a person, then 'Who?'

One answer often mentioned by visitors to the museum, is Freud himself: an externalized 'alter ego' or intellectual travelling companion. A kind of internal sounding board for his ideas, or a critic with whom to debate and engage in dialogue. There are many echoes of such a function in Freud's writing - the 'impartial person' in *The Question of Lay Analysis* for instance - replacing real companions and critics with whom Freud once debated. As he withdrew more from the world in later life, through illness and perhaps his own inclinations, he conjured up the battle within himself. So the chair can represent another Freud, an alternative point of view, slightly askew from the original and embodying the friendly antagonist who seemed so important to Freud's early intellectual development (Wilhelm Fliess, Carl Jung etc).

Some visitors have pointed to another function. It may have helped in his therapeutic work. Listening to patients with 'evenly hovering attention' is complex and demanding. Trying not to prejudge the issues or jump in too early with thoughts and interpretations places great strain on the therapist. On one level it is like trying not to think. Some high school students visiting the museum suggested that the chair safely holds Freud's intellectual capacities while he sits in his green tub chair behind the couch, engaged in the more passive activity of therapeutic listening. Thus he is able to lose himself in his patient's world, and 'bend his unconscious like a receptive organ' to the unconscious of the other person. The chair then represents the 'critical researcher' part of himself that has to be temporarily abandoned or suspended in the therapeutic work of psychoanalysis.

Most often, however, visitors assert that the chair represents the mother. Behind every great man there is a woman, they say, and Freud was no doubt of a similar opinion. As his mother's favourite, Freud always felt he owed his own success in some measure to her love. That debt of gratitude is implied at the close of Freud's brief essay *'A Childhood Recollection from Dichtung und Wahrheit'* (1917): '...if a man has been his mother's undisputed darling he retains throughout life the triumphant feeling, the confidence in success, which not seldom brings actual success along with it. And Goethe might well have given some such heading to his autobiography as 'My strength has its roots in my relation to my mother.' The chair, then, may represent the basic grounding and sense of security found in a mother's love. The arms of the andromorphic chair encircle the sitter and hold him safely. The seat supports him and provides a firm basis from which to venture out to explore new horizons, like a toddler venturing forth in the playground. Freud's adventures were in his mind. He devours his books, chews over ideas and has a thirst for knowledge as a metaphorical echo of the early feeding relationship. Yet were we to consider the matter as Freud did, we would look for the conflict. The arms that encircle can also smother; the seat that supports can immobilize; the debt that is owed eventually must be paid. Thus we find Freud's admission of his ambivalence to his mother which is perhaps inescapable for any man. On the one hand there is the filial piety of his weekly Sunday visits; on the other hand Freud expresses his feeling that her death aged 95 brought him an increase in personal freedom. The recognition of such ambivalence was not always clear in Freud's writing. Often he seemed to idealise the maternal relation as a 'pure' and conflict-free sphere. At other times (in *'The theme of the three Caskets'*, *'Leonardo'* etc) he fully recognised the destructive and perverse potential in the maternal relation.

Thus we can picture the baby Sigmund in the lap of his mother, one leg draped over her arm, his head thrown back, his elbows jutted out in the posture of his peculiar reading position, trying to escape... from an embrace he desires.

But perhaps he is not so much on as in. A visiting student once had the uncanny feeling that the chair was the inside of the mother's body, and this seemingly unlikely train of thought can be pursued with reference to Freud's work. If the chair is an index of Freud's intellectual creativity, it is precisely a concern with the insides of the mother's body to which Freud ascribes that capacity. In his essay 'The Sexual Theories of Children' Freud attributed the first philosophical investigations of the child - where do I come from? who am I? what do I know? - to the traumatic arrival of another baby; that is to say, the externalised contents of the mother's body. The child is not a 'born philosopher' in Freud's view, but prompted to his investigations by the potential threat of a rival for the mother's affections. Freud's essay on Goethe, quoted above, in fact describes a story of three year old Goethe throwing plates out of the window on the birth of a sibling. Freud says that the crockery represents babies which Goethe is trying to eliminate from the home/womb. Similarly Freud eliminates all rivals from his maternal space and occupies the chair alone in his thinking - just as he leaves no room for other people's books on the crowded surface of his desk.

An alter ego, a container of a split-off thinking part of the self, a maternal support, a womb. The chair can have many meanings for which we can find evidence in Freud's writing, in cultural history and in our own experience. Another possibility which many visitors have raised is the chair as the father. Some say it is shaped like a phallus. If we continue with our assumption that the chair is instrumental in Freud's scientific writing - the difficult process by which thoughts are conceived, given birth to and externalized on the page - then we can expect a paternal function to play a pivotal or seminal role. Knowledge is traditionally handed down from father to son - women's knowledge has been devalued in the history of human culture - and in many cultures is held sacred and secret. Just as Freud's father presented him with the family bible as a rite de passage for his coming into adulthood, so the ritual transmission of knowledge has often been associated with the entry into manhood. The secret knowledge is regarded as dangerous and surrounded with taboos. In 'ahistorical' societies it may involve the killing of totem animals, or the wearing of animal skins. The metaphor of insemination may be concretely enacted in ritual, just as it was in the Gymnasium of ancient Greece.

There is always a tension involved for both fathers and sons; fathers want to maintain control over the sons, but for the culture to continue they have to pass on the secret knowledge. Sons want access to the source of male potency, but they also want to escape from the shadow of the fathers. Fundamental issues of identity are at stake - being the same or being

49

different; following tradition or going further - which find expression in both the pleasures and the difficulties of creative thinking and writing (see Ron Britton 'Making the Private Public' in *The Presentation of Case Material in Clinical Discourse* (1997): also Freud *A disturbance of memory on the Acropolis* (1936)

Having spotted the possibilities of maternal and paternal symbolism, the next (and final?) logical step is seldom taken by visitors. Why not mother AND father? If any creative process requires two things to come together in the mind, perhaps this coming together is modelled, as Bion suggested, on the primitive phantasies of the mother and father in sexual union. In this interpretation, Freud becomes the conduit for a creative process going on 'outside himself'. Touched by genius, and touching us, it is fitting perhaps that this process may have been as unknown to him as to the many visitors who contemplate this 'bizarre' object today.

If these interpretations seem far-fetched let us remember that when we recognize Freud's chair as a person', most chairs, including our own, have 'backs', 'legs' and 'arms' and, metaphorically at least, are associated with the human body. Moreover, throughout history, chairs - thrones of kings and the seats of learning etc. - have been imbued with ritual significance and power.

L'eclipse Virginia Margerison
[Courtsey of E.Stina Lyon]

Several years ago, a friend of mine bought a portrait of Freud and hung it in his study. 'What do you think,' he said, in a proud voice that also sought support for spending money on an indulgence? 'That'll keep you honest', I quipped.

The memory of that brief moment drifted back as I thought about Freud's eyes, while perusing an interesting collection of reminiscences of Freud, gathered by Hendrik Ruitenbeek (1973)[i]. Many reported their impressions of Freud upon first meeting him, and in particular noted his eyes. 'His most striking feature ... was the forward thrust of his head and critical exploring gaze of his keenly piercing eyes,' said Joan Riviere. 'The half-peering and half-piercing gaze beneath the heavy brows showed a power to see beneath the surface and beyond the boundaries of ordinary perceptions' (pp. 129, 130). '[H]is steady and keen eye seemed to miss nothing' (Martin Peck, p. 186). 'His dark, brilliant eyes penetrate beyond your mortal flesh' (Maryse Choisy, p. 292).

These observations focus upon Freud's penetrating gaze, as if he were looking inside one's protective skin, seeing to the heart of oneself. But people also looked into him. There they found humanity, utter seriousness and truthfulness. 'I was struck by his general simplicity, and above all, by the seriousness of his look, which I found more brooding than penetrating' (Emil Ludwig, p. 213). 'Yet his face [despite his struggles with age, disease and pain] retained the expression of strength, clarity and truthfulness' (Paul Federn, p. 217. 'I looked into his warm and expressful eyes, and felt as if a hand had touched my head – the pain had disappeared' (Bruno Goetz, p. 266). 'Behind rather thick spectacles were eyes that were magnetic and gave a reassuring feeling of great kindliness' (Roy Grinker, p. 181). 'His penetrating attentive eyes had not only the simplicity and innocent clear-sightedness of a child – one for whom nothing is too small, and nothing either common or unclean – there was also in them a mature patience and caution, and a detached inquiry' (Joan Riviere, p. 130).

Many of these accounts were reminiscences from a long time after meeting Freud. The question they raise, therefore, is not whether they give an accurate account of Freud's physiognomy. Nor is it whether Freud's eyes penetrated the shell of ordinary life with which we surround ourselves. The question is how we see ourselves.

---

[i] All references with the exception of Freud, are from this book

This question is akin to the self-reflection that one might pursue in prayer, in portrait painting, in philosophy, in writing, yet it is radically different. It is different because the axis around which one turns back to oneself is another person. The reminiscences of meeting Freud, softened over time, were self-reflections, but from the vantage of Freud's eyes.

One can imagine that these self-reflections were compounded with fantasies about Freud himself, and also judgements. What kind of a man looks in this way? 'I was always intrigued, when looking at his picture, by his dark, penetrating eyes, and wished for a long time to visit this strange man' (Emil Ludwig, p. 213). And this wish to look into the one who looks into oneself extends to the phenomenon of a psychoanalytically informed culture. 'His familiar picture as the sage of Vienna, sitting seriously and in somewhat Olympian fashion behind his desk, peering at us with searching and critical eyes, hides as much as it reveals of the phenomenon Freud, that largely transformed and created today's world' (Frederick Hacker, p. 325).

We are led to ask, how do we see ourselves in the eyes of someone who is devoted to seeing clearly but without moralism? Indeed, what kind of morality might develop in a culture in which one could see clearly without moralism? What kind of self-awareness might develop in a culture in which self-awareness is valued in itself, in which inwardness is for oneself, rather than appropriated for tyrannical purposes? How do we see ourselves in a culture that has been permeated by psychoanalysis?
What comes across about Freud from these various reports are utter seriousness, inquisitiveness, kindliness and a well-tempered durability in the face of adversity. And if these virtues seem to be contradicted by an authoritarian streak and a single-minded defence of psychoanalysis, then it remains significant that a wish for such virtues was concentrated into looking at this man. It also highlights a curious feature of the psychoanalytic process. There are two moments when the setting – the use of the couch – makes analyst and patient available for looking: the beginning and the end of the session. The rest of the time, looking is pure fantasy. Just as the visitors to the creator of the talking cure made a point of describing how he looked – I intend the ambiguity – so too does the psychoanalytic patient attend to how the analyst looks. And just as Freud's visitors felt seriously, deeply, patiently, innocently, inquisitively – but also overwhelmingly – looked into, so the psychoanalytic patient is, in fantasy, held transiently, at the moment of meeting and of separating, in the glance of the analyst, as an exemplar both of a new morality and a powerful force that might undermine the very sense of self.

Vision is the most representational or objectifying sense, a distancing sense that confirms our conviction that the world is made up of objects out there. And yet it also works as a vehicle for projection and projective identification, in which looking puts the looker inside the looked-at. The moment of looking is therefore likely to undermine objectivity by confusing looker and looked-at. Freud's visitors were presumably intensely curious about him, perhaps to get to the root of this thing called psychoanalysis, but experienced their intense Inquisitiveness as Freud's dark penetrating eyes, boring into them.

How often do the initial and the final glances set fantasies going, which are buried in the first words or lost into the outside after the end of the session? Curiously, the fact that the 50 minutes in between these two glances are without looking intensifies the fantasies of looking. In ordinary social situations, looking around can bind the looked-at other into the everyday world, just by moving the glance around and thereby associating objects with each other. But in the analytic session, the first looked-at other immediately withdraws from view and cannot be associated with the everyday world by linking one looked-at object with another.

We could follow this line in many directions, tracing what is done to this first looked-at object. I want to refer to just two. Firstly, for some patients, the confusion has been achieved by the time the session begins. The first speaking is then from the narcissistic posture of having appropriated the analytic space. Secondly, they begin the session on the basis of a theft by their penetrating eyes, and therefore an inability to make use of a session without extreme anxiety. Self-reflection through the axis of the analytic other is therefore concentrated into both an inquiry and an inquisition.

In his obituary of Charcot, Freud said that 'he was, as he himself said, a *"visuel"*, a man who sees' (Freud, 1893, p. 12). In replacing Charcot's hypnosis by following the patient's free associations, Freud moved analyst and patient away from seeing to speaking and listening. Yet, uncannily, he may have accentuated a primitive visual transference, in which the innards of the patient have been occupied by the eyes of the analyst – eyes that are, in turn, projections of the eyes of the patient. This visual transference concentrates self-reflection (a visual image). It becomes, not only a method of inquiry, but also an instantiation of the self-reflection of its culture, informing objectivity, representation, conscience and morality.

References

Freud, S. (1893) *'Charcot'*, S.E. 3:9–23.
Ruitenbeek, H. (ed.) (1973), *Freud as We Knew Him*. Detroit: Wayne State University Press.

The embodied analytic couple (An interactive space)
Alcira Mariam Alizade *(Buenos Aires)*

This writing is just a game, a kind of play across words in order to try to express the universe of gestures and actions that take place in and between the sessions, behind and beyond the couch.

No analytic rule, no strict analytical setting can avoid the primary natural fact of the crucial experience of the encounter of two human beings bearing each one a body. These bodies speak their own peculiar language and send their own messages. The presence of the participants open up a wide field of unknown and invisible events in the midst of analytic rules and beliefs.

Let´s have a look at those unavoidable events that develop in a session. Expressions, gestures, movements. Projections or realities? Impossible not to move, to make some noise, to sneeze , to laugh, even to stand up ... A patient imagined I had a small house behind the couch where I made myself comfortable while I analysed.

The office has an atmosphere, a kind of inorganic body. It may be luxurious but poor at the same time or unexpectedly uninteresting. Sometimes splendorous, iluminated by an inner sun. The space is inhabited by the analyst´s soul and also by the invisible presence of the different patients that visit it daily. By analyst´s soul I mean the energy, the capacity of empathizing, inner strenght and personal qualities. Sensuality spreads in the analytic room. The voices touch both the patient and the analyst, corporal exchanges run through the analytic space. The patient goes to the restroom, he-she stands up and keeps on talking while walking. The couch stays temporarily empty and the analyst waits. Mind

The private phone suddenly interrupts the session... a third person enters suddenly... the patient is sorry about this unexpected call... or explains how important it was to get the message... he forgot to turn the phone off. Impossible to get healed through bodily inhibition... the hands move around while telling a dream ... the hands draw images in the air... an outburst of anxiety... the heart beats quicker or, why not, an outburst of laugh. The uncounscious is there, within the walls that surround the dyadic couple Neurosis walks in and forth,

One patient listens and talks of the perfumes of the ambiance... she is highly perfume-oriented. Smells and perfumes evoke remembrances and feelings. Particularly when she enters into the office. Another patient is

55

sitting in front of me. No couch during this period of her treatment. She loves shoes and always makes comments on mine. She looks around the office looking for changes, her mind and her body work close to freedom, she is almost healed.

Each encounter becomes a creative art piece. Sometimes the analytic atmosphere stays rigid, nobody moves, nobody talks, merely quite silence. The analyst behind the couch searches for a strategy or just encourages calm to develop out of the reign of words. The analyst conquers once more its own territory...the inner setting becomes the most important element of the analytic process. *Behind and beyond the couch* we find people passionately playing and struggling in order to accomplish healthy inner movements.

Beyond the Couch – not a body of thought

Sharon Stekelman *(London)*

I'm always amazed when I'm told that that this or that analyst works ten or more hours a day – largely seeing patients.
Firstly - I wonder why. Financial reasons must play a part, but what more? Secondly, I wonder how. This is because I find seeing patients intensely interesting and absorbing, but also immensely demanding on my own emotional and intellectual resources.

The hovering attention and the necessity to allow ones mind to roam and to be pulled back, the need to hold action and reaction are all part and parcel of work of a very particular kind. I know that I need to vary this experience with other quite removed activities so I have a life beyond analysis, which I also think influences the way I work and I think keeps me in better shape mentally and physically. Back to the 'why'. Why do we become analysts?

There must be a whole range of reasons – both positive and negative - curiosity, power, the need to relate to others – again for a variety of reasons, some negative and others more positive. But maybe ultimately to know ourselves better and to know ourselves in many and varied relationships so we may find the feminine/masculine, child/adult, sane/psychotic facets of our own nature.

All of this exploration is continuous, but there is also a need to stay in touch with the world outside and around the consulting room, which is where our patients spend a great deal of their lives. So I shop, use public transport, go to the cinema and theatre as no doubt many colleagues do. In addition I dance, walk, play badminton, paint and enjoy a more complete body-mind experience. Part of knowing oneself is in knowing ones own physical self, reading the signs from ones body and being in tune with it ('the first ego is first and foremost a body ego'). This is an area that analysts do not write much about, but I suspect that we are informed in our countertransference responses by physical sensations as well as by the images and phantasies that are stirred up by patients.

Seriousness and Humour

Psychoanalysis is a serious subject. Humour may evoke laughter, but this thinly conceals an underlying seriousness. Moreover, the very mechanism whereby a serious matter is hidden, denied or trivialised may be regarded as an important motive of humour. This is because humour offers the opportunity and permission for the ridicule of such serious matters as religion, death, sexuality, aggression, politics, racism, illness etc., not simply philosophically, but with laughter. For instance, an otherwise solemn or sacred subject is made the subject of derision and this attracts, indeed culturally permits, laughter.

In *Jokes and their Relation to the Unconscious*, Freud (1905) referred to "the gift of humour" but he also noted that humour and jokes may frequently be offensive or threatening because of the way serious matters are blatantly disrespected. When it comes to psychoanalytic technique, analysts, with some justification, have regarded humour with suspicion, since the line between use and abuse is narrow. Kubie (1971) warns against bantering or belittling humour, hostile, defensive or distracting humour, humour that makes it difficult for the patient to believe that the analyst is serious, and especially humour aimed at drawing the patient's attention to the analyst's humourous facility. These are all counter-therapeutic techniques and as such are abuses of humour.

On the other hand, the total absence of humour, or an analyst who cannot laugh spontaneously at certain moments during a treatment, might have an adverse effect. A humourous intervention may be constructive and liberating if the comment approximates an interpretation, especially a transference interpretation, but without the humour reducing its impact. For such an interpretation to be effective, the analyst/patient relationship must be of excellent quality. However, even those analysts who regard humour as potentially helpful or facilitating rightly recommend its use only sparingly.

The British comedian Ken Dodd was perceptive of Freud's contribution when in a much-lauded quotation he brought together humour and seriousness. Reflecting on the difficulties endured by a stand-up comic in the days of Music Hall, he said, "Freud's theory was that when a joke opens a window and all those bats and bogey men fly out, you get a marvellous feeling of relief and elation. The trouble with Freud is that he never had to play the old Glasgow Empire on a wet Saturday night after Rangers and Celtic had both lost".

It is unlikely that Dodd was aware of the problem of the use and abuse of humour in the psychoanalytic situation. Yet, he put his finger on the essence of the difficulty in recognizing that there is a special moment when a well-timed joke could bring relief and elation. However, on that rainy night in Glasgow facing a depressed and angry audience, that moment was not available. The psychoanalyst's interpretation is subject to the same conditions when offered to a patient, so depressed and angry that even a hint of levity may be experienced as traumatic.

More specifically, the taboos of sexuality are often bypassed in jokes by setting them in other generations. Here are a pair of contrasting anecdotes which when placed under analytic scrutiny reveal and confirm an important unconscious source common to both:

The first is... *"the story of two elderly nursing home residents in adjoining wheelchairs. An old woman insisted that she could tell an old man's age despite his scepticism. She challenged him to let her prove her ability. When he finally agreed to let her try, she said she first had to hold his penis. After fondling it several minutes, she announced that the man was eighty-seven years old. Astonished by her accuracy, he asked how she could tell. "Easy," she answered, "you told me last week."*

The second is... *"A 5 year old boy says to his 3 year old sister, "I found a contraceptive on the veranda", to which his sister replies, "What's a veranda?"*

In order to be tolerated appreciated and understood, humorous anecdotes require the listener to have the capacity to be surprised. Reik (1935) postulated that surprise was the essential ingredient that made a psychoanalytic interpretation effective. He also drew attention to the role of surprise in wit. Reik's understanding of the parallel situations was as follows: the first response is one of shock (not necessarily in conscious awareness) which is quickly followed by release of affect (relief in analysis, laughter in wit). Certain patients anticipate every interpretation so as not to be surprised. Equally, there are people who anticipate every "punch" line, never allowing a response of uninhibited laughter. Both groups have vigorously reinforced their repression barriers, possibly because of narcissistic vulnerability but always at great personal cost.

In the veranda story, the initial shock (surprise) is due to an intensification of inhibition aimed at reinforcing repression (a little girl of 3 is not supposed to know about sex, let alone contraception), which is then released in the form of laughter. We laugh at the story because children *should not have reached* the stage of being wise to or excited by sexuality. We laugh at the "old-timers" story because they *should have long passed* that stage. These stories, originally presented for humorous purposes, had in common displacement of sexual activity to another generation: in the first to the younger generation, in the second to the older. We deny the danger by suggesting the joke be on the sexuality of another generation. The humour is thus legitimised.

Placing the stories side by side reveals a possible root of the displacement beyond that of merely shifting sexual activity from our own generation. The shift *of* generation reveals a concern *about* generations. At the shared root is the resistance we all have to being able to imagine *our parents* performing sexual intercourse. Thus the ingenuity of the old lady who finds a way to enact and enjoy what is plainly sexual, effectively breaches the repression barrier because the displacement away from the parents is on to the still less likely grandparents.

Alongside childhood concerns with the differences between the sexes and the riddle of where babies come from lies the common denial of the active sexuality of one's own parents. In contrast to the way that we would all like to keep our parents apart, in viewing these stories we benefit from bringing the separated pair together. However, the shift of setting to children and grandparents speaks to our anxieties over the sexuality of parents. Our analytic understanding of other serious life issues, such as religion, aggression, death and so on, may be equally enhanced by the application of that complex developmental achievement which we call humour.

References:

Baker, R.S. (1993) Some reflections on humour in psychoanalysis. *International Journal of Psychoanalysis*. 74:951-960.
Freud, S. (1905) *Jokes and Their Relation to the Unconscious*. S.E.8.
Kubie, L.S. (1971) The destructive potential of humor in psychotherapy. *American Journal of Psychiatry* 127:861-866.
Poland, W.S.(1990) The gift of laughter: on the development of a sense of humour in clinical analysis *Psychoanalytic Quarterly* 59:197-225.
Reik, T. (1935) *Surprise and the Psychoanalyst*. Kegan Paul, London.

Solitude in the Psychoanalytic Journey

Jhuma Basak *(Calcutta)*

In 1599, when the Elizabethan audience heard a raving soul in King Lear uttering - "Who is it that can tell me who I am?" - little did one know then that there would come a time about three hundred years after Shakespeare when evolution of a science will emerge in the history of mankind whose engagement, till to-day, comprise a study and understanding of this single statement made by a man on the verge of insanity leading to the hidden cave of the human mind. Therein lies the genesis of the psychoanalytic journey whose quest for the vision of truth is interminable and unquenchable. Perhaps there itself lies both the ecstasy and the agony of it. On one hand the sheer joy of discovering the mind's immeasurable nuances, conflictual desires, wealth of passions, while on the other comprehending for the first time to such depth that,

> *'Life's but a walking shadow, a poor player,*
> *That struts and frets his hour upon the stage,*
> *And then is heard no more; it is a tale*
> *Told by an idiot, full of sound and fury*
> *Signifying nothing.'*

The purpose of psychoanalytic exploration is precisely the significance within such 'nothing'. Through this journey a certain integration of psychic life is sought where the essence of solitude plays the part of an inevitable residual element of a mature ego. The constant and simultaneous play of both Eros and Thanatos in the analytic experience perhaps helps the ego to glance into the vicissitudes of life to gain enrichment and leaves it forever intoxicated with marvellous discoveries, at times frightening though often simply exuberant.

The essence of solitude is inherent in the psychoanalytic experience both for the analyst and the analysand. As Charles Hanly so rightly puts it, 'At the core of the being of each person there is a solitude in which he is related to himself. Truth resides in this solitude...The ground of genuine analytic work in the analyst is his attitude of respect for this solitude.' It is when these two cores of solitudes (of the analyst and the analysand) interact, respect and submit to each other that the process of real internalization sets in. The individual technique of the analyst determines how he guides his analysand along this path of solitude and reaches that 'core of the being'. However, in order to really enjoy this quality of solitude, to reach that state of 'bliss of solitude', one must traverse the labyrinth of infantile anxieties and the later uncertainties of life while undergoing the analytic experience. Nevertheless, in the experience of this solitude during the analytic journey - the analytic dyad provides a fundamental basis, manifested in the transference-countertransference encounter, to mutually share between two egos this essence of solitude. At an abstract level it is closest to that 'core of the being' through both verbalization, highly charged silence and other non-verbal communication that fills the analytic space with such meaningful eloquence. Interestingly, the greatest difficulty encountered following this shared analytic dyad is the ego's capacity to dwell in this solitude in reality all alone. Under such circumstances the only sharing of such deep emotions is possible by an ability to internalize this dyad, chiselled out by the Unconscious according to the fashion of the original, ideal dyad of the mother-child relationship. The innumerable reality tests may at times still be too overwhelming for the ego when it again experiences that similar childhood desperation of helplessness against reality and destiny. For example, the uncountable wars down civilization (as well as the present global war against terrorism) and the ego's irresistible apprehension regarding destruction and death. The ego has also to learn the tenacity to bear being a helpless witness to consequences of such human atrocities. Its struggle with reality never ceases. That is precisely the work of a well-developed, mature ego.

The creation of a unique personality, individual in progress, which began with the analytic experience, is a process-in-continuum till the last day of one's life. In this sense analysis is truly interminable. That 'core of the being' is in a constant state of 'becoming'. The more one gets in tune with this core, the more one realizes the acute pain of loneliness involved in the ego's process of psychic integration. On the one hand the deep wish to traverse the whole course of the analytic journey with the analyst because of an intense love involvement created by the uniqueness of transference-countertransference phenomenon; while on the other, the recurrent attraction for immediate material and physical pleasures that are readily available in reality persists. Here, one remembers Hegel's understanding of the tragic state of a character - as if it is caught in a 'collision of equally justified ethical aims'. But, this new emerging individual tragic man can wade back no more - he has to continue the process set forth by the analytic experience and live life to its brim. Be it loneliness, war or death, he is to experience the 'jouissance' of tragedy in life as so brilliantly portrayed in the works of Sophocles, Euripedes, Shakespeare, to name only a very few timeless maestros of the world.

In one's effort towards this process of psychic integration especially within a particular cultural milieu which is strongly influenced by fundamentalist religious and political motives, one unfortunately experiences the pangs of a certain aesthetic isolation from the community. But once the mind has tasted freedom what chains of religion, politics or even culture can bind it to conformity, even if it has to suffer such frightening isolation. Perhaps one has also to learn to deal with this aesthetic isolation which is a unique product of the present cultural context and city that I happen to come from. Though this place (Calcutta) has an eighty-year history of psychoanalytic presence, it is ironical that the struggle of an individual analyst should still comprise the establishment of the psychoanalytic profession itself besides his own professional struggle. There have been too many bifurcations and distortions in psychoanalysis here even before it had time to form a nest in order to settle down. Due to the lack of a certain scientific orientation regarding the subject among people in general Calcutta, unfortunately, has still not been able to create a particular ambience conducive to the development of psychoanalysis. Needless to say, from Freud's time till today, psychoanalysis as a science has faced many a rebuff from various sections of the society, and most strongly from the religious and political sectors of the world. Though not a new phenomenon in the history of psychoanalysis or for any committed psychoanalyst, the degree of this rebuff here makes it significant enough for consideration. Sadly enough it is not easy to be scientific about human feelings, beliefs and passions. In *Thoughts for the Times on War and Death*, Freud talks about the need to look at human emotions as a scientist and not to remain a 'sentimentalist' on these issues. As so poetically elaborated by E. Mahon in his play, *Anna and Sigmund at the Rue Royale*, Sigmund says to Anna, "When my tears fell on parchment, I studied them! I invite you to do the same."

Living up to Freud's invitation to study one's heart-rending tears is definitely not an easy task to accomplish. Neither is it easy to travel the solitary path of 'the vision of truth'. The quality of honesty required for acquiring this kind of insight about one's mind can draw inspiration from biographical studies of Freud's life and works (especially necessary for generations like ours who unfortunately missed having the direct experience of the spirit of Freud's time and personality). Only by an uncompromising attitude of the mind in its validation of one's inner truth in solitude can one hope to attain the psychic integration for which this quest began in the first place. And yet, in spite of all such trials and errors, efforts at understanding life and death, struggles against reality discord, aspirations and failures at creative sublimations, one must most humbly confess in genuine dedication to that solitude of the core where truth resides that "with all this sweated lore, I stand no wiser than I was before".

References

Freud, Sigmund (1915) *Thoughts for the Times on War and Death. S.E.* 14

Hanly, Charles (1990): The Concept of Truth in Psychoanalysis.
    International Journal of Psychoanalysis, 71:382.

Mahon, Eugene (2000): Anna and Sigmund at the Rue Royale. *Journal of American Psychoanalytic Association.*, 48:1624.

Ongoing-everyday language and psychoanalytic concepts
Jan McGregor Hepburn *(Northumberland)*

> As Sweet
>
> *It's all because we're*
> *so alike-*
> *Twin souls, we two.*
> *We smile at the*
> *expression, yes,*
> *And know it's true.*
>
> *I told the shrink. He*
> *gave our love*
> *A different name.*
> *But he can call it*
> *what he likes-*
> *It's still the same.*
>
> *I long to see you,*
> *hear your voice,*
> *My narcissistic*
> *object choice.*

[Serious Concerns by Wendy Cope 1992 Faber & Faber]

I recently heard the poet Wendy Cope on the radio say that her friends call her 'the shrink marketing board'. I suppose it is not surprising that I should find her poems so refreshing and interesting, but this is a particular favourite just now as it speaks to me about something I am much exercised with 'between sessions and behind the couch' What do we actually say to patients to undo repression and bring the unconscious to light?

I still find it a challenge to think about the applied theoretical concepts, in language that I think my patient could understand. Whenever I read a paper or book now I find I really want to know what did the author actually say? How did the author translate their theoretical understanding into words recognisable by the patient?

When Freud wrote about the *Psychopathology of Everyday Life* it was the idea which was so illuminating and exciting, and it is still exciting

64

today, but now I am occupied with perhaps more mundane matters- how do I translate this for those who need the insight pre-digested?

My first thought is that perhaps it hardly matters what we say. If we speak to the unconscious directly, the unconscious will be able to understand. But I fear that this may be rather magical thinking. In Melanie Klein's account of her analysis of Richard, for instance, she seems to have said a very great deal, and to have made little concession to his age or any resistances which might not respond to a direct challenge. However, for myself as an ordinary psychoanalytic psychotherapist, I have not found this to be very possible in everyday practice. Words themselves carry great significance; they can be experienced in a variety of ways- as concrete things, weapons, food, comfort, a conduit of understanding or a barrier. Of course the negative feelings evoked have to be addressed, but our patients need to be able to come, and to listen. Badly chosen or clumsy words are not necessarily experienced in the spirit in which they are meant, and I have become more and more interested in the way the words themselves can be used as objects.

I have realised that working with a new patient sets off a process of teaching a new language, as well as learning the patient's idiom. I had previously been solely concerned with trying to understand how the patient was communicating, but I find that this only works with patients who have sufficient emotional language to understand the concepts. As we widen our scope and take patients with more diffuse and complex difficulties, it seems to me that it is up to us to learn how to talk to them.

When I trained, we were told that we should make an interpretation when doing an assessment to see whether the patient could work. Now I am much more interested in whether the patient knows of the existence of the unconscious. This would not necessarily mean anything about their suitability for treatment, but tells me whether I will have to find words to explain what the patient does not know. Otherwise the patient is liable to say, with varying degrees of irritation, "no, I'm not feeling that". Equally, I have found patients to be so offended by unexplained allusions to infantile processes ["you're saying I'm childish"], transference interpretations ["why do you always bring it back to yourself"], and my drawing attention to projections ["what an insult"] that they have stopped listening. Obviously the unconscious cannot stop listening, but it can erect higher and higher defences when it perceives an attack. Even those not otherwise paranoid can experience my words as an attack, and that my feeling attached to the words can be quite misread.

65

What is distinctive about our way of working is the interpretation of the unconscious, and we know that this is what is mutative, in the end. I am particularly interested in how others have put these interpretations into everyday language for their patients, if indeed they have. So I am thinking, reading and tempted to collect *mots justes* and felicitous phrases, and doing my best to suggest some to others in case they might be useful. I am also trying to remember that words do not mean what I chose them to mean when I am engaged in someone else's inner world. True relating, as distinct from a kind of merger, requires a shared language: my patient and I have to find a language together. This is why I like Wendy Cope's poem. She reminds me that ours is not a language which can be readily understood in a truly helpful way without translation, and that unlike the telepathic twinship of narcissistic object choices, relationships necessitate verbal dialogue.

Mother Tongue and other tongues

Judit Szekacs *(Budapest/London)*

In 1946, another Hungarian, immortal expert of cultural-psychological 'adult observation', master of satire and professional immigrant George Mikes writes in his How to be an Alien:
'In England everything is the other way round...If a continental youth wants to declare his love to a girl, he kneels down, tells her that she is the sweetest, most charming person...and he would be unable to live one more minute without her This is a normal, week-day declaration of love. In England the boy pats his adored one on the back and says softly:'I rather fancy you, in fact.'

Love is a normal 'weekday' word in Hungarian, a difficult one in English – though the beat generation did a lot to make this word speakable. Simple words. You will find the same words in different tongues – but do they really mean the same? The one in your mothertongue will be embedded in early feelings, bodily sensations, phantasied and experienced archaic connections; the whole culture and style of primary object relations. These will provide the affective context for our 'internal etymological dictionary'.

The Hungarians say, 'the nation lives in its language' (Nyelveben el a nemzet). Let alone nations, a psycho-analyst for sure does and if one decides to live in another country, work in a second language (quite often with people in the same or similar position) while struggling with the loss of mothertongue one will soon realise that guiding aspects of verbal orientation are shattered or lost and it is on the level of basic assumptions that the world needs to be rediscovered.

I came to live in London in 1990.
I was not a refugee, 'just' an emigrant, moving to another country.
Leaving was my own decision, a cumulative act of transgenerational dynamic forces wrapped in 'free choice'.
It has not been easy, but eventually we arrived at the other side. Soon I started to see patients in London. The difficulties began – literally – at the door. The Hungarians shake hands, in London people do not. The prophetic words of my ex-tutor from the Tavistock Clinic have often echoed in my ear: 'never mind if you still do it, the worst thing that can happen will be that the patients realise you are a foreigner before you open your mouth.' Yes, I am a foreigner, and being a foreigner is a matter of fact. And so are a number of my patients.

What is the language we speak to communicate when verbal forms and structures are deconstructed? Which Stage of Development in the Sense of Reality – to quote Ferenczi – does one revisit when words don't carry their meaning because they have lost their affective-emotional charge?

For a long time I had the diffuse feeling that in my second language I was working from a different part of my body and my mind, somewhere in the zone between object representation and word representation. Never in my life before was I able to work with borderline patients so naturally and well than in the first couple of years in my new language. Having achieved a better grasp on living speech this gate has closed once again.

Working with 'English patients' has created a strange counter-transference situation: what I experienced was a peculiar sense of mutual holding due to the sensation that the patient is holding the therapist on the level of speech. This is not Ferenczi's 'wise baby'; this is a synchronicity of mental functions and affective exchange, an oscillation in the analytical space between present and past unconscious on an operational level. The image I used to describe this constellation was Magritte's surrealistic Madonna: a child mother holding an adult baby.

As time goes by the analyst becomes safer, better oriented and structured in the new language and this new verbal self will fit more seamlessly with the old parts of his/her personal and professional identity. Like an idyllic state, one feels proud and relaxed, the illusion is that you managed not only to have arrived in your new world but that you own the words and grammar again, and this blissful moment lasts until the time the first patient comes who speaks your mothertongue.

This is how it has happened in my case.
Tamas had been in analysis with me in Budapest several years ago. We had finished our work then, but later he felt he would like to take a second look at certain areas of his life. Being a very successful businessman he could arrange a two years assignment for himself to stay in London – partly to be able to come back to therapy with me. I was pleased to see him. What I was not prepared for was the wave of joy that has swept through the consulting room during the first session in Hungarian after so many years. I tasted words and phrases like long forgotten delicacies, enjoyed the poetics, syntax, the plasticity and creative potentials of Hungarian grammar, in one word: I was really in my element! At the same time with my next patient in English I was less than pleased to realise that my English was gone. The grammar went upside down, I was searching for the appropriate phrases, became hesitant and insecure and was translating in my head yet again – something I had given up long

ago, at the time when I began not only to speak but think and dream in English.

This second analytical honeymoon with Tamas has lasted for some time. I became aware of the unconscious sources of joy while working in a mind-set belonging to my mothertongue. Simultaneously I also started to see my defensive manoeuvres against mourning the loss of my original language and culture; images and ideas that would not speak for themselves any more.

During these formative years in a multilingual therapeutic world I experienced how exploring and working through language-barriers standing in the way of self expression and understanding leads to finding better symbolic translations for diverse mind-sets. This enables us to uncover the dynamics of unrecognised individual and social trauma of changing context, which is a crucial aspect of all migration.

At this time something else has also happened which was relevant in opening up internal and external gates: I found myself in the company of other colleagues of many tongues interested in and struggling with similar problems. Together we started the *Multilingual Psychotherapy Centre.* We found ourselves in a peculiar transitional space where images, thought-objects and the others (people) could offer themselves for being created. Language proved to be a very useful metaphor for understanding-misunderstanding and non-understanding. Translations and translatability, movement and change. Sharing and solitude, isolation and being with others.

I am not alone and lost anymore.
I have even been 'naturalized'. Mikes, the humorist thinks that:
'The verb *to naturalize* clearly proves what the British' (and let me add, that this is the word other English speaking nations, like America, also use to this very day) 'think of you. Before you are admitted to British citizenship you are not even considered a natural human being'...

I am now a double citizen, which is a formidable metaphor for what I really feel I am: psychoanalyst with one brain and two minds.

On the Move
Ruth Berkowitz *(London)*

The move from my old to my new consulting room, just a few minutes walk away had few of the usual features of moving house. There could be none of the wait and see how this looks in this corner, or how that looks on that wall. This had to be planned with precision because when the day came to begin work in the new room, everything had to be in place. So it is and has to be with the therapeutic setting, where the patient is held, in part, by time and space, a space which during the therapy becomes a reliable external world for the patient. There is the painting of the road leading who knows where, which becomes at times a place to wander into, away from the intensity of the therapy and the transference. There is the little cloth doll with her baby on her back ("Will you bring my little putski?") So everything must stay in its place, even errant books need attention ("Have you always had that book there?") The patients, therefore, were prepared by me for the move, time to mourn, time to be angry with me. My preoccupations were with them with the upheaval, the disturbance of this reliable arrangement.

I gave little thought to the place of the setting in my own internal world, I, myself, was a part of my patient's setting, reliably there and available to do the containing, the taking in and digesting of the disorder and disorientation, which was then to be served up to them in palatable and manageable form. A presentiment of my own disorientation was hurled at me when I first locked myself into and then out of my new consulting room, the evening before I was to begin working there. The keys did not fit the lock An emergency locksmith came, quiet and reassuring. The door had dropped in the hot weather.

The first moment of meeting the first patient in the new room was strange. We were in a different place in relation to each other and the room being smaller meant we were physically closer. Where did I stand while a jacket was being hung up? As the session began, there were some landmarks, the picture with the road leading who knows where, I realised was reassuring to me. However, the pictures which had been on the left-hand side of the couch were now on the right hand side. The familiar rug, the patterns which had at times been the interconnecting web for free associations, was now strange. The patient was now on my left instead of being on my right. When the session ended, I fumbled as I stood up and the ritual leave taking which over time takes on the formality of a highly choreographed dance, fell apart and we were like a couple stepping on one another's toes.

There was not only the visual strangeness, objects in different places, the light falling across them in new ways, the sounds were new. Never before had the consulting room felt so like a skin, a membrane between the internal and external. There was no longer the familiar sound of buses drawing up at the bus stop and the window rattling as the engine of the bus throbbed before it moved off again. There had been the hum of traffic and the sound of voices, background to the therapeutic work and the therapeutic setting. Now footsteps and voices were closer and in the experience of the change, felt threatening. There were anxieties that someone or something would burst through this membrane which held me and my patients.

While I worked with my patients' sense of loss, the move evoked my own sense of loss, of leaving home, of migrations, underlined by the finality of a move such as this. Not only they, but I too was at times, in mourning

In this strange, sometimes twilight world of the therapeutic encounter, we find ways of holding ourselves sufficiently to be of use to our patients. Our growing knowledge of uses of the countertransference and countertransference enactments, and our theoretical knowledge at times can serve us well. Perhaps we need to add, at least, our own use of the therapeutic setting as a stable, reliable, enduring framework which we lean on and without which we may not only feel vulnerable, but also experience a profound sense of loss.

Changing Rooms

SusanBudd *(London)*

I moved my practice to two new consulting-rooms in 18 months. I worried considerably beforehand about this; in the event, it was less traumatic than I had feared. I will try to discuss some of my and my patients' reactions to the moves, but I have also some severely practical advice to give to those contemplating this experience, and I will interpolate this in italics as a kind of counter-point.

The first consulting-room had been an architect-designed, purpose-built side-annexe to what most of my patients realized must be my home. The second consulting room, in which I worked for 15 months, was a rented room in a house where all the rooms were rented out, often on an hourly basis, to a variety of therapists. The third room is in the outer part of my new home in a large mansion-flat, accessible only by walking through gardens. With each move, the room became smaller, and the arrangements for access, waiting, and using the cloakroom became less ideal. All three rooms are within 10 minutes walk of each other, but to both me and my patients, the small changes made between routines of getting in and out of the room, how to get to it, and what the nearest shops are like, matter a great deal. And so does the greater distance from the nearest underground station, and increased difficulty in parking.

The second move was to a room too small to accommodate my Balans chair. These chairs, which look like large clumsy rocking-chairs, are a godsend to many analysts. They take the weight of the head off the spine, and stop the blood pooling in your ankles. Without the chair, I try to remember to do my exercises between sessions. Walk around the room on tiptoe; rotate your feet, clockwise and anti-clockwise; flex them inwards and outwards; and lie flat on your back on the floor for 15 minutes at the end of every day, head raised 1"on a book, arms by your sides, knees slightly raised, spine as flat as you can. Relax. Trust me, it really works.

All my patients had been with me for some time before the first move, and I did not take on any new ones. This fact, I think, considerably reduced both my and my patients' anxiety. In my experience, disturbed patients in the early stages of treatment are acutely sensitive to any change in the external environment, and all changes are experienced as catastrophic, because there is as yet no sense of the analyst's mind as being reliable, holding and containing. Once this has been established, external change is easier to bear. It did not seem to be only those who had suffered early real losses who mourned the first consulting room most acutely.

I knew three years ago that a 'For Sale' sign was about to go up outside the house. The week beforehand, I told everybody that I would be moving after the summer break to a new consulting room which was two minutes walk away. It felt much more of an effort to tell some people than others. As would be true of any other evidence of changes in the analyst's private life, some patients tried to ignore it, beyond establishing that I would definitely still go on being there; others were more or less openly curious. On the wall of my consulting-room hangs a patchwork quilt – a log cabin design, from Appalachia. Several patients asked if the quilt was coming too; they needed to know that they would still have this important transitional object.

One patient thought afterwards that moving during the long summer break, not having seen the new room first, had made things much harder for her. She had had to worry about it all summer, although she understood perfectly well that she was really worried about whether I would be the same person, who felt the same about her, in a new place. I was convinced by this, and moved for the second time just before a break so that people knew quickly that they could find me again, and could see the new room. It could be argued that I should not have acted in this way; by reducing anxiety, rather than analysing it. I don't think that the one precludes the other. Nor did I think that changes in my life should impinge upon my patients more than they had to.

The environment of the second consulting-room was far from ideal. For the first time, my patients were having to share the main entrance, waiting-area and cloakroom with other people, and we were aware of other therapists in the house. Several people remarked ruefully that they realized they had previously been able to ignore everything and everybody else during the session, and now we could hardly do so. Some did find it really hard to bear, but others rather liked the change. One felt that the smaller, humbler premises made us seem on a more equal footing, and when I had moved yet again, we realized that he had liked the impersonality of the hired room. His mother had been frustrated and unhappy, and had hated her home, and their happiest times together had been spent in cafes and tearooms.

The windows of this room looked out onto a school. I enjoyed the Ivesian cacophony of the music rooms, and the girls walking to and fro, squabbling and giggling. For some of my patients, it revived the terrors of the playground, and for others, the loss of the children that they had never had. Because I did not feel that the school or the rest of the house were my responsibility, I was able to cope with equanimity with

73

impingements which would have disturbed me in my own home, and was able to analyze the impact of them more easily. In some ways, the situation took me back to my student days; I made coffee from a kettle on the floor, ate bananas out of paper bags, and cursed when my milk disappeared from the communal fridge. But in the end, it began to get me down; and when I arrived one day with someone for an assessment in tow, to find a complete stranger in my room, who had been in the habit of getting in and using it for a waiting room, I finally snapped.

I had wondered whether I would be able to see patients in my new home. In particular I had worried about the piano overhead, on which the talented little girls upstairs practised so assiduously. But I decided that I had to move my consultingroom, and Dr. Rafe Orlowski, of Arup Acoustics, took time off from advising on large concert halls and came to look at the problem. The solution turned out to be piano cupmounts – dense, high castors which dampen noise transmitted downwards through the fabric of piano legs and floor – and a false ceiling, for which he gave careful specifications. Many thanks to him, and to our kind neighbours Yumi and Waldemar Januszczak.

But the main shift was internal. I felt increasingly confident that I had to move; and that in the end, analysis only requires a quiet and private space with two people in it. If there was no waiting room, and if it was somewhat awkward getting into and out of the consulting room, it could be surmounted and got used to. We all seemed to have learnt something; the second move was less upsetting than the first. Although, as one patient remarked, I initially seemed to be rather more worried about the arrangements than she was, nonetheless she seemed to accustom herself easily to a shift which had been difficult the first time around. She was right to comment on my perturbation. During this time, the familiar pattern and rhythm of psychoanalytic work was the only unchanging part of my life. As I emerged from this period of turbulence, I felt grateful to my patients, and to the discipline of analysis.

In retrospect, I think that it is important not to become over-responsible. The ideal arrangements with which I had started had been a great help and support to me and to my patients for many years. But in the end, we could live without them, and in the process we all learnt something.

THE INFANT & THE BABY WITHIN:

At the Window *Jeni Couzyn*

In your neck
the heart of a trapped bird
fast and light.
In your eyelids a shoal of tiny fish
swept downriver as backwards swirling
you swim to sleep.
Each day a new game:you shake your head
then I shake mine
and we laugh. Sunlight fills your room.
Knuckles and feet
knees and elbows and hard skull
all the bullying bones in you
still soft and green
lie sleeping, dreaming
in a world before hurt.
Your tongue and eyes and brain
potential killers
innocent still of their harm
but your mouth that early learner
has two bright teeth
like needles. A fresh snow falls.
A new year floats into our house.
Already you can tear flesh.

[With thanks to Firelizard for permission to reprint 'At the Window']
(*A Time to be Born*, Firelizard,1999)

'Baby sister'
Courtesy of Astrid, 4½

Infant-Parent Psychotherapy: working psycho-analytically with the infant in the consulting room

Frances Salo *(Melbourne)*

In the infancy field it is increasingly recognised that it is no longer sufficient to treat the mother's depression, the infant and the mother-infant relationship also need therapeutic input to ensure optimal outcomes for the infant. Working psychoanalytically with the infant in the consulting room affects technique in that the analyst may need to respond physically to the infant and to work with the parent's feelings about this as well as any internal discomfort about not working in more traditional ways. The infant's distress can only be communicated somatically, and with a distressed mother *and* a distressed infant in the room, we need to be aware of how much more the body does the feeling and thinking in this interaction than in adult work. As our emotions have a bodily counterpart, one question might be what does a woman clinician bring to this work, and linked with this, whether there are gender differences in women's experience of the affects in this work?

1. A more physical experience with the infant present

Direct work with the infant is usually done in the presence of the parents and does not replace working with their representations but is seen as additional to it. Having the infant present may seem to complicate the process if she wants to engage with the analyst who is talking with the mother, for example, if she raises her arms to be lifted by the analyst. But it is now acknowledged that at times the infant needs a therapeutic intervention herself. Direct work is conceptualised as altering the infant's representations, and may be very subtle, relying considerably on the therapeutic effects of gaze and play. Outwardly it may seem to consist of little more than facial or hand gestures, and imitating the infant's vocalising or play. The therapeutic factor, as in adult work, is the analyst's thinking about the infant. We work actively at making a connection with the infant. If you hold out a toy so that even a very young baby can hold, and then gently pull back, the baby has an awareness of someone who recognises her agency, and she can begin to sense it for herself, which is extremely significant. Ann Morgan (cited in Thomson-Salo & Paul, 2001) commented that: 'what I think is important about helping the mother see this link, is that it allows a space in which something can appear: in the mother's mind a thought, in the baby a beginning of a preconception'.

The mother's feelings

There has often been concern by clinicians that working with the infant will be resented by the parents or result in mothers feeling guilty or inadequate. Our experience has been that the parents' feelings about it are usually positive. They recognise when their infants are depressed and that the situation is urgent for them and usually want help for their infant. Recently other clinicians have begun to move in this direction. Dilys Daws (2000) described her practice as changing and that whereas she used not to hold the infant, she is now doing so more.

2. Working quickly with countertransference and projective identification

Infant-parent psychotherapy is usually short-term because of the fluidity in the parent-infant system and the infant's extraordinary responsiveness to intervention. The clinician needs to be comfortable working with the mother's primitive material and the infant's non-verbal communication. She relies on being able to quickly read her countertransference responses, including those of a female body, and of projective identification, where the mother engages those qualities in the other that she wants to disown. It is also how the infant communicates uncomfortable affects. With 'no language but a cry' the psychosomatic 'language' is the first language of the infant. At this time when the mother's psychic state may be in disarray and the infant in distress, how much more likely is it that countertransference responses will be more on the borders of psyche and soma? Many women clinicians describe physical responses while doing this work. They have been surprised at finding themselves overwhelmed with hunger after visiting a depressed mother or assessing a young child who tried so hard to be so pretty, so good, so engaging. One clinician said, "it's a gut feeling, the baby's distress becomes mine, it's very powerful, I began to feel what it was like to be the baby, and then to feel sick."

Countertransference is particularly relevant where the clinician makes an emotional contact with the infant in order to bring about change, and uses more physical ways of relating than clinicians have in the past. Attuning to the infant's affect if she is despairing or angry immediately conveys to her: 'I know what you feel because I feel it too', and you can often see an immediate response. But perhaps playfulness in its widest sense has the greatest capacity to give the infant hope. What, then, is evoked in women clinicians when intuitively they choose a particular way of relating? What does the infant bring of their femaleness or maleness, and how do they relate to women or male clinicians? Is there a particular way that infants relate to male clinicians as they distinguish that their father or other men are different from their mothers?

3. The gendered analyst

I wonder if we may have ignored the relevance of the clinician's gender, as we may also have been relatively blind to the infant's gender, treating female and male infants as if there were no difference (Jordan, 2000).

It is likely that mothers are *primed* for projective identification because of the nature of birth and early child raising. Carrying the baby in utero starts off the process of being sensitively in touch with her communication of raw emotional states and transforming them. Fathers, too, will be able to draw on their own experience of having been a baby, to perform this function. What may be different about mothers' capacity for identification and projective identification is that they have carried the infant in their body, and their communications to one another have been known for a long time in the most basic bodily way. They have worked on their projective identification function for years, carrying the infant, '*my* baby', in their mind. A mother can then function with only very delicate things coming from the baby in the beginning.

It is also likely that women clinicians have ready access to this underpinning biological sensitivity when working with mothers and infants. How much, then, is countertransference gendered, and have we been relatively blind to the different physicality with which women and men respond to feelings aroused in them?

Conclusion

Infant researchers have illuminated how the experience of relating powerfully affects both partners neurologically and therapeutically. We therefore need to be mindful of what we bring as a gendered clinician.

References

Daws, D (2000) *Conversations with the author* WAIMH Congress, Montreal

Jordan, B (2000) Gender, Politics and Infant Mental Health *The Signal 5: 1-5*

Seligman, S. (1999) Workshop in Australian Association of Infant Mental Health Conference, Melbourne.

Thomson-Salo, F. & Paul, C. (2001*).* Some Principles of Infant-Parent Psychotherapy. *Australian Journal of Psychotherapy, 20: 36-59.*

Acknowledgments

For their part in extending my thinking I would like to thank in particular Campbell Paul and Ann Morgan.

Issues from the Floor – some dilemmas for the therapist in Parent-Infant Psychotherapy   Tessa Baradon *(London)*

My interest in the parent-infant relationship was shaped by the Baby Observation I did as part of the my training. It was of a baby and her mother who had lost her first infant one year previously. Thus the vulnerability (represented by the dead baby) and the resilience of her babies (represented by the infant I observed) were in the forefront of the mother's preoccupation. It reminded me of a photograph of my close friend in childhood, in which she featured with another little girl. I never quite understood whether this was a montage of pictures of two different daughters, one of whom may have perished in the Holocaust, or if it was two different pictures of my little friend. My curiosity in what these girls represented to her parents was intense.

In 1997, a proposal I had made for 'PIP', a Parent and Infant Project at The Anna Freud Centre got off the ground. The brief was to provide services for families with attachment disorders, to train professionals in the field of infant mental health and to further clinical research in this area. In the first few years, the families referred had children aged 16-24 months. By that age, the labelled 'patient' is usually the child – with a variety of taxing behavioural problems. However, research data and clinical experience regarding development in the first year favours very early intervention, and there has been ongoing, proactive work by PIP with referring professionals to identify relationship difficulties within the first few months. Consequently, in many cases the age of the infant at referral to PIP has dropped to under 6 months.

Working with very young babies, where structures and representations are still in formation, holds much hope. There are moving moments where the parents respond to their baby with new recognition and pleasure despite their personal pain. The Adult Attachment Interviews conducted with the parents reveal that many are in the 'disorganised' or 'unclassifiable' categories, their lives characterised by trauma (interpersonal - e.g. severe abuse, or political - e.g. refugees from genocide), unresolved losses, or chronic mental illness. Much of the work thus focuses on the intergenerational repetitions of terrorised and abusing relationships.

The work takes place on the floor: parent(s) and therapist sit on large cushions, with the baby placed on a baby mat between them. The predictable boundaries set by the patient's couch, the therapist's chair, even the furniture of child psychoanalysis, are not available. Physically and symbolically, the therapist is involved in the raw emotions between parent and infant as they unfold and encompass her.

The baby's presence in the therapy is crucial for the work. I want to suggest that the presence of the baby also heightens the countertransferential issues for the therapist. The therapist is faced with shifting and often contradictory identifications. On the one hand the adult's narrative is compelling and the therapist's preoccupation lies in this. On the other hand the baby's dependency and vulnerability create a sense of immediacy and urgent responsibility for, and towards, the baby.

Shona was referred with postnatal depression when Elias was 10 months. It quickly become clear that Shona had periodically suffered extreme depression throughout her life (in relation to the abuse and neglect of her childhood) but, with Elias' birth, her previous patterns of flight could not be mobilised. In the first session, Shona sat hunched in corner, completely silent. I was deeply moved by her intense pain. Elias was very separate from his mother, and played undemandingly with a toy. Some weeks later, Shona's rage prevailed in the session. She entered the Centre shouting that she had reached the end of her tether, and in the room she threw objects around. Elias looked very frightened. Shona stood over him and screamed that she wished him dead as she did want to be his mother anymore. The emotional tone was very intense for all of us. In attending to both baby and mother I felt there was an emergency around their survival.

In subsequent sessions I found myself unable to broach with Shona the actual words she had used. Working through the impact on myself, I felt caught up in a wish of my own to scotomise the murder expressed towards the baby. It was as though through being a witness I was also a collaborator in the brutalisation of the baby, and thereby I was beset by mother's guilt and shame.

This incident also raised the issue of the therapist's own hierarchy of beliefs and Achilles heels. In cultural and ethical terms there are questions of how, for example, to accommodate differing childbearing practices with basic assumptions about infant's needs? Tensions may be played out within the system – say in pressure, from the family or agencies, for a black worker to be allocated to a black family, or a religious family to be seen by a therapist of the same faith.

I was doing a Court Assessment on a teenage African mother who had injured her baby. The allocated social worker requested that a black colleague of mine join the work with me, questioning whether the needs of a black family would be met by a white therapist working in a white, middle class institution. I agreed to the arrangement for

81

institutional reasons, although in this case there was a clear process of psychological unfolding in our work, and I did not feel particularly challenged in the countertransference.

At the end of the assessment my colleague made the following observation: In retrospect she realised that she had identified with the black social worker and had unconsciously monitored me in relation to the family. When she felt that they were genuinely accepted by me for whom they are, she relinquished her vigilance and felt they would be safe with me.

At issue here was the question of riven identifications, that took the form of racial sensitivities. The black family was perceived to be at risk of victimisation by me as the infant was by her young mother. In this case, the process within the therapist of maintaining empathy in the face of violence to the baby was enacted in the network.

Working as a therapist with a responsibility to the judgement of Solomon ("to whom should this baby belong") is onerous and painful. In these cases the personal aspects of the professional relationship between the family and the therapist are central. I have found working in a team has greatly facilitated the process of reflection and we are also learning to consider our personal attitudes towards race, class, religion and culture. Sometimes this is a conscious process, but transference and prejudice come into the relations between colleagues as much as into the work with patients. An open dialogue within the team is rooted in taking the risk of making available one's personal thinking for exploration by the other, and thus parallels the leap made by the babies and their parents in engaging with the mind of the therapist.

Treating Anorexia Nervosa: Ghosts in the Paediatric Ward or a Fetus in a New Womb?

Hisako Watanabe *(Tokyo)*

Lying down on a couch is an act of faith. One does it with curiosity and apprehension when starting one's psychoanalysis, assuming the analyst to be a reliable companion to an exploration of one's inner world. If it all goes well one finds this recumbence to be an experience of entering into the womb of psychoanalysis: one's thoughts and feelings of painfully lived moments, ghosts of the past so to speak, become scrutinized and inseminated with a new understanding.

Lying down on a bed for a child with severely emaciated anorexia nervosa must be a complex experience. It requires authentic faith on the part of a doctor to convince her of the need to rest her body while she is totally engrossed in her omnipotent control denying even her basic demands of life. As a child psychiatrist working in an open general paediatric ward in Tokyo, Japan, I recognize this act of lying down as a crucial sign of nonverbal agreement by 50 anorexic children who revived through our inpatient treatment programme.

On 2nd August 1993, the day I was invited back to the paediatric department as a full-time faculty staff on my return from London, I met in lobby of the Keio University Hospital paediatric ward a severely emaciated girl, looking like a skeleton in pyjamas, shuffling about with a venous drip infusion stand. She had only just been transferred from another hospital after an abortive treatment, but was already puzzling the pediatricians because she was stubbornly refusing to eat or rest. For a moment I thought I had come across a ghost; a ghost of our rapidly modernized society.

I approached this emaciated girl asking if she would let me give her a physical examination. She agreed but insisted there was nothing wrong with her body, although she had cold hands more common with an older person. Only when I got her to count her own weak pulse of 45 did she show even a glimmer of concern. When her heart rate remained unchanged when a handsome trainee applied the stethoscope, I insisted she give her poor weak heart and cold body a final chance to rest. Much to the staffs' amazement, this blunt intimation of death induced her to listen.

This marked the begging of my work with anorexic patients. Over the past eight years I have trained altogether 122 first-year trainees giving them first-hand experience in residential treatment concurrently with pediatric training. With the trainees as primary care workers, consistent intensive care, such as giving three spoon-feeding sessions each day, was prescribed for all anorexic patients. This girl became the model case on

83

which we based an intensive routine, enhancing sensitivity in the trainees to the unmet infantile needs of their patients.

Despite her verbal protest this girl gradually complied with lying down for two hours after each feed. These post-feeding hours were most upsetting for her and thus the most dangerous. I attended her until she settled down and closed her eyes. We spent hours together in this position, close and yet apart, with my observing her from behind. This reminded me of my own analytic sessions where I could feel the presence of a listening ear while I pondered on my own like a floating fetus in the mother's womb.

After a while, I asked her whether what her mother had said was true that she had never been naughty as a child. She fell into silence. After several days, as I was again sitting silently at her bedside, she opened her mouth and uttered. 'You asked me if I remember having done any mischief when I was small. Well, I have been thinking about it and remembered one incident when I had a real fight with my elder sister. She stole my paper magic wand, which I got as a present in a magazine package. I was so proud of it that I was boasting about it and my sister took it away and broke it. I was furious, I could not forgive her. So I attacked her with all my might.' Then she fell silent.

It struck me that this defiant, aloof girl had taken in my questioned and had searched into her past for a memory of mischief. The heightened tone of her words sparked me into realizing that she had something to say to me. I said that perhaps, for her, this state of anorexia was her magic wand, which freed her from frustration and sufferings as a perfect, but lonely girl. The magic of anorexia nervosa was something, which she had discovered on her own, perhaps for the first time in her life. What the anorexic state provided her was first, a new power over not only her domineering parents but also over the medical staff. The second magic she found in the anorexic condition was that hunger created omnipotent feelings through secretion of endorphin in her brain. She could not afford to lose this magic. Perhaps, to her, I was the intruding sister who took away this magic wand. 'You must be furious at me,' I said 'for having taken away your magic.' I observed her as she listened intently and fell into a thoughtful silence. She stayed calm for a long time. This process laid the foundation for our long-term relationship, which continues to this day. Lying down is an inevitable posture we take at the beginning and end of each day as well as at the beginning and end of life. It is a basic physio-psychological configuration harbouring a wealth of potentials for growth and healing. It is a resting posture, surrendering oneself to a passive mode that actually leads to an active participation in a joint search for a new self. Psychoanalysis makes full use of lying down and the paediatric ward uses it in daily setting. For my anorexic patient lying down in the paediatric ward meant entering into a fetal stage of a joint journey.

84

Brief Psychotherapeutic Work with Parents and Children
Sheena Polett *(Cheshire, UK)*

The NHS Adult Psychotherapy Service where I am Consultant Psychotherapist offers brief psychotherapeutic help to families in difficulties when their children are under 5 years old. Presenting difficulties include complaints about a baby's crying, feeding difficulties, oppositional behaviour, post-natal depression, overt attachment problems, a father's difficulty in handling his infant as a result of having experienced abuse in his own childhood. Families are referred by Health Visitors, GP's, Child and Adult Psychiatry and Community Psychiatric Nurses. Often other forms of help have failed.

Psychoanalytic, systemic and cognitive behavioural treatments are available, as families vary in which approaches they can use and in which order. No matter how we work, it is our capacity to think and work analytically which helps the families and ourselves to bear the intense primitive feelings underlying these difficulties, to understand the meanings of their suffering and facilitate change.

Our brief analytic approach is based on that of the Tavistock Clinic's Under 5's Service (Daws, 1989) with elements from Selma Fraiberg's long-term work with very disadvantaged families (Fraiberg et al, 1980). Fraiberg's team worked to dispel 'the ghosts in the nursery', the projections onto the child from the parents' internal worlds. They emphasised how traumatic events in the parents' past had been managed by identification with the aggressor, so that, whether or not they were remembered as facts, affective memory was unavailable, dooming the traumas to be re-enacted between parent and child. Fraiberg stated that the parent could not 'hear her child's cries' until her own were heard. For that to occur, the therapist had to be attentive to the splitting of the transference and prompt in addressing the negative transference. We find it essential to pay close interpretative attention to those and to the split off object relationships in the parent-child relationship.

I offer a family 6 sessions to think with them about their situation. The whole family is invited but I work with whoever comes, keeping absent members alive in our conversations. My focus is on the parent-child relationship and freeing up space in the mind(s) of the parent(s) for the child(ren).

I seek the meaning of the presenting difficulties through free-floating analytic attention to the family's verbal and non-verbal communications and my countertransference. Over 6 sessions I hope to learn about current difficulties, an ordinary day, the stories of this and previous children (born and unborn), the stories of the parental relationship and previous important partnerships, the family stories of each parent and the current partner, who may not be the baby's father.

No formal history is taken. The stories tumble out as they come - jumbled, fragmented, constricted, full of gaps. I acknowledge feelings that are expressed and look for those that are missing, wondering aloud how something may have felt for my patients. Often the missing feelings are terror for the survival of baby and parents and negative ones towards the baby and parenthood - feelings of which the parent is very frightened and ashamed.

Non-verbal behaviour affords understanding which I can share with the family. Three year-old Andy, unable to reunite a doll's torso and head, placed them imploringly in my lap, showing his anxiety about Mummy's mind and his wish that I would mend her. After worriedly watching Betty repeatedly ignore her twins' dangerous antics, I could voice her belief that her life was over unless they died. Out-of-control Calum's anxiety about a new baby in his parents' minds entered our sessions by his insistence that none of us could attend to anything but his demands.

Keeping analytic attention on the parent-child relationship and the contact I am allowed with it requires discipline but pays dividends. Parental preoccupation with self, partner, marriage or child is often defensive. Shortly after recounting how she brings Jess into the marital bed to avoid sex, Fiona spoke at length about the toddler. Eventually, I realised this had diverted us from thinking about how Fiona had regained consciousness after delivery to find she had been oblivious to new-born Jess for hours. It dawned on me that Fiona feared that engagement with a third person would leave Jess unattended and at risk, as Fiona had been by her own mother's preoccupation with her ill sister.

We often find unmetabolised trauma connected with conception, pregnancy, birth, postnatal period or previous pregnancies. Frequently, there is loss - of necessary time as a couple before parenthood, of old identities, normal conception, a foetus, the imagined pregnancy and delivery or the imagined child. A partner or parent may be far away, estranged or have died.

Full up with loss, a parent has no room for the baby. Preoccupied with concerns for the infant's survival and growth, a mother has little room for her own struggles. Also, for the parent's unconscious, it often seems that it is the loved baby who has injured her and is stealing her life.

86

Occasionally, violent retaliatory feelings against the infant are painfully evident. Usually, however, the parents are left desperately warding them off by splitting and projection onto whatever suitable and safer target is available.

After a terrifying labour, prolonged bitter preoccupation with obstetric care or with evoked memories of childhood abuse can serve this unconscious purpose. Mostly the attacks are turned against the self, causing depression and sometimes risking suicide. When the partner is the target, intractable marital difficulties may ensue, especially if an idealised parent-child relationship resists therapeutic efforts. Even so, if the parent(s) can engage, brief analytic work can usually help alleviate parental depression and the presenting problem in the child.

Our work has taught us that all too many psychotherapy referrals of individual adults or couples are disguised and long-delayed presentations of difficulties which arose when a family was beginning or a child was born. We now adapt our adult psychotherapy intake procedure to offer such families brief parent-child work. This includes offering the option of a prompt screening visit, when the referral letter raises our suspicions.

Only analytic thinking and supervision helps us face and contain these intense feelings and the attendant anxieties. Using such an analytic approach at this crucial stage in personal and family development has great therapeutic and preventive potential.

References

Daws, D, (1989) *Through the Night: Helping Parent and
        Sleepless Infants.* London. Free Association Books.
Fraiberg, S., Adelson, E and Shapiro, V (1980) Ghosts in
        the Nursery: A Psychoanalytic Approach to the
        Problems of Impaired Infant-Mother Relationships in Fraiberg, S
        (Ed). *Clinical Studies in Infant Mental Health. The First Year of
        Life.* Tavistock. London and New York.

Infant-Parent Psychotherapy: Creating an Optimal Relational Space
Elizabeth Tuters *(Toronto)*

In this paper I will describe the way we work in the Infant and Family Assessment Treatment Team, Infant Program (0-4), at the Hincks-Dellcrest Children's Mental Health Centre, as it has developed over the past decade. When we first began we worked primarily with the parents' representations, observing behavioural interactions, with the focus on positive aspects, parental feelings and projections. We used the traditional Fraiberg Model (*Ghosts in the Nursery*), Interactional Guidance and *Watch, Wait, and Wonder*. Throughout these therapies we become aware that infants quickly developed a relationship with the therapist and our work transformed over time to where the infant became more central within the relational space of therapist, parent, and infant. Recently we have found similar approaches described by Norman (2001) and the Melbourne Infant Mental Health Group (2001). What follows is an explanation of how we understand the way we now work.

From the contemporary psychoanalytic Self Psychology, Inter-subjectivity, and Relational theories, we have taken the concept of sustained empathic enquiry; whereby the therapist attempts to understand, reflect on, and relate to the inner world of the other, in this case the relational world of infant and mother, from within, understanding the seeking systems of both. The therapist has knowledge of attachment theory, theory of child development, affect and motivation, and knows the central psychoanalytic concepts of the unconscious, transference/countertransference, resistance, psychic conflict, and defense. The therapist recognizes the importance of play in creating an optimal relational space, works within the intersubjective field and knows that self-regulation arises out of mutual regulation. She knows how to relate to both infant and mother and that each will develop a transference relationship which will transform their current relationships.

The therapist is focused on communication - the gaze, vocalization and distress regulation in the infant's play. She stands both outside and inside, in the relational space, to gain access to what is operating within the infant-mother system and causing the difficulties. She works directly with the infant and the mother to enhance their relationship and while understandings the mother's past, does not necessarily work with it, but works in the present - the here and now.

Sam, age 3, was referred because of angry, unpredictable outbursts at day care, attacks on peers and staff. In the first session

Sam lay on his side on the floor, running a car back and forth, while his parents talked to the therapist. Mournfully he asked "Do you remember me Mommy? - Do you remember me when I'm at school?" 11 minutes passed before mother answered. "Of course I remember you".

Sam was telling us about his difficulty feeling kept in mind by his mother when she was present and absent. Sam related easily to the therapist, who understood his need to be thought about. The therapist was able to use her knowledge of development and her relationship with Sam to help mother become more interested in her son.

The therapist affects the field by being a present, new transference object of understanding for both clients. She has knowledge of the intersubjective relationship between infant and mother being composed of representations of interactive experiences of each being with the other. The unresolved issues of the mother are carried into the interrelationship with the infant. Her subjective world interrelates with the innate capacities and biologically-driven adaptations, competencies and accommodations of the developing infant, which affects the development of his or her subjective world, which in turn reacts to and affects the mother's subjective world.

All of this impacts on and affects the therapist's subjective world, and her responses impact on both the infant and the mother, and on the infant-mother relationship. The therapist has an acute awareness of the fundamental nature of the early dyadic relationship in determining the emotional well-being of the child.

The therapist felt sad after the third session with Sam and his mother. She experienced Sam's interest and delight in having the therapist interested in his affective state, and observed how flat and disinterested the mother was in her son's expressions. It seemed the mother was depleted. The therapist and child enjoyed moments together, and the therapist wondered if the mother would fall in love with her child when she could experience him delighting in relating his feeling states to the therapist.

The therapist knows the mother's wishes and desires are to have an infant who will be free of all of the conflicts inherent in the mother's past, yet unconsciously the mother will attempt to meet her own needs through the infant. She unwittingly carries unresolved issues into her relationship with her infant. The baby necessarily cannot meet all the mother's needs; in fact, by being present he or she exacerbates these states within the mother. The therapist understands the impact of the past yet works directly with the infant and mother in the present.

She is aware that maternal conflicts are enacted within the infant-mother relationship, which makes the role of the therapist pivotal. She enters the dyadic intersubjective field sensitively so the mother will not perceive the intervention as criticism. She explores the mother's subjective world, being mindful of the power and vicissitudes of resistance and defensive structures needed by the mother to protect her vulnerable self.

> *During the history-taking the therapist learned that Sam had suffered a dog bite on his face at 1 year of age, which required hospitalization. As the therapist explored this event, Sam showed interest and asked his mother to tell the story of the dog bite. He watched her face intently as she spoke, climbing onto her lap, then hugging and kissing her. The next session Sam brought a stuffed toy, a blue dog with spots on its cheek. He played happily with his mother and the blue dog, the mother following his lead, with the therapist helping when there was a disruption. Mother and Sam were enjoying being together through play, discovering the affect attached to the trauma, a mutual remembering in the present.*
> *As the mother experiences the therapist's attempts to understand her own affective states, she is able to feel understood and cared for. This enables her to relinquish her unconscious, unrealistic expectations and hold on her infant to meet her reawakened and unmet needs as they become enacted in the therapeutic relationship. The mother joins the therapist in understanding the individual developmental needs of the baby as a separate being, with his/her own sense of initiative, agency and history, experiencing herself to be in a relationship with an other, which is mutually reciprocal and satisfying. This process is experienced by both the mother and the infant in the present, through the relationship with the therapist in the created relational space.*
> *Sam and mother play together with the dinosaurs, baby dolls and the blue dog, each very aware of the therapist's presence. When the time is over, both infant and mother are reluctant to leave, as if the space created cannot yet be taken within them to the outside.*

It is imperative that therapists know about their own resistances, unresolved issues, fantasies, desires and defensive structures when intervening in early infant-mother relationships. The therapist must be prepared to think about and reflect on the affect of his/ her own subjective experience to find the attuned affective moments with both the infant and the mother. The therapist's capacity to reflect on what is not able to be known by the infant-parent dyad forms the critical aspects of this therapy. Infant Observation seminars are central to developing this reflective stance from within. Our Infant and Family Team uses both live observation and viewing videotapes of sessions, which functions in a similar way to the Infant Observation seminars focus on reflection.

When we work with infants and their families we continue to learn about ourselves. Encountering the difficulties within ourselves can be of great benefit for all, when we create an optimal relational space for infant and parent.

References

Fraiberg, S. (1980). *Clinical Studies in Infant Mental Health.* New York: Basic Books.

Muir, E. (1992) Watching, waiting and wondering: Applying Psycho-analytic principles to mother-infant intervention. *Infant Mental Health Journal,* 13: 4, Winter, 319-329.

Norman, J. (2001) The psychoanalyst and the baby: A new look at work with infants *International Journal of Psychoanalysis*, 82:83-100

Salo, F. and Paul, C. (2001) Some principles of infant-parent psychotherapy. Ann Morgan's contributions. *The Signal* WAIMH Newsletter. Jan - June (14-19).

Tuters, E. (1988). The relevance of infant observation to clinical training and practice: An interpretation. *Journal of Infant Mental Health,* 9: 1, Spring, 94-104.

Tuters, E. (1996). Dyadic circularity in the mother-infant relationship. In Abosh and Collins (Eds.), *Mental illness in the family* (pp. 154-161). Toronto: University of Toronto Press.

Tuters, E. and Doulis, S. (2000) Observation, reflection and understanding: The importance of play in clinical assessment of infants and their families. WAIMH *Handbook of Infant Mental Health*, Vol II. Early Intervention, Evaluation and Assessment (Eds.) J. Osofsky and H. Fitzgerald. J. Wiley & Sons, 2000.

Tracing the world of an eight-year-old adopted boy to its roots in infancy
Gudrun Bodin *(Copenhagen)*

Psychoanalysis has had a difficult time in Denmark and not until the past decade has an interest arisen in the theories of Melanie Klein, child psychoanalysis and the observation of infants. It is, however, precisely Klein's theories and my training in infant observation that lie at the heart of my understanding of an eight-year-old boy and have enabled me to write about it to Danish colleagues in order to develop an interest in psychoanalytical thinking. My other motive for wanting to contribute was a feeling of great gratitude that I have been so fortunate as to share in the knowledge that is comprised in psychoanalysis, and which has enabled me to understand the boy that I will now describe.

Bo's parents contacted me because they were worried about and did not understand the boy's occasional outbursts of anger. Without apparent exterior cause, Bo would have a temper tantrum and completely lose control over himself. Afterwards, it was impossible to talk to Bo about what had elicited the tantrum. Bo himself felt unhappy and shameful about the outburst and could not explain what he had thought about and reacted on. Bo was adopted to Denmark from an orphanage in Vietnam at the age of 11 months. Bo was the youngest child of four of a very poor family. His mother died when he was six months old. The father, who was handicapped, had been unable to care for all his children, and Bo had consequently been placed in a orphanage with a view to adoption.

Bo is a beautiful, Asian-looking boy and he came to the first session together with his father. My first impression of Bo was of him sitting on his father's lap while his father was reading aloud to him. It looked like a nice, warm father-son-relationship. Bo had been prepared to be alone with me, and I started our conversation by telling him what his parents had told me. Bo sat silently with his head bent, not looking at me. On one of Bo's trouser legs a small patch had been sewn to cover a small rent in the fabric. When I began to speak, Bo started to work frantically on tearing off the patch, and when he succeeded in gaining access to the rent underneath, he put his finger through it and jerked at it so that the hole became bigger. It was as if Bo, who was otherwise well-dressed and well cared for, wanted to make me aware that there was something about him that was broken and not OK.

Bo's early history became present as I experienced his wordlessness and saw how he tore at the hole in his trousers. But at the back of my head were also experiences from an infant observation that I myself had undertaken. The little girl I had observed weekly for more than a year had

92

reacted as if she had "forgotten" her mother and could no longer recognize her when her mother returned after having been away from her in hospital for twenty-four hours. If the little girl had reacted so strongly to being without her mother for twenty-four hours, how, then, would Bo have experienced losing his mother when he was a baby of six months? It was not only his mother who had disappeared. He had lost his entire family. For the small child Bo, something had really broken, which made me say that I believed he felt that something was broken inside of him, and that he told me about it by tearing at the hole in his trouser leg and making it bigger. My comment made Bo increase his efforts. He became rather exalted. I suggested that he could not bear that something was broken, it made him anxious and afraid, and then he had to make it break even more. It might be like when he had his tantrums. When he felt that something was broken inside him, he made it worse and could not stop himself.

My comment that Bo might feel that he could not stop himself when he felt that something was broken inside him elicited a change in him. From being absorbed only by tearing a hole in his trousers, apparently without noticing me, Bo looked straight at me, there was life and a glint in his eyes and smiling, he said something like "Fifa". There was contact, and I experienced Bo like a baby who really wanted to tell me something important. To my suggestions of what "Fifa" might mean, Bo shook his head, but suddenly he jumped high in his chair and said "Fifa". Then finally I suggested that it might be a word in Vietnamese, and that he wanted to tell me something about the time when he was a small baby in Vietnam. Now Bo began to burp and make great efforts to provoke burps as well as farts. At this I suggested that Bo wanted to tell me that he felt he was a filthy baby that had all sorts of things coming out of him. Burps and farts. Now Bo started to jump so high in the chair as if he thought that he could jump it to pieces. I said that Bo seemed to think that he could ruin my chair and furniture. Since the agreed time had now passed and I knew I had to end the session, I said nothing to Bo about my idea that he saw himself as a dangerous, filthy baby who could destroy and poison me with his burps and farts, just as he believed he had destroyed his mother. But I said to Bo that I would talk to his parents about him coming back so that we could continue our work. Bo said, now in words, that he would like that. This marked the beginning of a therapy that is still in progress. It may turn into a child psychoanalysis. In Denmark, we see a growing willingness from the authorities to grant financial aid to child psychoanalysis, just as they do in the other Scandinavian countries.

The Experience of Infant Psychoanalysis is a Surprise

Johan Norman *(Stockholm)*

To work with infants is to work with feelings and emotional bonds, and often the experience of what is taking place in the analysis surprises the infant, the infant's mother and the analyst. Naturally this feeling sometimes exists with older children and with adults as well, but in my work with infants I think that I encounter a special quality—an open, naked sense of surprise.

It is perhaps with a feeling of surprise that the reader of this chapter notes that I use the wording 'infant analysis'. I was surprised myself when I noticed that I was thinking along those lines. I had had a first session with a 6-month-old little girl, whom I called Lisa, and her extremely depressed mother[1]. Lisa's mother was so depressed that she gave no emotional response. I had the feeling that Lisa and I were in the same hopeless situation, so I turned to Lisa and spoke directly to her. For several months Lisa had avoided her mother's glance, but to my surprise she looked me straight in the eye and paid attention to me when I was talking to her. Lisa seemed surprised that I was giving her my unreserved attention. Talking to her seemed very simple and natural. At the same time I felt it a bit strange to be talking to Lisa in my ordinary voice, thinking and expressing myself in my usual way, as if she could understand what I was saying. Lisa's mother did not seem to notice what was going on because she was so deeply depressed, and this made me less self-conscious.

Since Lisa was attentive and curious, I went on talking, like a verbal caption to what I observed in the room and was aware of within myself. Lisa could not resist the temptation to open an emotional link with me. It was possible to establish a relationship between the infant and me, and I realized that something familiar to me from earlier beginnings of analytical relationships was going on in my mind. This involves relaxation and concentration at the same time, free-floating attention and expanded awareness. A mental space is created for the infant as analysand. I was the infant's analyst and she was my analysand. Her contact with me seemed to reactivate Lisa's relation to her mother, and with every step toward receptivity on the part of her mother Lisa's emotional storm intensified. Her mother was forced to wake up from her depression and had to struggle to hold Lisa and contain her rage. Lisa's and her mother's mutual rejection was transformed into emotional links. The first time Lisa and her mother allowed their eyes to meet they both seemed very shy. They looked at each other for a long time, at first completely silent. Then both of them looked very surprised. It was a strange moment, as still as if an angel were walking through the room.

Lisa and her mother regained a warm, secure relationship. At the same time her mother's depression abated. Our work was intensive—four sessions a week for four weeks. My experience with Lisa was of crucial importance in my future work with infants and their mothers. It was with surprise that I was able to formulate what I had been thinking: The infant is my analysand; I am her analyst; and at the same time her mother is in psychotherapy.

Quite recently I began to work with another 6-month-old infant, a little boy, and his mother. I will call him Ossian. The boy didn't sleep or eat, whined and complained all day and all night. When Ossian was 3 months old his parents became extremely upset after being informed that the boy had a symptom that might indicate a chronic disease. It took two weeks for them to get a more objective, and not so frightening assessment of the risk that the illness would develop.

During the first consultation with Ossian and his mother I became aware of the following sequence of events: Just when Ossian and his mother turn their attention to each other and start an affectionate dialogue Ossian suddenly flings out his arms as if someone has stung him painfully, as if he has been frightened. Then he slings away his pacifier and his comfort rag. He whines and whimpers, not really crying out but just complaining. He avoids his mother's eye and is inconsolable for a long while. This sequence is repeated in the session.

We began our work immediately and had four 45-minute sessions a week. I could see that the boy had attacks of breaking the emotional links and was emotionally confused. Paradoxically this emotional turbulence occurred just at times when the contact with his mother seemed to be at its best.

Even during our first weekend break, a striking change occurred: Ossian slept at night, was eating and was happy. His mother had immediately realized that Ossian at three months had been affected by the feelings that had so upset her in connection with the frightening information she had received about Ossian's possible illness. She understood that her fear was still there. At the first session after the weekend Ossian seemed to have grown and he was happy. But during the session his emotional turbulence recurred again and again. On one occasion when he had just started to calm down after having whined and complained for a long while, he did not let go of his eye contact with me. He sat on his mother's lap looking at me so I went on talking about what I thought I understood. He was very calm, lying still, and attentive. Sometimes there was silence. Ossian looked at me the whole time, so I continued. This went on for 15 minutes! The feeling of surprise that both his mother and I had felt passed into astonishment and finally into a quiet wonder. Then Ossian did something I had never seen before: While he held his head still, turned toward me, he turned his eyes to the side as far as he could so as to get a glimpse of his mother, in whose lap he was sitting. Then he turned his eyes to me again. I commented that I realized that he was trying to get a glimpse of his mother, and the dialogue continued ... Ossian repeated his attempt to get a glimpse of his mother in the same way, looked at me again ... and then turned his face directly toward his mother, looked intently at his mother ... and fell asleep. I went on talking and suddenly there was a rapid movement of his eyes under his closed eyelids. He was dreaming.

After three weeks of analysis, everyday life in the family was restored. The family took a 10-day vacation abroad and everyone was happy during the holiday. Back in analysis again, Ossian continued to express unhappiness; rejection of his mother and emotional storms recurred — but only in the sessions. Sometimes when Ossian had recovered from one of these storms, he looked at his mother and at me in astonishment, as if it were a surprise to him that he could land in this state of mind again and another surprise that he had suddenly recovered. After less than three weeks there were no further signs of his attacking the links. We worked four times a week for a total of six weeks. Then our work was finished.

And I ask myself: Isn't this a mystery?

---

[1] I have described this work in the article "The Psychoanalyst and the Baby: A New Look at Work with Infants." *The International Journal of Psychoanalysis, 82:83-100.*

Part II: <u>BEYOND THE COUCH</u>

APPLICATIONS OF PSYCHOANALYTIC UNDERSTANDING IN SOCIETY

Poem written while travelling in the Metro eating hot <u>croissants</u> and listening to a group of men <u>san papiers</u> from Senegal playing their drums on their way to a demonstration on a Saturday early morning and the rain in Paris wouldn't stop

> Let's face it,
>
> > a quiet life?
>
> No,
>
> > come on!
>
> *That* ain't for us.

Gregorio Kohon (from *The Style of Desire*, unpublished)

ORGANIZATIONS:

Group sculpture by British psychoanalyst Eric Rayner

'The characteristic feature of the social defences system, as we have described it, is its orientation to helping the individual avoid the experience of anxiety, guilt, doubt and uncertainty. As far as possible, this is done by eliminating situations, events, tasks, activities and relationships that cause anxiety or, more correctly, evoke anxieties connected with primitive psychological remnants of the personality'.

[Isabel Menzies Lyth, 'The Functioning of Social Systems',
p.43 in Containing Anxiety in Institutions, FAB, 1988

'On The Wings Of A Song' – Melanie Klein's concept of the Paranoid-Schizoid Position and the problem of values in Society
Elliott Jaques *(Washington)*

I have been engaged for the past 55 years in consultancy research on how to develop healthy social institutions. This work has taken me into governmental organizations, industry and commerce, health and social services, the Church of England and the US Army. The first 20 years of this activity I combined this work half-time, with a half-time practice in child and adult psychoanalysis.

A first major discovery was that psychoanalytical and group dynamics concepts and theory did not have the practice value I had assumed in understanding how to assist social institutions to improve. The problems of social institutions turned out to be caused by poor organization structure and poor managerial and other working processes. It was pathology in these social systems that produced apparent pathological behaviors in their members, and not individual pathologies that produced the stresses in the institutions. I say 'apparent' pathological behaviors, because many of the problem behaviors were the result of ordinary reasonable attempts to survive under difficult organizational circumstances.

There was, however, one concept from Melanie Klein's work that turned out to be of major importance. In the course of my work with social institutions I became aware of how fundamentally important it was for people who had to work together in managerial organizations to be able to trust each other. They did not have to love each other, or even to like each other, for you did not choose who you had to collaborate with in getting your work done. Your colleagues were produced by the vicissitudes of the selection process, and you had to find ways to work together effectively.

It turned out to be impossible to overcome the problems of working relationships by exhorting, or training, or counseling people to behave in a trustworthy manner, or to give them experiences in group dynamics and group processes. The reason turned out to be the simple fact that the organizational systems themselves generated mistrust, and made it necessary for individuals to protect themselves while at the same time doing their best to work and to work together to get the necessary work done.

Let me give a few simple examples. Group dynamic experts have advised the setting up of self-directed teams using group decision making and earning group bonus pay. The fact, however, is that managerial systems are based upon individual employment contract, individual recognition and career development, and individual accountability. Group teams and decision making absolutely confuse everything and everybody because it is unclear who is accountable when things go wrong or who gets the credit when things go right. Stress and manipulation are rampant.

In the same vein who should be held accountable for results, what authority managers should have, what factors should be taken into account in selection, how many layers there should be and why, what is leadership really about, and countless other problems, leave individuals to sort things out as best they can, work together as best they can. I have had the great privilege of seeing, and coming to admire and respect, the constructive and creative side of human nature that tends to be obscured from us in the psychoanalytical situation. For people really do make these systems work, and they do manage to work together, in spite of the difficult conditions.

But one other finding has emerged. For people to be able to associate, we really do have to be able to trust each other. In situations where we have been able to help organizations to modify their structures and systems, so that they provide for clear accountabilities, mutual authorities, just methods of recognition and fair differential compensation, and many other things besides, the people find themselves in a situation where they can trust each other, because the systems can be relied upon to require behaviors that are trustworthy.

Constructive behaviors take most and flourish as though on wings of song. Behaviors change 180° overnight; and certainly without any change whatever in personality makeup. Morale and productivity, both, take great and sustainable upward strides.

I then became aware of an important application to social situations of Melanie Klein's picture of infant development. Mistrust and suspicion, and trust, (paranoid-schizoid position), underlie love, hate and ambivalence (depressive position) developmentally. So it is in the social world. The basic glue that holds humanity together and ensures human species survival (and, indeed, all species survival), is our ability to rely upon everyone everywhere, stranger and neighbor alike, not to decide on their own account to do anything that would harm anyone else. In order for this trust to hold, we have to be able to rely upon our genetic endowment supported by our laws and rules and regulations, to rule out such behaviors

It is when we walk down a badly lit street at night in a neighborhood where we do not trust the policing, that we experience how much we rely upon this kind of mutual trust. Terrorist acts are acts against this basic glue of mutual trust that bonds us together, and so strikes terror into our hearts.

The etymology of justice is joining or bonding. The etymology of injustice is the breaking of bonds, and gives us the term injury. We do not have to love, or even to like each other to get along. We do have to be able to rely upon our genes and our laws to provide a social life that extends from our homes and neighborhoods right across the world, if we are to live in a world free from the mistrust that can stir the deepest remnants of the paranoid anxiety with which we took our very first breaths. To have sufficient opportunity to like and love as well, is a wonderful bonus.

Ubuntu – From the consulting room to the vegetable garden
Astrid Berg *(Cape Town)*

Prologue

The place is Cape Town – the oldest city in South Africa, at the tip of the African continent. The writer is a child psychiatrist and Jungian Analyst, born, bred and educated in this country. The position I hold is that of a senior consultant and lecturer in the Department of Psychiatry, University of Cape Town and I am also in part-time private analytic practice. The narrative that follows is about an important part of my professional life, probably the one that is impacting more deeply on me than most of my other commitments. I have not tried to separate out facts from feelings and personal views, but have allowed them to interweave as the story unfolds.

The word *ubuntu* appearing in the title needs some explanation. The Xhosa proverb *Umtu ngumtu ngabantu*, literally meaning 'a person is a person because of another person', is a concept that is common to all African traditional cultures. It describes the emphasis that is placed on the close relationship between the individual and the group. Personal development is a progressive incorporation into the community and is given expression by the various rituals at the different life stages. The western 'I think therefore I am' is replaced by 'I participate therefore I am'. (Schutte, 1998) The term *ubuntu* thus signifies our common humanity. Implicit in this is the notion of sharing with others, of what has been termed 'vital participation'. (p.55)

Entering into the unknown

It was 1995 – the year after the first democratic election in South Africa. The new country was in its beginnings and it was perhaps not by chance that the first conference on Infant Mental Health was held in Cape Town. This turned out to be a most stimulating and productive event and it was the start of many creative endeavours in Cape Town. A large research project in conjunction with Reading University, UK on intervention in post-partum depression was started and is ongoing. Then there is the University of Cape Town Parent-Infant Mental Health Service which I initiated and am responsible for. This clinical service is for children under 3 years old and is based in two places: one in Rondebosch, where the Children's Hospital is situated and which draws on a wide socio-economic spectrum of patients. The other is in Khayelitsha, the largest informal settlement outside of Cape Town. It is here where the real challenges lie.

The work in Rondebosch is much like I imagine work at any Child Psychiatry Unit in Europe. There is a reception area with staff, consulting rooms, playrooms, and a steady team that fills the building. The patients are seen as per appointment, the week is scheduled to the hour for every person working there. Regular team discussions are held where case material is presented in detail and where academic input is part of the course. It is reliable, predictable, and known. It is embedded in the long history of similar units all over the western world.

Khayelitsha offered none of this for me. I had to start from the beginning, I had to engage in a process, the complexity of which I had not envisioned.

Khayelitsha is a sprawling township, about 11km from Metropolitan Cape Town, adjacent to the International Airport. It lies in the so-called Cape Flats – an outstretched area between the mountains of the Peninsula and those of the lush winelands of the Cape. It has spectacular views onto both sets of mountain ranges, but on the ground the soil is poor and sandy, it is water logged because of winter rains, desert like and dusty because of summer winds. Its inhabitants are Xhosa speaking people who have moved from their former 'homeland', now the Eastern Cape, to the city in search for employment, better education and health care. Mostly the family, especially the elders, remain behind in the traditional homestead while the young people, young mothers flock to the urban areas. Housing is in make-shift shelters, which, as time passes may be turned into houses made of bricks.

As one descends for landing or passes on the highway, from the Airport into the City, one sees these shacks – thousands of them, close to each other. They all seem the same, and one does not really want to look and is grateful for the concrete fence that has been erected to prevent people from crossing the road. It is easier to ignore and drive by swiftly. In the apartheid days 'white' people were not allowed into these 'black' townships. The reasons for these laws were complex, but were motivated psychologically by a drive for power, based on an unconscious sense of inferiority of the self that manifested in the fear of the other. The other, as a recipient of projections, became condensed into one undifferentiated mass of blackness. A dark skin colour became the signifier for a host of psychic attributes: mental inferiority and primitiveness in the widest possible sense of these words. Thus external laws had to be made to keep these perceived threats to 'white' civilisation at bay. The brutality and thoroughness of the laws of the apartheid government were such that this split was successfully perpetuated externally as well as internally.

It was only when I entered Khayelitsha in 1995 that I became fully aware of how much I had incorporated this racist split. Apartheid had been an effective system indeed. The withdrawal of projections has been an ongoing process for me and with it strong emotions have come to the surface: emotions of fear, shame and guilt. I have had to acknowledge these within myself and I am sure that this process is one that people in South Africa have had to go through and are still going through.

Fear of otherness was manifested concretely in my complete unfamiliartiy of the geographical design of Khayelitsha. Going into such an unknown area meant facing physical uncertainty on many levels, including being violated in one way or another. It also involved having to face the poverty which I had only read about in newspapers and had preferred to ignore. When, after a while, I came to know the area and some of the people living there, my fear soon gave way to shame that, as an educated person, I had been completely ignorant of my fellow citizens' life style, customs and values.

I recall one Tuesday morning in the beginning when I was walking with my co-worker, Nosisana Nama, along the street the one side of which had shops selling all sorts of things – from meat to clothes to taped music. On the other side was a children's crèche and a little boy was peering over the wall, calling out something in Xhosa. I heard a man on the opposite shouting back at him and the child ducked. I was told that the little boy had exclaimed "Look, a white woman". The man had chided him, saying "She is your mother".

This interaction moved me deeply – here was this older man, who had known the inhumanity of apartheid, and who was accepting me as a person and teaching this young child to do the same. In African tradition anyone who could be another person's parent in terms of age is addressed with the respectful term of *uMama* or *uTata*. He was telling this child not to look at skin colour, but at the position of the person in terms of age, and to act according to that. There is much to learn for us in the western, so-called 'civilised' world.

Finding a space

During all of my time in Khayelitsha – from 1995 to the present – I am accompanied and led by 2 special women: Nosisana Nama and Nokwanda Mtoto. Both are Xhosa speaking and deeply connected to their ancestors and traditional values. They act as my guides and mentors and together we learn from each other. There is mutual respect and trust and together we have had to go through some difficult times. The most intense of these was our naïve attempt at setting up a community resource for mothers and their infants in a renovated shipping container. Structurally altered containers are a frequent sight in the township – they act as telephone houses, meeting places, offices. We bought one of these from a woman, called by her clan name of Magadebe, who was running a crèche – she did not use the one container and we thought it appropriate to be situated near a place designated for the care of handicapped children. The money used had come as a gift from my family abroad, and in our trust of Magadebe, did not ask for a receipt. Initially all went well – after we had a night time burglary, we appointed a night guard and paid him, as well as Magadebe, a monthly sum of money —for his services and for the municipal rates for using this piece of land. My daughter and her school friends even painted the container with bright flowers. We had an inaugural ceremony which was a colourful occasion. We used it as our office once a week, and during other times it was used by other organisations who wanted to inform mothers about various issues – such as the safe use of paraffin. So, it seemed ideal.

However, gradually it became clear to us that Magadebe was a woman with trickster traits who was exploiting our good will. She told people that the container was hers, and denied that we had paid a large sum for it. Other unpleasant, plainly untruthful allegations were made, such as that we were withholding funds we were thought to have from the community. We felt increasingly fearful and vulnerable, so much so that Nokwanda, who lives near by, started having bad dreams and was fearing bewitchment. I was very worried and after her house was gutted with fire in December 1998, I decided it was time move. The feeling of paranoia that was evoked was real and came from deep layers of the unconscious plus of course very real outer danger. Through all of this, Nosisana, Nokwanda and I worked as a team. We understood Magadebe to be greedy, entitled and prepared to tell lies in order to obtain as much money and material possessions she could lay her hands on. Such behaviour can evoke the notion that she or others could bewitch us – a concept that needs to be taken seriously, because it can be a real threat to life.

I told the above to the head of my Department of Psychiatry at the University and he advised me not to go into the area for the time being. Nosisana, who does not live in Khayeltisha, shared this view. In January 1999 she went in alone for the first time to feel out the atmosphere. It was only when she reported back to me that everything seemed to be fine, that I returned.

We decided that the best way forward was to continue our work in one of the official well-baby clinics where infants are brought for weighing and immunisation. These are mainly staffed by nursing sisters. We eventually settled down in a clinic called *Empilisweni*, meaning 'good health'. This is situated in one of the sub-sections of Khayelitsha called 'Harare'. This place feels safe, protected by the community and larger municipal structures and above all, is staffed by nurses who are professionals, but who care deeply for their people.

Looking at this process from a deeper perspective several issues arise. There were many times I asked myself why I was continuing wanting to work in this area. For many 'white' people living in Cape Town going into the township in the first place was, according to them, asking for trouble. I had heard this often enough. When I was then confronted with all these difficulties, these fears and predictions of unrealistic idealism seemed to be confirmed. The opinion that our western values of right and wrong, of boundaries between professional life and personal life, between the individual and collective were not compatible in a community where seemingly other values, other rules were adhered to.

What continued to motivate me on a conscious level were several factors. I regarded the above view as a pejorative one, one that was of the stereotyping kind reminiscent of the past. Cultural differences certainly do exist, the interaction with others, the dance one has with them is to my mind much more complex, more differentiated than the western styles I am used to. Much more power lies in community relationships, in the interconnectedness between the people than in the individualistic society of Europe and Northern America. What we experienced with Magadebe was an unfortunate incident, one we could have had in any society where there was so much poverty and deprivation.

Then there were the people I had come to know and respect – Nosisana and Nokwanda, as well as nursing staff and the mothers with their babies. They had become an integral and essential part of my life. I could not imagine being without them. At another level there is the wish to connect with the African culture, to be enriched and learn from age-old traditions, particularly those of ancestor reverence. In part this is a making-up for lost time – when in the first half of my life I was prevented from engaging with African people on this level – because of the political situation in the country and my own lack of awareness of what was happening. It is of course also about guilt and reparation, but there is more to it.

In my Europeaness I have lost my own connection to my ancestors, to a deeper universal rootedness. The separation anxiety that is so prevalent with

Western mothers and their babies, is almost non-existent in traditional African culture. I do think that this has to do with that linking to the clan and to the ancestors that is present for every individual from the very beginning of life. The person is merely part of a much larger whole – this notion is profoundly reassuring and accounts for the sense of equanimity that I come across, time and again. This is not resignation or depression, but a knowing of a greater order in which the individual is embedded. While I am mindful of the danger of romanticising the other culture, of stereotyping and generalising in an idealising way, I do experience this sense of harmony as a deeply embedded part of the collective psyche. This is of course not to deny or minimize the conflict, the pain, the deprivation that exists in daily life.

The *Mdlezana Centre, ubuntu,* and the garden

The word *Mdlezana* was chosen by Nosisana and Nokwanda. It is an old Xhosa word that depicts that time when mother and infant are one, are inseparable. It comes close to the Winnicottian term of 'primary maternal preoccupation'. One room at the Empilisweni clinic has become the *Mdlezana Centre*. On a weekly basis we are present and mothers and the staff have come to know and trust this regular rhythm. Very often the clinic is busy with a great number of women and infants sitting and waiting. The patience, the sense of order in seeming chaos is what strikes so many visitors from abroad. The babies and toddlers seem calm and contented – there is none of the anxiety present that is often so evident with my 'white' patients.

We are faced with a wide range of problems, often of a physical nature and of late increasing numbers of HIV infected mothers and babies. Underlying the majority of cases however is poverty and its sequelae of helplessness and despair. The depression is manifest in both mother and child. We have developed various means of dealing with this on a clinical level and within ourselves, but here I wish to bring one theme – namely that of *ubuntu*. As stated earlier, this African concept runs deep within the psyche. Like all human attributes this one too has positive and negative aspects to it.

With the income generated from well-off patients that are seen at the Parent-Infant Service in Rondebosch, I manage to pay both my colleagues as well as have cash and food on hand for the mothers. While I am mindful that the latter goes completely against any analytic principles, the giving to others of what one has oneself is syntonic with African culture. In practical terms this means that we give the mothers money to attend appointments at the Children's Hospital. Apparent non-compliance there mostly has to do with not having the financial means to pay for the taxi fare to go to the Hospital which is situated in Rondebosch. In our 6 years of experience with this practice, we have had very few mothers who have abused our good-will. Almost all of them use the money to get themselves and their children to the appointments In addition, when extreme poverty is evident, we give the mother a food parcel, which consists of maize meal, beans and sugar – staple food for the family. While the quantities are not large, it is a gesture from our side and we make it clear that this is not a 'hand-out', but given in the spirit of *ubuntu*. It is accepted as such and because we do this together, I never feel that it comes from the premise of the 'white' woman giving to the poor 'black' women. In a traditional culture where much is manifest in the concrete – such as the rituals of various parts of the life-cycle – the actual giving of something, no matter how little, means that we really do care. Words of empathy and containment are not enough.

However, in myself I felt that something else needed to be activated. While the positive side of sharing, of giving away of what one has is something that has been lost in western culture, there is the negative side of passivity that is constellated through this custom of trusting that the collective will provide. My European background, my own parents' determination to make things better for themselves through hard work, made it difficult for me to accept the apparent resignation I felt in so many of the mothers, particularly the very young ones. The idea of the mothers doing something with their hands that would also feed themselves and their families took root. After a consultation with a local gardening project, I discussed our idea with the head nurse of the clinic. As is so often the case in Khayelitsha, she said she had had the same vision for her clinic for some time and was thus very supportive of the idea of making a garden around the building of the clinic. With money donated to me from colleagues from the USA, our dream was realised. At present the clinic garden is like an oasis amidst the sandy soil of the area. Vegetables of all sorts are growing and our gardener is a devoted man, who is frail because of Aids and Tuberculosis, but is grateful for having a task. It has been disappointing that the mothers themselves have not engaged with the work as hoped – the reasons for this are many, one being the fear of stigmatization that they would be seen as HIV sufferers in the community. The next step is to open up the garden at the back of the clinic and give each mother a patch of ground. Perhaps the relative seclusion from the outer world, and the fact that they have this piece of land is their own to cultivate, may motivate them in the way that we had hoped.

Going on

The weekly mornings spent in Khayelitsha have become part of my life. They are never predictable. All I know is that Nosisana and Nokwanda will be waiting for me and that the clinic with its staff will be bustling with mothers and babies. Who I will see and how many, is not foreseeable, although mothers have become increasingly reliable in keeping the appointments given to them. The garden continues to grow – the potatoes by at least five centimetres per week during the summer. What will happen to them is still open.

A part of me wants to organise the garden, hurry the process and make things happen, but I have learnt patience. Collective forces, conscious and unconscious, are prominent in this community and I respect them. I have come to go with the flow, take opportunities where they present themselves, and hold back and wait when doors seem closed. Perhaps acceptance of things, trusting that they will work out has become part of my psyche too.

Reference

Shutte, A.(1998). Philosophy for Africa. UCT Press

Very brief psychotherapy? An approach to managerial assessment
Olya Khaleelee *(London)*

There are a number of reasons why an executive might come for a psychological assessment, including selection for a new role, development either in the current role or in order to re-think career strategy and, finally, crisis intervention.

On this particular occasion, the person being assessed was a 40-year old Finance Director of a subsidiary of a large financial services group. After a period of high performance, James had within the last 2-3 years been performing unsatisfactorily. He was now being moved to another role, which was seen by his superiors as his last opportunity to regain his former high standards. Failure to do so would lead to him being dismissed. We felt under a certain pressure to help him.

Using a multi-faceted, psycho-analytic approach we - my work partner and I - expect to achieve a reasonably accurate understanding of an individual's personality. We are interested in how personality development, influenced by formative experiences, has affected career choice and leadership capacity. The assessment day consists of four exercises and two discussions, with up to an hour of feedback and discussion of the test results. A further meeting is scheduled to discuss the report and its implications for career strategy and personal development.

The exercises include a family sketch, looking at the individual within his or her family system. We are interested also in the pattern of livelihoods that come down through the generations. Later, within the context of the oedipal, 3-person, assessment setting, we discuss the individual's formative experiences in detail, much as one might do during a consultation when referring someone for psychotherapy. We are interested in their experience of growing up, how they perceived the personalities and values of their parents, the quality of parenting received, and relationships with siblings. We try to understand how these experiences, including educational progression (or lack of it), have affected their development.

The core of the assessment process is an exercise called the *Defence Mechanisms Test*. This was developed by Kragh (1955) using a perceptual process beyond awareness. Using a tachistoscope the assessee comments on a number of pictures, which are flashed up very quickly. The technique identifies and measures the defence mechanisms the individual intuitively mobilises to protect himself or herself from stress.

108

Much research has been carried out since then applying the test in various settings. Essentially, it provides a profile of the individual's emotional development over time and pinpoints within a reasonable time range, significant features of their development and where defences have arisen. We generate hypotheses about whether this person is an early or late developer, how resilient they are and how well or little defended.

Further hypotheses are formed about the effects on functioning at work, which is explored in an intensive discussion about working life. For example, whether someone is a good initiator, perhaps entrepreneurial, often related to fast early development, or whether better at consolidating work, related to more regular emotional development, will affect how they function during times of organisational change and growth. Their managerial style is discussed, including how the person believes their strengths and limitations are perceived by bosses, subordinates and peers. This is combined with their perceptions of how they are viewed by significant people in their personal life.

This information is further integrated with their results from a problem solving exercise, which explores intellectual capacity. We develop ideas about how logical, intuitive or analytical the person is, whether they prefer to operate at the detailed or strategic levels and how much confidence they have in their intellectual ability. Finally, a Colour Test explores current conflicts and provides data about personality characteristics such as ambition, drive and doggedness.

Taken together, the exercises and discussions provide a fairly complete picture of the individual from different perspectives. The understanding we gain from this is then offered back to the person. This frequently generates a flash of clarity whereby the pattern of the person's life suddenly comes together before their eyes. At that moment they can see what has happened to them and why.

With James, it became clear from his test results and our counter-transference reactions to him, that he was a man of capacity who for unconscious reasons was now trying to fail. The evidence was presented to him and he was able to make the connection between his current performance and the professional failure of his father when he was the same age. The resulting shock made him face the reality of his own situation and enabled him to make a choice between using his capacities fully or failing as his father had done. He was enabled to take the first course and we were told a few months later that his performance in the new role was outstanding and thought was being given to promoting him to MD of the subsidiary from which he had been moved.

This makes the assessment a powerful transformational instrument, akin to a brief psychotherapy intervention. Many managers who engage with this process feel that they have stood back and taken a good look at their lives. From this, various decisions emerge. It is not uncommon for the person to have subsequent role consultations to enable them to retain and use their insight in order to bring about changes in the way they function at work. Or they may, in addition, enter therapy in order to deal with old problems stemming from formative experiences, which are still affecting them as managers today.

References

Khaleelee, O and Woolf, R. (1996) Personality, life experience and leadership capability. In: *Leadership & Organization Development Journal* 17/6: 5-11.
Kragh, U. (1955) *The Actual-Genetic Model of Perception-Personality: An Experimental Study with Non-Clinical and Clinical Groups.* Lund: Sweden, University of Lund, Thesis.

Finding the familiar objects   Michael Sebek *(Prague)*

Gate keepers (the immigration police, customs officers, doormen etc.) are holders of real and magic power. There are also gates which are nearly closed, like the Iron Curtain was. Can people get in? And how to get out ? And are there any 'gates' in the psychoanalytic treatment?   What is going on in gates ?

After landing in the U.S.A. several years ago. I had to be checked as usual by an immigration officer. He looked at my visa and said that the kind of my visa somehow did not fit to the purpose of my journey which was residence at the Austen Riggs Center. Then he asked what Riggs was because the logo of Riggs (in the inviting letter) did not indicate it. My reply was : 'a psychiatric hospital'. This suddenly allowed him to become an informal authority. He said his wife worked with drug abusers, and so he had no other objections and let me go. Unfortunately, in the next 5 minutes I was in trouble. Customs officers discovered a small sausage in my luggage and in front of me threw it into the garbage. They wanted me to pay a penalty of $50. One of officers asked me if I was from Prague, and then he added his parents were from Prague also. He let me go without paying anything. These two very much related stories can be interpreted in various ways, but I am interested mainly in two qualities: (1) the process of changing of the external, formal and powerful authority into containing, erotising, informal authority which is flexible but at the same time not being able to keep rules and laws sharply; (2) a desire to find a similarity between own internal objects and external objects, or internal objects in others.

Both stories when they are retold have some dream-like characteristics. For instance, it can be stated that I could enter the U.S.A. because somebody's wife who I never met[saw] worked with drug abusers. And I did not pay a penalty because somebody's parents lived in some past in the same city as I did. Furthermore, my sausage was dangerous for the American people. These people were saved thanks to the customs officer who threw the sausage into the garbage. Nevertheless, these (acted out) primary processes, beyond the practice of the law, are an important part of identification based on separation of good objects from bad ones. Fortunately, I was chosen as a good object by both officers thanks to my fortuitous capacity to mirror or represent their good objects. My dry sausage, being by definition the bad object, finished its existence in the trash can.

A British analyst Roger Money-Kyrle (1947, 1978) who belonged to those in the past who were also interested in social processes, wrote the following:

'..... *If these two, the inner and the outer object, do not closely correspond, society becomes for us something other than individuals in it; and if the gap between them is a wide one, we may abandon the individuals for the abstraction; or rather seek to control them, in a compulsive and omnipotent way, for its supposed benefit. In an extreme form, this lack of conformity between the inner and the outer object leads to the totalitarian fallacy that the welfare of the abstract state is best served by sacrificing the welfare of all its concrete citizens.' (p.204)*

Looking back to both aforementioned stories, the state officers representing law and powerful authority could become less oppressive when they found some similarity between them and me, or if they succeeded in finding some of their internal objects connected with me (being an external object to them). It is also the way any totalitarian authority can become less totalitarian. Money-Kyrle indicates that growing differences between internal and external objects provoke a totalitarian omnipotence and compulsive control. I think this is the important component of the genesis of what I call the totalitarian object (Sebek, 1996,1998).

Money-Kyrle's thoughts about a gap between internal and external objects indicate indirectly an existence of a very important aspect of our internal life: some urge to find in external reality what we consciously and also unconsciously expect, and what is derived from internal objects and their relation. When we meet a new external object, we try to identify something familiar to us, which is either discovered by perceptual processes, or it is projected from our internal space. A sense of similarity can be of a psychotic quality when projective processes prevail. I do not exaggerate when stating that probably all individuals under normal conditions strive to change their external objects to be more similar to their internal objects. So far the external world mirrors the internal one, or gives a sense or meaning to the psychic reality. The gap between external and internal objects can be diminished by the process of identification, and by projections and introjections in so far as these are a part of the identification process.

In summary, finding the closeness of some similar (in reality or fantasy) objects is the easiest way how to set up a meaningful relationship, a new psychic structure kept in the long-term memory. Maybe, the immigration officer might remember me some time through his wife 's work with drug abusers, and the customs officer might remember some

112

time not only me but also my sausage because his parents came to the U.S.A. from Prague.

No doubt, psychoanalytic encounters and the work in the dyad is also strongly influenced by the tendency to diminish a gap between the internal world of the patient and the internal world of the analyst. Shortly, there is also some necessity to get through 'gates'. Although the analyst' s disclosure as a technical tool is under current debate among some analysts, there are ordinary 'disclosures' in each session which consist in manners of speech, peculiarities of gesture, style and richness of interpretation and changing moods of the analyst to which the patient already learned smoothly to register and respond. And when the patient has discovered that his/her analyst like to listen to dreams, he/she knows one of 'gates' through which to get into the analyst.

Anyway, the concept of transference is basic for understanding the tendency of the patient to create a familiar world in psychoanalysis. Potentially, the analyst is able to take over the historical and actual role of the patient's internal objects. In fact, I suppose that this tendency to diminish the gap between internal and external objects goes beyond what is conceived to be the ordinary transference, because it is the aspect of normal everyday relations, for example, the closeness of the sexual pair when referring to genital identification involving simultaneous and intense identification with one's own sexual role and the object's complementary role during the sexual intercourse. Normal adults have a capacity for entering and becoming one with another person.

The big difference or gap between internal and external objects (or objects of other persons) creates a tension and may have a totalitarian solution in social relations. A general libidinal tendency to diminish the gap between objects of individuals by finding some familiar objects is an important building stone of all human relationships starting from birth. Also, psychoanalytic relations between the patient and the therapist are characterised by the convergence or also divergence of object relations, which goes beyond the ordinary transference and countertransference.

References:

Money-Kyrle, R. (1947) Social Conflict and the Challenge to Psychology *British Journal of Medical Psychology,* 31:198-210
Sebek, M. (1996) Fates of Totalitarian Objects. *International Forum Psychoanalysis* 5:289-294
Sebek, M. (1998) Post-totalitarian Personality – Old Internal Objects in a New Situation, *Journal American Academy of Psychoanalysis.* 26:295-311

Organizing an international psychoanalytic conference: the Babel of languages, cultures and theories

Jorge Canestri *(Rome)*

The organisation of an international psychoanalytic congress or conference is an activity that we carry out alongside our normal analytical practice, and those of you who have undertaken such a task know how many problems there are to be dealt with. Some of these may be of such importance and interest that they exceed the realm of mere anecdote and personal exertion; I have therefore thought of contributing to this volume with a brief consideration of the problem of communication among analysts.

My experience is based on the organisation of the 42nd Congress of the IPA, Nice 2001, in my role as Chair of the Programme Committee, and also as Chair of the Working Party on Theoretical Issues of the E.P.F. But in reality, as often happens, my concern about this topic has roots in my own personal history. I was born in Argentina, Spanish was my mother tongue, and my psychoanalytic training was carried out in the Spanish language and culture. Analytically speaking, the Institute of the Argentine Psychoanalytic Association was for a long time mainly Freudian-Kleinian, but between 1960 and 1975 it enthusiastically incorporated Lacanian ideas and those of French psychoanalysis in general. When I emigrated to Italy I discovered the Italian language and incorporated it into those that I already knew; but above all, I had to assimilate another literary, scientific, philosophic and psychoanalytic culture.

Working in two continents with patients from different countries and in different languages has certainly made me particularly sensitive to the problem of the passage from one language and culture to another, just as writing about psychoanalysis in different languages and for a variety of dissimilar publications has made me aware of the problem of trans-cultural communication. It is true that a translation is always and in any case possible, but it is also true that the problems are not limited to translation. Let us begin from here.

In the presentation in the IPA Newsletter *International Psychoanalysis*, vol. 9, Issue 2, 2000, of the Scientific Programme of the 42nd Congress, I wrote that the problem of language conditioned the choices and therefore the exclusions that the Programme Committee had to make. I quote: "I think it is useful to know that simultaneous translation (criticised by many for its sometimes inevitable approximation) represents a third of the Congress budget. As usual the plenaries will have simultaneous translation, and so will two of the afternoon panels. In which language if not English should almost all the other activities be conducted? It is clear that today English represents what Latin did in Europe up until and beyond the 17th century; that is, a language for exchange and mutual understanding within the field of culture *that cannot, however, take the place of the mother tongue when discussing clinical or conceptual differences*. For this reason some colleagues declined their invitation to participate in certain activities where they would not be able to speak in their own language. Where possible the Programme Committee has created some of the panels or workshops in other languages, but this solution cannot be generalised as it would favour incommunicability between different cultures. One language—one culture does

114

not wholly correspond to the truth, but it is fairly clear that there is a connection between language and psychoanalytic culture". I have quoted this paragraph of the presentation because the problem discussed in it arises again in every international conference as well as in the activities of the E.P.F. The problem is of minor importance in the other two regions of the IPA as they are almost monolingual (Spanish and English for Latin America and North America respectively, with the addition of Portuguese and French, but with a good reciprocal comprehension when not perfect bilingualism).With the intention of going more deeply into the question of cultural and linguistic differences and their weight in our practice and theory, a panel on 'Psychoanalysis Across Cultural and Linguistic Differences' was organized for the 42nd Congress. In this panel the participants began to reflect on topics that are, in my opinion, fundamental to our discipline, especially now that it is expanding towards countries, languages and cultures that are very different from the Mittel-European culture in which it was born. Several years ago (1971) Takeo Doi, in his fascinating *The Anatomy of Dependence*, introduced us to the meeting/clash between cultures, and to the conceptual as well as practical problems that arose as a result of the union of Japanese culture with psychoanalysis. However, the presenters of the above mentioned panel quite rightly drew attention to the lack of specific psychoanalytic contributions referring to the conceptualization of cultural and linguistic problems, with few exceptions.

As I said before, if the problem were limited to the translation between different languages, or to the incidence of cultural differences in theory and practice, it would be less worrying. However, within the international psychoanalytical community there is a growing awareness of a difficulty of communication between analysts that is, to a certain extent, independent of the language or culture to which they belong, as it is noticeable even between psychoanalysts who speak the same language and come from the same analytical tradition. Concerning this point H.Smith (2000) wrote that tribal dialects are spoken in an obvious clinical and theoretical confusion of languages in international conferences and meetings. Some of these obstacles in communication can certainly be attributed to a curious difference that can be seen in our attitude as analysts: we have a careful attitude of listening to our patients and we lose it when we dialogue with our colleagues. This awareness is nothing new. W.R.Bion was already writing about it in some undated notes (probably around 1960) in his *Cogitations*:

> "Language has been invented; translation can be achieved; musical and mathematical notations exist; men compose and paint. And now psycho-analysis attempts to elucidate the barriers and links that hinder or promote the relationships that require a capacity for communication. Nevertheless, the success of psychoanalysis lies so far not so much in bringing communication nearer, as in showing unmistakably the feebleness of our methods of communication even in the communication of disagreement. But this does not touch a yet graver issue, namely the problem of communication with our successors, for it would appear on the surface that if we cannot communicate with our contemporaries, we are even less likely to be able to communicate with our successors. If this communication cannot be made, the future development of analysis is imperilled and the successful discoveries made so far could be lost to the world" (p.173).

This paragraph identifies some of the knots to be unravelled when considering the problem of communication. Certainly, I cannot do more than mention them; the interested reader will follow Bion's notes and add others of his own. Let us see what development Bion suggests. If we give the name 'communication' to the link between related objects, in order to solve the problem of the confusion that arises in scientific controversies we can hypothesize recourse to various therapies; for example, says the author, to the simultaneous translation (as at international congresses) or to a rigorous mathematical logic. These therapies prove to be somewhat ineffective; there exists an "impotence of the disputants who show an inability to meet each other's contentions because they cannot communicate thesis or antithesis" (p.173). Why? Bion thinks that such a link exists in mathematics or in music, and personally I am inclined to think that this is so. Mathematics functions– in this case whether one has a platonic or non-platonic vision of the discipline is of little importance; it adheres to reality and can be communicated without difficulty to anyone, in different cultures and across generations. The loss of information that may occur due to the passing of time or through changes from one culture to another is negligible. This is not so in psychoanalysis. Bion wonders whether this could be due to the fact that the psychoanalyst fails to record a certain material because it is obvious to him, because it is part of his cultural environment and is therefore taken as acquired. The changing of culture or of era could render it incomprehensible or lacking in sufficient information.

This observation tangentially touches on the matter I mentioned above. But the main question is *"What should be the content of the psycho-analytic communication?"* Probably, says the author, in order to adequately face up to this point we should have a methodological concept that is alien to science. Not even the concepts deriving from the conceptual revolution produced by quantum mechanics would be of much help in giving an account of our experience. I cannot sufficiently emphasize the importance of this observation: it seems paradoxical, but psychoanalytical institutions and psychoanalysts themselves, although exerting themselves to refute the theses of those who question the 'scientificity' of psychoanalysis, have shown very little care and interest in trying to define which model of science psychoanalysis should refer to. What appears to be missing, with the due exceptions that confirm the rule, is an appropriate epistemological reflection concerning the specific object and its statute (Canestri, 2001). Without it, communication, whose central importance in the scientific method is repeatedly emphasized by Bion, will always fail in our discipline.

Bion suggests that the analyst, like the navigator, should make use of an artefact whose characteristics would exonerate him from the described interferences, i.e. from changes in convention and culture. In order to safeguard from confusion, this expedient should be used in analytic practice as well as in communication with others, and would allow to embody what one wants to communicate in a 'notation that is precise and permanent' (p.175). But this solution, with which in theory everyone would agree, soon reveals its limitations. We are all familiar with Bions' love of logic and his desire - clearly expressed in *Elements of Psychoanalysis*: '... the elements I seek are to be such that relatively few are required to express, by changes in combination, nearly all the theories essential to the working psycho-analyst' (p.2) - to force thought and practice into univocal formulations. In order to do this the elements must be invested with fixed values. The result of his efforts is condensed in *The Grid*. It is not difficult to identify in the definition of the elements the essence of old and prestigious philosophical research: from the *Dissertatio de arte combinatoria* by

G.W.Leibniz (1666) to the *Begriffsschrift...des reinen Denkens* (1879) by G.Frege. It is interesting to observe that Leibniz, unaware at the time of writing his thesis (of which the quoted Dissertatio is a re-writing) of the demonstrations of the geometrists and only discovering them later, writes: 'By reflecting more intensely on this study he is referring to the methodology of combinatorial analysis deduced from the *mos geometricus*, I arrived by necessity at this admirable observation: that one could certainly excogitate an alphabet of human thoughts and that from the combination of the letters of this alphabet and from the analysis of vocabularies formed by those letters, all things could be discovered and judged.' (G VII: p.185). In his *Elements*, Bion invokes Euclid's Elements. I cannot dwell longer on the affinities of the projects by Leibniz, Frege and Bion, who have a methodological antecedent in F. Bacon (Canestri 2001), but they are certainly fascinating. Remaining strictly in the psychoanalytical field, I must recall a similar attempt made by J.Lacan with the theorisation of his 'mathèmes'. Also in this case, fixed values were assigned to symbols that were needed to express through combinatorial analysis 'all the theories essential to the working psycho-analyst'. Lacan's pretension of writing proper algorithms with these formulae (mathèmes) was perhaps more radical than that of Bion, but in my opinion, in both cases the project came up against an aspect of psychoanalytical practice that had been underestimated. For the algorithms to function, the value or meaning of the symbols used in the combination must be univocal, as whoever is familiar with the functioning of computers based on Boolean logic will certainly know. Any vagueness or slipping of the meaning of the terms used makes it impossible to form the algorithm. It so happens that psychoanalytic theories and concepts (and naturally the vocabularies needed to name them) are studded with a wide variety of meanings that inevitably increase, inasmuch as the theories with which the psychoanalyst works in his daily practice are to a large extent private and preconscious. We must thank J.Sandler (1983) for giving an accurate and convincing theoretical status to this reality. He, in fact, makes a distinction between 'official theories' and 'private theories'. Official theories are the offspring of the psychoanalyst's academic training, while private theories have a more complex and varied origin. When the psychoanalyst, in his clinical experience, enters into contact with a wide variety of problems and with the effects that these produce on him, 'he will preconsciously (descriptively speaking, unconsciously) construct a whole variety of theoretical segments which relate directly to his clinical work. They are the products of unconscious thinking, are very much partial theories, models or schemata, which have the quality of being available in reserve, so to speak, to be call upon whenever necessary' (p.38).

Clinical experience is not the only source of these private theories, as I attempted to demonstrate in a work concerning this matter written in honour of Sandler (Canestri, 1999), but for our present purposes it is sufficient to consider it as being the principal source. As Sandler emphasizes, the 'private, preconscious theories or schemata' are internally contradictory and certainly not usually valued very highly in scientific circles. As we all know, this does not stop them from existing and us from using them. However, these theories do not only have a negative trait; in the above mentioned work, I have said that they may and usually do have a heuristic value also. But there is an evident risk deriving from the recognition of the heuristic value of 'private theories': an inevitable increase in theoretical pluralism and in the babelization of the language of psychoanalysis i.e.

an effect contrary to that proposed by Bion. An equally inevitable consequence is the increase of the difficulties in communication between psychoanalysts, and this was the harassment of myself (and of others) in the organisation of an international psychoanalytic conference.

Here we have the classical question: What do we do about it? Firstly, it is clear that we cannot deny reality simply because it would be nice to follow 'logistical' routes that are more suggestive and epistemologically more correct. It is equally true that Bion's warning concerning the central importance of communication in scientific method and the danger of seeing our discoveries disappear if this communication is not guaranteed, must be taken very seriously. A therapeutic measure that is certainly important, but less so if we consider the problem in its totality, consists in at least specifying the sense (meaning, use, limits) in which certain concepts are used and the relationship that they have with a whole concept or particular theoretical model. As an example I quote R.Britton (1999) in the introduction to his book *Belief and Imagination* when he states how, within a Kleinian model, he will use the usual concepts of projective identification, Oedipus complex, depressive position, etc., and with what meanings. But we must move towards a wider solution that takes into due consideration what has been said before. We must come closer to the reality of our clinical experience as it really is, with its inherent and irreplaceable subjectivity, with the use that we make in it of our own person and of our 'private theory'. What is private cannot be the object of scientific research until it is made public: 'i.e. undergo transformation in the observer that enables them to be communicated to another...this process, which I call public-ation...' (Bion, p.119). Making public, studying the methodology for doing so in a manner that is faithful to the reality of what we must communicate, is the task that awaits us. The translation, the careful consideration of the cultural - and linguistic - differences, the logicized notation, the accurate description of the models we use, the construction of a common language, the exploration of the private theories and their transformation into publication - these are the routes we must take if we seriously want to effectively communicate the substance and the discoveries of our discipline to ourselves and to others. There is a difficult task ahead of us all, and not only those who organise international scientific events: that of creating a commonality to be the basis of our scientific communication.

References

Bion, W.R. (1963), *Elements of Psycho-Analysis*. London, William Heinemann.

_____ (1992), *Cogitations*. London, Karnac Books.

Britton, R., (1998), *Belief and Imagination.Explorations in Psychoanalysis,* Routledge.

Canestri, J. (1999), Psychoanalytic Heuristics, in P.Fonagy et al (eds) *Psychoanalysis on the Move. The Work of J.Sandler*. London, Routledge.

_____ (2000), The Scientific Programme of the 42nd Congress of the IPA, Nice 2001 IPA*Newsletter International Psychoanalysis*, Vol. 9, Issue 2.

_____ (2001), La ressource de la méthode. *Revue Française de Psychanalyse TomeLXV*, 67-80. *Numéro Hors Série : Courants de la psychanalyse contemporaine. Sous la direction de André Green*. Paris, Presses Universitaires de France.

_____ (2001), Changing Scientific Ideals and Idols in the History of Psychoanalysis. *Psychoanalysis in Europe. EPF Bulletin 55,* 139 –146

Sandler, J. (1983), Reflections on some relations between psychoanalytic concepts and psychoanalytic practice. *Int. J. Psychoanal.* 64, 413-425

Smith, H. (2000), Towards an international dialogue: North American reflections on the Santiago Congress. *Int. J. Psychoanal.* 81, 307-312.

Above and Beyond the Couch: Psychoanalysis and Spiritually-Based Conflict Resolution

Susan G. Lazar *(Washington, D.C.)*

As a dynamic psychiatrist and psychoanalyst for more than 30 years, I have been immersed in a developmental approach as a way to understand human conflict and human growth. Now I find myself extending and expanding this accustomed way of thinking in an approach to fostering international peace. At this stage of my life and career, in addition to my practice and teaching, I have taken on the responsibility of serving as the Executive Director of the Friends of Erevna International Peace Center. This organization supports the development of a new spiritually-based, ecumenical peace center on the island of Cyprus.

The approach of the Peace Center includes aspects that are consistent with a psychodynamic understanding. Prior to meetings between members of groups from areas of conflict, the socio-cultural and historical issues behind the origin of each conflict will be investigated so that the values and sensitivities of each side will be understood. Then each of the participants from the opposite sides of a conflict will be separately interviewed to understand the specific personalities before bringing them together. Once brought together, the work is to create empathy within people from each side of conflict situations for the experience of those on the other. The vision is to create increasing bonds of mutual understanding with which participants will return to influence and inform both the attitudes and the policy at home.

What are some of the similarities between a psychoanalytic point of view and the spiritually based approach of the Erevna International Peace Center (EIPC)? Both rely on a focus on motives of individuals and groups to arrive at an understanding of conflict, intrapsychically, interpersonally, and between groups and even nations. Both approaches would also agree that there is a developmental hierarchy of motives from less to more mature. For example, a Freudian hierarchy would describe a progression from oral to anal to genital aims with the implication that the earlier levels of motivation are more focused on self and personal survival and then move on to levels of self-regulation and autonomy and finally achieving levels of motivation with loving aims directed to others beside the self. Similarly, the Eriksonian conceptualization, elaborating and adumbrating the basic Freudian hierarchy, describes a hierarchical progression of stages from Trust through Generativity and ultimately Ego Integrity. Of course, Melanie Klein also describes a development from a paranoid-schizoid position that is primarily protective and defensive of the self alone, through a stage of gradually resolving ambivalence toward others, to a depressive position of guilt over the harm one has caused to others, to a higher level of reparation and concern for the others in one's life.

Similarly, the spiritual approach of the EIPC considers motives on a spectrum reaching from less to more mature, from more centered on the survival and safety of the self, stretching to concerns of safety and well-being of first one's group, then one's nation and allies, and eventually to motives that value and embrace the survival, safety, well-being and optimum development of an increasingly expanding circle that includes all of humanity.

In addition to being interpersonal and psychological, the approach of the EIPC also rests on principles that are spiritual and of a nature that historically psychoanalysis either does not touch or has viewed as not legitimate. These basic assumptions include that
    1) People are subtly but literally connected to one another and influence one another.
    2) Our thoughts, feelings and intentions have an impact in and of themselves. This fact has been demonstrated by research data.
    3) Both a spiritual approach and evidence from research suggest that human beings have a multi-faceted, subtle, but literal interconnection such that whatever we do to another we ultimately are doing to ourselves.

Rigorously designed studies from a number of institutions including Stanford and Princeton Universities have provided startling scientific evidence for the fact that people's thoughts, feelings and intentions have a literal effect on one another and on the world around them. The impact of human intentions on the health of distant human subjects has also been demonstrated in a recently published study in the Archives of Internal Medicine. These facts and the evidence behind them run counter to received psychoanalytic wisdom that would refute the power of feeling and intention alone. Nevertheless, this power is reasonable and understandable within modern models of the universe that explain action at a distance by taking into account the property of nonlocality. These models of the universe also underscore principle #3, namely that both a spiritual approach and evidence from research suggest that human beings have a multi-faceted, subtle, but literal interconnection, and that because of nonlocality, whatever we do to others we are ultimately also doing to ourselves.

Within psychoanalysis, I believe that the reality of the impact of unexpressed, unspoken thought, feeling, and intention has not been clearly addressed or understood, except perhaps in the literature describing the power of transference/countertransference relatedness and the communication between the unconscious of analyst and patient. How this communication is conveyed has been left as an unknown.

However, now that literal interconnectedness and mutual influence, both for better and for worse, have been demonstrated in a modern scientific way, we can see that the way people focus on specific goals can have a powerful impact. There is the implication that a growth in the maturity of one's goals will have an effect on the world at large, eventually potentially moving societies beyond aims of brute power, possession and domination of one group at the expense of another to deeper issues of a shared peace based on a shared concern for the interests of all. It is envisioned that an increasing body of people trained in the new approach to conflict resolution will return to their homes in areas of conflict and influence others around them.

I believe that one recent inspiring example of the impact of peace seeking citizens on national policies is the outcome of the Turkish and Greek conflict over the small, rocky island of Imia in the Aegean. As one distinguished scholar and practitioner of conflict resolution, the Greek Cypriot Professor Maria Hadjipavlou, expressed it to me, the women in both countries contributed to a peaceful resolution of this conflict by forcefully and publicly objecting to having their children killed in a "stupid war over a rock."

Very importantly, in this new post September 11, 2001 era, it has been pointed out by those who study the psychology of the terrorist mind, the war on terrorism in which we are currently engaged is fundamentally *a psychological war between competing world visions and human goals.* Surely, at no time in history has it been more urgent to create an expanding consciousness of our interconnectedness and mutual responsibility to combat the self-righteous fundamentalist forces that seek to impose their will or to destroy those who disagree.

At the Erevna International Peace Center, a spiritually based approach to conflict resolution strives to assist people in conflict to realize who they really are beyond the immediate social, political or religious issues that separate them. There is also an implication that their true nature endows them with the potential to reach beyond these more immediate issues to deeper ones of their common humanity.

An important principle is that the level of motivation of each party is crucial to any measure of success. Each party must be sincerely ready to create peace or the entire effort is pointless. It is always preferable to have

121

allies and friends than to continue in a state of enmity. To improve the level of motivation, it is also important to appeal to the deepest interests of parties in conflict. These are often concealed underneath more common, material, but ultimately more superficial concerns. The EIPC will ask the most basic and important questions, including these: What is important in this lifetime? What is it that creates enemies? What is the importance of material things compared to obtaining happiness and security? What has been gained so far by virtue of fighting? What more is it possible to achieve by creating peace? It is also important to understand clearly the agendas of third parties, (often other countries with motives of power, influence, economic advantage and domination), who are invested in the continuation of conflict in specific areas and who manipulate behind the scenes to perpetuate it.

The role of the Erevna International Peace Center will never be to take sides. Its unique approach to conflict resolution lies in its aim of touching the specific sensitivies of each side and understanding and dealing with them in a deep and meaningful way. In addition, to this most important conflict resolution activity, the EIPC will also be a place for other peacemaking groups to meet and a place where our own unique spiritually based approach will be practiced, will be taught in our educational facility, and elaborated in our international conferences.

This work will take generations, if not centuries. To fail to address it because it will not be completed in our own lifetimes would be selfishly neglectful on the grounds of our narcissism. Every piece of social progress takes focus, dedication, hard work and time. This most important work of peace, based on the fundamental equality and connection between all human beings, will not be accomplished without our working on it, and it will surely not even begin until we ourselves actively set it in motion.

LIVING WITH VIOLENCE

The Interrogation*
Who is screaming in the night
Who is dying in the forest?

Lightening is the question
Sparks dance from your eyes
Terror is the price, pain
the prize

Who is screaming in the shadows
Who is trembling in the darkness?

Words are the meat you eat
Words are your water
Time is forever
Death is the comforter.

Who is safe in his body
Who is safe in the forests?

In the beautiful forests are wild flowers
Are birds' eggs, sunlight
On the wind leaves are moving
Old the trees.

Who is screaming in the forest
Who is screaming in the forest?

Jeni Couzyn from affidavits written by 14 prisoners charged under the Terrorism Act, South Africa, August 1971.

[Thanks to Bloodaxe books for permission to reprint The Interrogation (Life by Drowning , Selected poems of Jeni Couzyn, Bloodaxe, 1985)]

Working in the setting of violent behaviour

Siobhán O'Connor *(Belfast)*

When invited to contribute to this work, I had a momentary revival of an old reaction. The invitation referred to my 'special experience'. I suspected that my 'special experience' referred to the fact that I am a psychoanalyst and psychiatrist working in Northern Ireland, a place renowned as a setting of violent behaviour.

In the past, when asked about working in Northern Ireland, I had regularly answered that Psychiatrists do not have a great experience of the effects of the 'troubles', unlike our surgeons, who are experts in trauma. In fact this was the prevailing opinion among researchers until relatively recently. Most of the victims who had symptoms of Post- Traumatic Stress Disorder did not consult psychiatrists, except in a medico-legal capacity. Perhaps the lack of available psychotherapy services played its part in giving a false impression. The deficit in Child Psychiatric services in the region may have also contributed to the previous denial of the results of the violence on children. However, I think that other factors were more powerful.

When I was medical student the medical profession was only beginning to see the importance of the clinical signs of 'non-accidental injury' to children. Later, as a junior doctor, I remember signs of what I now know were indicative of sex abuse. Despite asking others their opinion at the time, I could come up with no reasonable explanation for the physical signs I had observed. This was innocence, at least on my part. I remember documenting the details thinking that, some day, the significance of the signs would be recognised. I remember it well, because in dictating one letter I said that a boy had a 'patulous' anus. The secretary had typed that he had a 'patch on his anus'. Privately, I had come up with the idea that maybe the boy was poking at himself to relieve his bowel problem, but it didn't seem a satisfactory solution.

I trained initially as a general practitioner, and worked in a deprived area at a time when the troubles were at their height. During the I.R.A hunger strike in the prison, I visited ghettos on both sides of 'the divide', with that special privilege given to family doctors. Barricades were lifted to let me pass. On one occasion, I drove into an area which was barricaded to keep the police out, and a parade of armed, masked men parted their ranks to let me through. My friends cautioned me, but it was exciting, and I did not want to miss what I hoped would soon become history. One night as I was driving through a troubled area on a house call, some youths started to petrol bomb a police land rover in front of me. I then realised the danger I was courting, the risk of becoming the victim of violence by accident. The history of Northern Ireland abounds with apologies to the families of people 'accidentally' killed or maimed.

Many years later, as a Consultant Psychiatrist, I chose to work in a 'locked ward', with violent patients. Consciously, I thought this a result of my having seen over-sedated patients whom I thought could benefit from a psychotherapeutic approach. Had my experience of Northern Ireland any relevance? In the course of preparing an analytic paper on the theme of violence, an analysand mentioned an experience her family had had during the more troubled period of the 1970's. She had not seen it as significant. Many of us in Northern Ireland tend to dismiss our own experience as 'not so bad compared to others'. But I now recognise this as a defense reinforced by the experience of the group, or culture.

I think that the culture or group experience is linked to the difficulties faced when trying to write or speak about violence in Northern Ireland. For example, a psychotherapist came to me with her fears about confidentiality concerning a patient directly involved by his profession with terrorism. He was under a real threat, and she was afraid that if anything happened to him she might be asked later about their sessions. She came to me because she felt that, as a Psychiatrist, I could help her regarding any legal issues that might arise. The details suggested that this fear was irrational. We were able to explore the counter-transference and how in her anxiety, she dismissed the real danger to herself. If terrorists were to monitor the patient's weekly timetable, they could be sure of one place he visited regularly at specified times. The patient was dealing with his own anxieties about the threat, by using projective identification to excite the therapist, at the same time as ignoring the advice of his colleagues and friends. The psychotherapist could not easily talk to colleagues about this patient, because the situation was dangerous. In a relatively small community, there are external forces that facilitate repression and denial.

I discovered that the work in the locked ward was over-stimulating and frustrating, for so much more could be done. How I deal with this frustration is by my involvement in the 'outside world'. I use my psychoanalytic perspective to teach and supervise within psychiatry, and my psychiatric experience to help psychotherapists. Perhaps one of the reasons that I can disengage myself from the cultural context, and shift perspectives, is that I spent my formative years in America. I moved to Northern Ireland at the age of seven. I have now moved from getting frustrated with the interest in Northern Ireland as apparently more violent or irrational than other places, to taking advantage of it, by writing from an analytic perspective about violence.

125

Frame and Setting   Moty Benyakar *(Buenos Aires/Tel-Aviv)*

My personal experience as an analyst who has participated actively in five wars in Israel and has had to assist those injured by terrorist attacks or other catastrophes in Argentina, has prompted me to research and develop different perspectives of the traumatic. As much from a metapsychological perspective as from that of the theory of technique.

Clinical Vignettes:

Meir's Case: an Israeli reserve officer called to duty during the Lebanese war. He expressed his intention to stop the sessions until his return. I proposed to continue our sessions during his times off duty with the firm conviction of the importance of preserving this space.

During these sessions the patient related how important it was for him to maintain this frame where he felt he could become himself, not to have to continue in the function of doing, but to be able to reflect. In one of the sessions he said: "here I stop doing what I feel I need to do for my people and my country, I am here simply for myself."

It was impressive to see someone who had been in trenches and shelters, be able to perceive the psychoanalytical framework as the place in which he felt mostly safe because he could count on himself. I have also confronted this type of situation repetitively in the Argentina of today, a country immersed in the violence product of an economic distortion, in which some citizens lose their sources of income, expressing that it doesn't make sense to pursue the analytic labor until they can solve their working and economical situation. Our conviction of the function of holding allows us to postulate the analytical frame as an elaborative paradigm in these types of disruptive situations.

Dalia's case: During the Gulf war, in which all Israeli citizens had to carry their gas masks box with them all day, she came to the session without the box, stating that for her these rules did not make any sense. This was for her a new expression of omnipotent and indiscriminate challenge, as if she were flirting with death. It was possibly her way of presenting her disavowal (*Verleugnung*) or the rejection (*Verwerfung*), or may be an expression of 'negative hallucination'.

I asked her to go back home and to bring her mask, in order to be able to initiate the session. With an expression of distaste and without any other comments she went out in search of her box. When she came back she showed her anger and complained about what I had asked her to do. Fifteen minutes after her return, the emergency alarm sounded, and we had to put on our masks and share the sealed room, adapted specially for this kind of situation, and thus we remained there until the missiles finished falling. This episode of real holding was elaborated during the treatment as a situation in which she felt truly protected. This protection did not have characteristics of reassurance, but enabled Dalia to start elaborating her childhood experiences of helplessness. She saw herself acting in an omnipotent manner rejecting and devaluing the figure of her parents. She characterized them as weak and impotent, lacking the capacity to develop adequate mediating functions, increasing the sensation of loneliness that invaded her, contents that were elaborated during the process of her analysis.

Based on these cases we can approach the relationship between frame, process and the analytical field. The main position of the paper is that the frame in situations of threat has two functions – one is to preserve the patient and the other to allow development of the elaborative process. A further issue is the special process of transference and countertransference that develop in situations when both the analyst and the patient are threatened in the same way. And finally, that these situations can serve as paradigms to re-think the way we establish the setting and it's difference with the development of the frame.

The psychoanalytical frame has been central to the development of daily clinical practice. It is a set of rules that determine an artificial standardized and regulated situation between analyst and patient. It presents itself as a framework of stability and coherence that is partially exempt from the impact of every day social demands. Through these characteristics we attempt to create a paradigm that enables the greatest deployment of processes and psychic contents to be approached and elaborated. In my clinical task and ever more in supervisions, it has been very useful to distinguish between the concept of 'setting' and 'frame. The special relation between laws, rules and norms constitutes the tool to face the difference between setting and frame. As a paradigm we can say that **Laws** are postulates which are not product of human modification. Each science has its own universal laws. In the same way that physics has Gravity as a basic law, psychoanalysis postulates as a law that man acts by unconscious processes with special dynamics.

Rules are man-made regulations presumed to be opposed to laws (for example the ten commandments are rules which tend to oppose unconscious laws expressed in human drives). **Norms**, emerge from the interaction between laws and rules. The norms are open to be elaborated and interpreted in the analytic process. By the interplay of those concepts in our field we can say that in the psychoanalytic frame we formulate rules that we belief adequate to facilitate the emergence of the

127

unconscious laws to be elaborated. Fixing the hour of the beginning and end of the session is one of these rules; establishing usage of the couch is another. This enables us to analyze the specificity of the norms deployed in every therapeutic relation.

After clarifying these three components we can approach the specificity of the **setting** and the **frame:**
Even though the concept of setting is often used synonymously with frame, I see its establishment as a specific activity. The English term 'to set-up' means to establish or to place in advance. The psychoanalytic setting must be the product of the analyst's conception of the laws of the unconscious, in what form they emerge and in what way they could be elaborated. The stipulation of the setting is established before the interaction between patient and analyst. On the other hand the frame starts developing from the very first contact between them. As this interaction develops, several kinds of phenomena start to appear, part of them conscious and situational and part unconscious and irrational, phenomena that tend to transform the 'setting'. It is extremely important to emphasize these changes, that generally seem justified from a factual point of view. As an analyst, and even more as a supervisor I can focus on the specificity of this process of transformation of the framework, only if I have in mind those rules established before the beginning of therapeutic work, that means the structure of the setting.

I make these statements because when we confront situations of crisis, social attack or wars and terrorism, there is a logical and natural tendency to alter those pre-established rules in the setting and to develop different frameworks. Faced with these phenomena we must have the basic tools to evaluate if our determinations are the product of the disruptive reality, or simply the product of our own anxieties with an inadequate perception of reality. In both cases the analyst have the two options open, he can maintain the established rules or may change them in a hasty way. This is the reason why we need conceptual parameters for our own evaluation, not to be exempt from mistakes, but to be more related to the dynamics of our own decisions. The implosion of the environment, in some cases, can be so abrupt that we must conceptualize and train ourselves adequately in order to be able to approach these events. In situations of war, terrorism and social disasters in which the stability of the environment is very weak, the rules of the setting, established by the analyst are of extreme importance. These rules are those which enable the framework to acquire the quality of preserving psychic stability in this elaborative and special field constructed by patient and analyst, that is the therapeutic space.

128

The frame has to function as a mediating and dynamic space, preserving it to remain static and protected from the surrounding reality. In situations where the rules are threatened, the authentic function can be sustained through a clear conception of the analytical task (as opposed to rigidity and non-discrimination which are product of obsessive tendencies, masked by the label of "what it is supposed to be done," based in an super-ego imposition).

In my opinion, this is not professional caprice, is an important factor in the progress of the daily clinical activity, particularly with high frequency sessions. I believe that constancy and solidity of the framework is what enables the deployment of psychic plasticity, in contrast to those who propose to adapt or extend the framework based on what emerges from the psyche of the patient. Together with this position and as product of the same conception, I recommend being extremely careful and sensitive to the reality the external world imposes on us when it becomes disruptive. Wars are characterized by psychic implosion and its product, in some patients, is the display of pathologies of trauma in its different variations. I propose facing the emergence of traumatic experiences through a solid frame that promotes containment, holding and figurative interpretation, as we do elsewhere. In the two clinical examples above we can see how much the framework has functioned as a transitional space. In Meir's case it could offer the possibility of sustaining the psychoanalytic approach and preservation of subjectivity, while allowing elaboration of the idiosyncratic, in contrast to the impersonal and indiscriminative features of combat situations. In Dalia's case, the analyst within the framework was presented as the person who could foresee the dictates of reality, preserving the patient's safety, but also, by continuing to elaborate unconscious content, preventing external events provoking destructive attitudes.

Working with survivors of political violence

Renos K Papadopoulos *(London)*

Bundled in a United Nations armoured vehicle in the asphyxiating heat of a Kosovan summer over a bumpy country dirt road (where a hidden landmine had blown up a car two days earlier killing its passengers), entering into an enclaved Serbian village and then squeezing into a tiny one-room house packed with wailing relatives of those killed is not part of the usual activities of an ordinary analyst. Admittedly, such a venture is not part of the usual activities of mine, either. However, although not very typical, this incident has been part of the work I have been doing for many years, in addition to my usual analytical practice and my work at the Tavistock Clinic and the University of Essex. This work has been about consulting to international organisations in connection with traumatised people as a result of political violence and war.

Nowadays, this kind of work, tragically, has a certain glamour about it and also it has become attractive to many therapists who wish to 'do something real' and useful and not remain passive in the face of the many eruptions of evil destructiveness in the world. However, getting involved in this kind of work for either of these two motives can create difficulties. Sheer idealism, however good and appropriate, would need to be coupled with professionalism along with all its implications. Otherwise, missionary and other anti-therapeutic discourses are activated. For example, I do not undertake any work of this nature without suitable remuneration. In other words, I see this as work and not as charity; as an extension and another form of my ordinary work, regardless of its extraordinary nature. Charity is something that I do by donating money to charity organisations which leaves me free to approach this work with the full attention of professionalism in a way that locates me in the field as a professional and not as a do-gooder. Moreover, I have found that it is equally important to approach this work within the same framework of 'ordinariness' and attempt to reduce (if not eliminate) the exotic elements of its external otherness. Essentially, I would argue that unless the outlandish parameters of the given situation are translated into specificities of the therapeutic frame and thus included in the conceptualisation of our work, they are likely to distract our attention and reduce our therapeutic effectiveness (Papadopoulos, 1997; 1998a; 1999a).

Another delicate issue concerning this work is the discernment of the concepts of neutrality and advocacy. One cannot work with survivors of horrendous acts of brutality without taking a stance against the perpetrators. Consequently, survivors need to feel that the professionals working with them understand their plight and are not uninvolved

130

bystanders. This violates the basic condition of therapeutic neutrality, unless we refine its definition. In short, it is possible to differentiate between individual perpetrators and their wider ethnic, cultural and religious groups to which they belong. As a matter of policy, I always try to work with survivors of both opposing factions, if feasible. I have found that it is possible to convey (in appropriately therapeutic ways) to the survivors my full support of them whilst not sharing their blanket dismissal of their enemy. Paradoxically, although survivors wish to own the professionals completely and have them on their side, they can also be relieved and experience a sense of safety if they realise that the very professionals who work with them also work with survivors of the opposite side. Moreover, in certain situations, professionals can be 'for' the survivors without necessarily being 'against' the perpetrators. Essentially, embracing the polarised perspective of the survivors in its totality cannot be therapeutic. It is therapeutically containing if the professionals distinguish between the suffering of the survivors and their understandably polarised political beliefs (Papadopoulos, 2000).

One of the main difficulties in this work is the way we position ourselves. In ordinary therapeutic frames, patients come to us referred by other professionals or by themselves within a well defined and understood referral network. Moreover, referrals are located within the 'societal discourse of the expert' (Papadopoulos 1998b), according to which there is a clear delineation of the exchange of services and responsibilities. However, most of the work with survivors of political violence in the field (and not in institutions and set services in the UK) lacks such clarity. More specifically, it is usually based on professionals going to people assuming that they need our services. Unless professionals undertake a detailed and judicious analysis of all the contributing factors and dimensions which create the frame within which our contact with the survivors is enabled, it is likely that the contact will be fraught with difficulties that would destroy any therapeutic endeavours.

One of the most important considerations in this work is the professionals' ability to distinguish the various overlapping epistemologies involved in order to avoid (a) pathologising human suffering, (b) psychologising socio-political dimensions, and (c) moralising the psychological or psychologising the moral. Without a clear delineation as well as a connection between these overlapping realms, along with their corresponding epistemologies, professionals are likely to fall into the many traps (metaphorical mines) that are scattered across the territory of this work. Our analytical perspectives create a strong predisposition to view such client group as 'traumatised' people and to overlook their resilience; this can have grave consequences unless it is examined properly and systematically (Papadopoulos, 1999b; in press).

131

Enthusiasm without prudence and attention to detail tends to cloud our perception and increases the chances for erroneous positioning.

Finally, attention also needs to be given to the closed system of the powerful dynamic of the victim-saviour coupling (Papadopoulos, in press). In addition to the intrapsychic dimensions of this dyad, it is important to appreciate its wider systemic implications. More specifically, if the survivor is seen exclusively as a victim, invariably the professional is likely to be positioned as a saviour and then both tend to team up against the violator/s. However, apart from denuding the 'victim' of his/her strengths, this closed triangle tends to perpetuate itself creating endless variations with different people in the same roles, e.g. the professional (saviour) may experience the survivor (victim) as his/her own violator when the latter keeps oppressing the former with increasingly more unreasonable demands; also, the victim-saviour couple may keep creating more violators that they will need to defend against, such as the managers of the relevant services and other individuals and bodies who do not offer the kind of unconditional support that the couple expects and tyrannically demand.

References

Papadopoulos, R. K. (1997) 'Individual identity and collective narratives of conflict'. *Harvest: Journal for Jungian Studies*, vol. 43, No. 2, 7-26.

—— (1998a)'Destructiveness, atrocities and healing: epistemological and clinical reflections'. *The Journal of Analytical Psychology*, vol. 43, No. 4, 455-477.

—— (1998b) 'Jungian Perspectives In New Contexts' in *The Jungians Today* edited by Ann Casement. London and New York: Routledge.

—— (1999a) 'Working with families of Bosnian medical evacuees: therapeutic dilemmas'. *Clinical Child Psychology and Psychiatry*, Vol.4, No.1, 107-120.

——(1999b) 'Storied community as secure base. Response to the paper by Nancy Caro Hollander 'Exile: Paradoxes of loss and creativity''. *The British Journal of Psychotherapy*, vol.15, no.3, 322-332.

——(2000) 'Factionalism and interethnic conflict: narratives in myth and politics'. In *'The Vision Thing. Myth, Politics and Psyche in the World'* edited by Thomas Singer. London and New York: Routledge.

——(In press) 'Refugees, home and trauma'. In *'No place like home'; therapeutic care for refugees*, edited by R. K. Papadopoulos. London: Karnac, Tavistock Clinic Series.

'Questions without answers must be asked very slowly' [1]

Sverre Varvin *(Oslo)*

Disruption and loss characterise the life of many refugees living in exile; disruption of the bond to family and culture of origin, the violent death of friends and relatives, disruption of culture-bound identity and, in the case of trauma, loss of the earlier healthy self and often loss of trust and hope including loss of hope for the future. Those who have undergone extreme traumatisation such as torture may in addition experience an impairment of their ability to integrate experience both cognitively and mentally. This has potentially far-reaching consequences regarding integrating traumatic experiences, mourn losses and organise their life in a new context. Many live in addition with a second dissociated or split-off internal reality concerned with their experiences of massive traumatisation in wars and prisons.

The traumatised refugee must adapt to an external reality, which is strange, and often confusing and an internal reality that is frightening because of intrusive memory-traces from atrocities. What we describe as posttraumatic conditions may be seen as survival strategies and adaptive solutions to continuing stressful internal and external situations. Many succumb under chronic post-traumatic conditions but one may also observe creative adaptation and accommodation i. In spite of unfavourable conditions, few resources and powerful psychological hindrances, many adapt to the new culture, learn the language and often new skills at the same time as they support an extended family. They become survivors in exile as they were during their persecution (Varvin & Hauff 1998).

Attempting to symbolise and work through aspects of the traumatic experience may give relief, but at the same time, it may provoke the unpleasant re-experiencing of meetings with the perpetrator. Increased ability to symbolise and integrate is therefore seen as helpful not only for coming to terms with a difficult past but also for the process of working for a better future. The past is experienced as present (Varvin 2000) but ironically, it is the sense of future that represents the problem. This time-pathology concerns the basic *sense* of time while the ability to foresee and hope for satisfaction and resolution of anxiety and frustration may be more or less foreclosed. Symbolisation and mentalisation may restore the sense and experience of time and thus restore the traumatised person's vitality and hope. However, to be able to hope, some vital questions seek answers. The unthinkable has happened, that which should not have been possible. A breach in the sense of continuity of being has occurred and a

---

[1] From Michaels (1997).

133

background of "the uncanny" has replaced the background of safety. Because it has happened, it may happen again, and, in fact, for many it happens again in nightmares or flashbacks. A patient told me, when you are exiled because of such atrocities, you always ask the impossible question "why". As Michaels says, such question must be asked slowly. They are indeed asked in many different ways in psychotherapy with extreme traumatised torture victims; often with despair and as a rule over and over again. The slowness is an empirical fact; it takes time to seek answers and more time to realise that one has to live without satisfactorily answers. Therapies are experienced often as long and strenuous struggles with mistrust, aggression, depression and fatigue. Nevertheless, slowly something may come, often as childhood memories and unexpected experiences of mastery and joy. At the end of a long and industrious therapy patient made a small accident with her car. To the therapist's surprise, she exclaimed with joy and pride that she really felt that this was her fault, "I did it, it was not forced upon me". At the beginning of therapy she was stiffened with anxiety, her whole life was anxiety and depression. She did not know anything else. Her trauma story was beyond imagination, and her lack of trust was severe. The question, "why did it happen?" had not been answered, but she had got a reasonable answer to the question "why not again?"

Between these points, was a long process towards ability to symbolise and mentalise emotional states and re-establish some connection with early good internal objects. The kernel of the traumatic experience is, according to Laub and Podell (1995) a break of the link to the internal empathic other. A void or a persecutor is experienced in its place or the body may take its place as a persecuting object. It is in the relation to an external other that a symbolising process may be started. What the patient seeks is some resonance in the other, another ear that will not close the gap, but listen in a way that opens for dialogues in the mind. The therapist struggles with helplessness in the face of the horror described, and this helplessness scares the former victim as it only reflects her own. When Celan could speak of 'black milk of daybreak', we were ready to understand some of the horror experienced in the death camps (Celan 1980). Similarly, when a patient of mine was able to demonstrate his silent scream experienced in his recurrent nightmares, I was able to understand some of the agony of the experience of not being heard, of experiencing the absolute loneliness before the executioner. A dialogue could then occur, first between patient and therapist, and later in his mind. These are the privileged moments where the dialogue starts. They are preceded, and accompanied, by the necessary attempt to 'see' if it may be true, 'it may not happen again'. And this time the question may slowly be transformed to the question: "will I again be let alone in the

134

face of the emptiness of the horror experienced and so vividly re-experienced in dreams and repetitions?". A complicated 'game' of finding the torturer or executioner ensues. By identification, the patient becomes the aggressor and by projective identification, the therapist may take the same position. Slowly the other as empathic, and oneself as autonomous, may emerge in cycles of hope and loss of hope.

References

Celan, P. (1980), "Death Fugue', ' in *Paul Celan: Poems selected, translated and introduced by M.Hamburger.*, M.Hamburger, ed., Carcanet New Press Limited, Manchester, pp. 51-53.

Laub, D. & Podell, D. (1995), 'Art and trauma.', *International Journal of Psychoanalysis.*, 76:991-1005.

Michaels, A. (1997), *Fugitive Pieces.* Bloomsbury, London.

Varvin, S. (2000), 'Die gegenwärtige Vergangenheit. Extreme Traumatisierung und Psychotherapie.',*Psyche*, 59(no. 9/10):895-930.

Varvin, S. &. & Hauff, E. 1998, 'Psychoanalytically oriented psychotherapy with torture survivors,' in *Caring for victims of torture*, J. M. Jaranson & M. K. Popkin, eds., American Psychiatric Press, Inc, Washington DC, & London, England, pp. 117-129.

When a patient kills

Angelo Fioritti *(Rimini, Italy)*

On October 24th 2000 at 1.00 PM I was driving to the Community Mental Health Center that I directed, on the way back from a maximum-security hospital in Reggio Emilia. Very unusually I had had lunch at home and very unusually I was so captured by thoughts about the special hospital that I passed by the Department and went along. I tried to turn back, but road constructions just started that day forced me to park in an unusual lot and reach my office from the back door. At that time I was just annoyed by these complications. I was unaware that they saved my life.

At the front gate of the department a patient of mine, let's say Franco, was waiting for me. He had just killed two persons and had a list of ten more, including me, a young resident collaborating with me, his parents and sister. All responsible in his eyes for "playing games on him". The next morning, after I bought the papers, I linked the two mysterious slaughters by pure chance to a weak association with him from a few words he had left beside one victim. I called his parents, alerted the police. He was caught three hours later and confessed his intentions to continue to kill. All happened just like being in a movie, with a sense of depersonalization which allowed me to keep cool and firm in such dire straits. I remember the sense of absurd fiction becoming reality when I jumped in a taxi leaving the police station and the radio aired the news about Franco being caught and the driver commenting *"well done!"*.

Since then not one single day has passed without thoughts and questions about this story. An inner dialogue made of rational examinations, emotional uprising, physical reactions has since been established between me and myself. Very few answers have come out and they are not worth being reported here. The only question I had put to myself several times before that event ("How would I react in such circumstances?") has now an answer. I have reacted *normally*, in so far as normality exists.

At that time I was very proud of my 15 years of intense practice without having lost a patient by suicide or having had a patient committing serious violence. I had always figured out that such events would have left me dispirited forever. And now this totally unexpected situation, in which all of a sudden a patient killed, and I and a junior doctor working under my responsibility escaped from his killing just by the grace of chance.

The second half of the story, having survived, dominated my reactions for months. Every morning was a given day; I woke up every day with an

136

undirected sense of gratitude and making efforts to concentrate on the beauty of every single piece of perception. I became more aware of my physical sensations and started to pay attention to many little pleasures neglected for years. My attitude got somewhat religious rather than manic, although I am basically agnostic in my spiritual views. The result was that I hadn't to cope with serious self-esteem problems for months. I passed without serious self-demeaning problems through a nightmare of police investigations, journalists'curiosity, patients' reactions, professional inquiries and institutional turbulence. I was much helped by my family and by my colleagues and their support was unanimous. My work was not dramatically affected by this event and neither was my career. As established before that episode I took over the direction of a large department two months later. All this seems very "normal" and functional, but I had never imagined I would react this way.

On December 18th 2001 the trial against Franco occured. It went on for 40 days, with its ritual of witnesses, prosecutors, defenders. Franco was finally sentenced to ten years of detention in a special hospital, the one I visited the day he killed. I discovered that I had very mixed feelings about him, to put it euphemistically.

That was when I came across the other half of the story. I had to give witness in public, to pass formal cross-examination by the attorney, the lawyers, the court. My words were reported in newspapers and I was "named and shamed" by them as "the one who knew and didn't stop the criminal lunatic". The support from my family didn't stop although initially they had difficulties in realising why I reacted so intensely one year after the real event, and the front of professional solidarity was not as strong as in the immediacy of the event. A few colleagues released ambivalent press interviews. There I found myself really alone with the irrationalities of two deaths and a community looking for someone to hold responsible. The situation got physical, with early awakenings coloured by ruminations about the facts, the trial, scenes of the murders, figuring out my patients' feelings on reading the papers, asking myself "am I up to go on working?" ... Finally I dreamed Franco killing me, one night. All this seems astonishingly predictable, it's all described in our textbooks as a pure reaction to stress. And again I had never imagined I would have reacted this way.

Slowly the papers have stopped publishing on this issue and step by step life is coming back to "normality" during the last two months. Now I sleep well and love writing again. Writing has always been my favourite way to adjust to unadjustable things. I am very grateful to Joan Raphael-Leff who gave me this opportunity to write about this fact. Immediately after her invitation to describe my experience I discovered that I was finding all possible excuses to delay my writing and every time I thought how to start my mind became dull. Finally I put something down about it. It came out flowing as a river.

There is no conclusion to these lines. I am sure this story will accompany me all my life long, as well as all tragic events I have lived and which have produced structural changes in my mind and personality. Which ones I will say in decades. I am also sure that reflections about the professional side of this experience will accompany me forever. But what strikes me today are two things. The first is how strange and difficult it is to imagine "normal reactions". The second is a frequent and surprising question: "On October 24th 2000 what (who) made me park my car in such an unusual spot?"

Will it ever go away? Abuse and trauma cannot really fill the world can it? Judith Trowell (London)

When I was a junior professional in training working with children, young people and families and later when I became a psychoanalyst and child analyst, help could be offered to adults or children and their lives would move forward on a more healthy trajectory.

But there was a social revolution on the way after Ruth and Henry Kempse in the USA wrote about Non Accidental Injury in 1962. This was followed by growing awareness of sexual abuse, and other areas of child maltreatment and then other traumas, civil wars, genocide and horrendous, natural disasters. Suddenly abuse and trauma seemed to be all around. Psychoanalytic work in the consulting room seemed to be enable patients to talk about extreme experiences or their uncertainty about what had happened.

Child work increasingly contained elements of abuse whether it was direct work, teaching or consultation. Analytic ideas seemed vital, how else could one understand violence, hatred and sexuality that was out of control? Experience inevitably grew but still there was hope, we could prevent these things happening if only we had enough resources and good training if we worked together and had good supervision. We knew how these processes lead to splitting and denial and how projective identification makes decision making so problematic. When different professionals are caught up with different family members, different organizations, re-enactment can be seen and addressed.

Slowly we began to see that all our psychoanalytic skills could not change the way society behaved. Then there came a request, supported by Unicef, to go to a Central American city to undertake a project with their street children. 6,000 children from age 6 to 16 live on the streets, sleeping rough, begging, stealing, working when they can, providing sexual services to tourists and passing lorry drivers and using solvents and some hard drugs. Was there despair, no hope at all? What emerged were charities and volunteers reaching out to these young people, providing health care, food, shelter and offering those who would accept it, rehabilitation. This consisted of providing group homes, facilities to learn to read and write, drug detoxification and therapy in a therapeutic community. They worked with and were hungry for psychoanalytic ideas, knowledge and supervision. Most of these children, prior to their lives on the streets, had been physically or sexually abused or witnessed the brutal murder of their families. And yet they were attractive, lively, intelligent children and young people who had potential and real hope for the future. The workers, dedicated and committed people who in their group work, their individual work, their organizations and their professional lives, were using psychoanalytic concepts with great courage. Returning to the UK inspired by them, gave fresh zest to our professional life and gratitude to the professionals and children visited. There needed to be a fresh initiative here.

One way of offering to increase psychoanalytic understanding that found support in our child protection agencies was the introduction of observation. It is well established as a valuable start for the psychoanalytic trainings. This aimed to use it as part of the assessment process and it has gained recognition as a useful contribution to understanding relationships. The following illustrations of brief examples from observations show the contribution that can be made:

A member of the team went to observe a four-year-old boy, four times in his home, because there were serious concerns expressed by his nursery class to Social Services, this is from the last two visits.

"David, as I entered the hall, invited me into his bedroom. This he shared with his older brother and sister. David had some little plastic toys and he used then to talk through. He explained they were not real monsters but had powerful weapons. Some had magic swords and some had guns. They started to fight and then they began to swear, bugger and fuck, and he repeated it was the monsters talking. His mother heard him, called him and took him to the bathroom. I thought she was going to clean his teeth as it was still quite early in the morning. He began to cry ………

Half an hour later he was still standing in the hall crying, I thought an upset, unhappy boy not for attention. Mother said to father why is he crying, "I only washed his mouth out with soap." David slid into the room and his father called him over and told him to open his mouth. He did and then came over to me pulling up a book and sat next to me and wanted to show me he could "read".

On the next visit Mother said David had trashed his room so she was keeping him confined to his room. He had not been allowed out from the previous afternoon except to the toilet. He tried to come out to show me a toy but was sent back firmly to his room and remained there during my visit. This young boy was seen as disruptive, aggressive and unhappy at school but in the family and individual sessions there was little of note until this observation material was brought up. The extent of the dislike and rejection of this child then began to emerge.

140

The observation material was included in the report for the court to show how the assessment process unfolded.

Another case, Peter aged three, was referred because he did not speak, was he becoming autistic, was he silenced, abused? There was great concern. Observation in the nursery and home followed.

"In the nursery, he did not speak as the children sat playing at the tables, cutting, sticking, doing puzzles. Then they had circle time on a mat on the floor and Peter sat looking excited and involved for the first time. The play leader began a singing and talking story and after a few minutes Peter suddenly started to sing quite loudly. It was the wrong place in the story and he was told sharply to be quiet. He did not speak again during this visit or the next. Seen at home, he chatted way to his mother in their African language and was a cheerful, friendly boy with frequent eye contact." Peter was struggling to master English and his new surroundings he was not being maltreated at home or autistic. He came off the Child Protection Register.

The observer in these cases had done their own observation training. They were amazed at what they saw and felt and how this helped us understand. Including the material in the reports raised many questions but was accepted as helpful. The counter-transference experience was incorporated into the 'opinion' section and not the interviews.

Psychoanalytic Observation provides a method that can be seen as a systematic. The conceptual framework is now well established. Well-trained observers who write up and then discuss their observations became excited as they discover the potential. Assessment can become almost mechanistic and whether the observations are done in the consulting room, the home or another setting, freeing the professional from the anxiety of having to give an opinion, can be surprising. The passion and enthusiasm for the work, of trying to think about and be in touch when the child comes to life again is obvious, and hope for a good enough outcome for the children and their families.

References:

Kempe C.M., et al (1962) The Battered Child Syndrome, *Journal of the American Medical Association* 181:17-24
Kempe, Henry & Ruth (1984), *Sexual Abuse of Children and Adolescents* Freeman: USA
Trowell J.A., (1999) Assessment and Court Work: The Place of Observation, *Infant Observation*, 2:91-102

The events of September 11th   Malkah Notman *(Boston)*

What to do in an immediate crisis, a crisis that is precipitated by major external events that intrudes into an analysis is a question that does not ordinarily arise within a psychoanalysis. The extraordinary events of September 11th undoubtedly have produced many unusual psychoanalytic situations. I will describe one and the thoughts I had at the time.

I have a telephone in my office which usually is turned to a position where only a light goes on when there is a telephone call so it does not disrupt the hour. On September 11th I was expecting the delivery of a refrigerator and after many attempts to arrange it I agreed to have the delivery people telephone me when they were on their way. I warned the analytic patient who was to come in that time period that I might briefly answer the telephone. Shortly after the hour began, on the morning of September 11th the telephone rang. I picked it up expecting notification of the delivery. Instead, it was my daughter who told me in very condensed terms that two airplanes had been hijacked from Boston and had crashed into the World Trade Center. At that moment the full magnitude of what had happened did not dawn on me but nevertheless my preoccupation with the event crowded out my attention the too patient's associations. I hesitated for a moment before deciding to tell him what had happened. I then told him what I had heard. It seemed clear that my attention could not be fully devoted to his material, and that we needed to share this knowledge to be in the same place. He was also not fully aware of the magnitude of what happened. At that moment it did not seem more major in its implications than other accidents or reports of other disasters such as plane crashes or earthquakes. Nevertheless it seemed clear to me that it must be an act of terrorism. My preoccupation of the moment also concerned the fact that the planes had left from Boston, and that there might be immediate danger to us here from other Boston targeted terrorism. Shortly afterwards there were two more phone calls from other people informing me of the same news. I then turned off the telephone and we were left to feel and express the impact of this on each of us.

The hour went on and the patient returned to his thoughts. Neither of us knew the further events at that time such as the collapse of the towers. There was shock but also compartmentalization of our reactions and it was possible to return to other matters briefly.

I wondered if I could have had any choice other than the decision to tell the patient the news. I felt too flooded with the impact of this event, not so much by full awareness of the consequences. Those were not clear at that nor did we realize there was such a huge loss of life, but just the fact of our being invaded and attacked by an "alien". There was another feeling as well; I felt I needed the presence of the other human being who was with me to share the experience but this also had another purpose.

There is a collaboration in undertaking and pursuing the work of analysis that also puts us in a special relationship to the outside world, not only in the microcosm of the transference-counter transference but in undertaking that project, of the careful attention to things of individual importance. In the moments before it was clear who had been the hijackers, my associations led to the bombing of the World Trade Center in 1993 and to the personal events of that year. The bombing was closely followed by my husband's illness and death several months later. So the intensity of feelings of loss and death was revived by the news, however brief that immediate association was. Without knowing the additional facts, it seemed that this attack probably had the same source. The alienness of the culture that the Taliban represents, the blind obedience to repressive religious beliefs and the enmity to individual liberty and to the kind of developmental concepts that psychoanalysis represents, put my patient and me into the same world of opposition to all these forces. We were in a different world by virtue of sharing the project of the psychoanalysis with its values as well as the larger cultural differences. It became important for me to support that collaboration, to in some way emphasize that we were in this kind of joint enterprise by the telling, as well as the need to communicate the information.

Much has been said and written since then about the trauma, the losses, the enormous shift in national consciousness caused by those events. Certainly I felt overwhelmed as did many others in contemplating what might be the consequences, including those of the actions of our own government. We have had an increased sense of vulnerability in the world. I think the way in which both the patient and the analyst share a culture, especially in the training situation, needs to be considered. This event underscored for me the ways in which the analyst needs the patient. The patients provide some validation and human contact through this sharing of the traumatic experience, and the recognition of shared vulnerability. There is also implicit recognition of the commitment to the values of self understanding and individuality that analysis represents.

I have since heard from other colleagues about their similar need to share with their patients knowledge of the terrorist attack and the shock, helplessness and anxiety this aroused. Particular transference and countertransference reactions are then woven into the response. In my case the fact that I spontaneously said it was my daughter who had called became an important communication of which the significance emerged later.

Other dynamics, such as the intrusion of my announcement into the hour, and the deeper meanings to each of us are gradually emerging.

Working Without a Couch and Without a Patient

Jack Novick *(Ann Arbor)*

Psychoanalysts have always stepped out of the consulting room, from the free clinics in Vienna and Berlin to Anna Freud's war nurseries. After years of volunteer efforts in our community a group of child psychoanalysts spearheaded the funding and building of Allen Creek Preschool, a psychoanalytic preschool in Ann Arbor, Michigan. Allen Creek is not a therapeutic school, but is defined by its psychoanalytic approach. The population is the same as at any ordinary preschool. The assumption is that psychoanalysis is a general psychology, that metapsychology is the language of psychoanalysis, providing us with the most comprehensive approach to both normal and compromised development. Our years of clinical experience with patients of all ages has reinforced our conviction that patients do not exist in isolation. They are part of a family and the reality of parent child interactions is the foundation of the complex matrix of internalized relations we find in our patients. Being a parent is the most difficult task facing all adults and psychoanalytic theory has the potential for offering crucial developmental help to all parents and children , not only those with overt and undeniable difficulties.

My wife Kerry, a child and adult analyst, is chair of the board and clinical director of the school. I am secretary of the board, chair of the research and development committee and a family consultant assigned each year to work with a family. We each have full time psychoanalytic practices, we are active at our local psychoanalytic institute, we write, lecture and do all the usual things that analysts do. But the preschool has become an absorbing additional activity and many of our unpaid hours are spent on various components of the school. We are not alone, as over forty psychoanalysts and psychoanalytically oriented mental health workers have volunteered substantial time as board, committee members and family consultants. We have estimated that in this small college town psychoanalytic clinicians donate 7,500 hours per year to the school and have been doing so for years. Working at Allen Creek has brought us into contact with a broader range of families than we usually see in our practices and with this have come many challenges.

So there we are, forty psychoanalysts out in the preschool community, working as psychoanalysts but without a couch and without a patient. The parents don't think of themselves as patients and they don't think of their children as having anything more than time-limited difficulties which they will outgrow. Even those who have children with diagnosed pathology do not think that psychoanalysis has any relevance. These parents are advised by their pediatricians or the internet to seek help from speech therapists or occupational therapists for developmental disorders. Most parents have little knowledge or experience of psychoanalysis. Many think of psychoanalysis as obsolete and discredited. There is an assumption that we will look for problems, pathologize ordinary functioning and seek deep, underlying motives for all behavior.

This assumption has a basis in reality as psychoanalysis has become a narrow theory of pathology rather than the classical theory of psychoanalysis as a general psychology of normal and pathological development. Working without a couch and without a patient has forced us to abandon the pseudo-scientific jargon of Stra chey's translation and find a language that is immediate, relevant, and encompasses the whole child -- strengths and positive capacities as well as conflict and potential for pathology.

This note on what I do between sessions is being written while sending out brief responses to the tragedy of September 11, 2001. These words of advice are sent to the parents and teachers. Parents have expressed their sincere gratitude for the help and support. They have sent the notes to friends, other schools, preschool email networks here and nationally, and the local newspaper. We have heard from teachers and parents at many schools and all have said how much they were helped by our messages. The notes we have already distributed related to protecting preschoolers from over stimulation, addressing their fear that the grownups, especially parents, are unable to protect them, and that anger is a useful feeling if accompanied by love. Anger without love is dangerous. Our last communication is entitled "Don't take love for granted." Each of these brief responses to the crisis, and further ones we will compose, contains classical psychoanalytic ideas about trauma, developmental phases, fusion , love, aggression, among other concepts. But the language we use is simple, direct and relevant to the immediate needs of parents, children and teachers.

The language of psychoanalysis in its original form was direct, evocative, forceful, and carried radical ideas that could be grasped and reacted to by a wide range of people. Working in the preschool world without a couch and without a patient has challenged us to refind and reclaim psychoanalysis as a powerful adaptive force to engage with and change large segments of the community.

145

Crisis Intervention with New York Children post-9.11

Christine Anzieu-Premmereur *(Paris & New York)*

I am a psychoanalyst living in New York. On September 11, 2001, I shared the emotional shock of all New Yorkers after the horrific terrorist attack that killed 2,870 people and let 2,500 children mourning a parent. I volunteered at the Pier 94 Family Assistance Center, where the "Kids Corner" became a psychological oasis for both children and parents

I would like to emphasize the role of playing with acutely traumatized children. Some of the children I saw there were apparently frozen in their frightening memories. Others were overwhelmed with anxiety, and some were already in mourning. In order to make contact and to offer an opportunity to talk about their experience and feelings, I chose to initiate playful activities. With each child, I began with some game involving reciprocity, trying to establish and a sense of communication and enjoyment. Game playing can facilitate benign regression and at the same time implicitly offer containment for feelings. Once a relationship was established around playing I was able to ask questions, and often found the children were ready to talk in this context of safety.

How to deal with intentionally inflicted disaster

Two twelve-year-old boys were jumping, running, laughing loudly in the children's' area. It was difficult for them to calm down, they didn't want to draw, and they needed to be hyperactive, in what seemed a kind of manic reaction. I initiated a game of soccer. While exchanging the ball, I asked them which kind of games they liked to play. They usually liked sophisticated games, advanced computer games for instance, but it seemed this day they wanted just to play like little kids; in a regressive process, they needed to play as if they were still toddlers. Usually in computer games they enjoyed aggressive scenarios and competition. But they didn't feel like it today. I wondered if they were feeling that their own aggression might be dangerous. I told them that being sure they were the strongest in a fight could make them feel more secure. Thus, I showed them how afraid they had been from their own aggression and asked them if it could have been related to the World Trade Center disaster.

They immediately stopped playing soccer, and started to build towers with bricks. This was a game without any sense of fun, a compulsive form of reenactment of the trauma. I commented on the repetition of the tragedy in their playing and the need to set up a very strong tower in order to overcome feelings of insecurity. In response to my thinking about their

146

play, they had already become more creative, trying to discover some architectural plan to build solid foundation for the towers. One of the boys using an obsessional style of defense calculated the number of bricks they needed and what it would cost to build a strong tower for real.

Then they told me what had happened to them: while walking to school from Battery Park, they saw the first plane hitting the tower. Their fathers had gone crazy, making them run and jump onto a boat. Now, they were living in a hotel, they didn't have an apartment or a school anymore, and the parents were fighting and screaming everyday. Family dynamics were altered; in the wake of the disaster, distress rose, increasing the threat of violence, making the children witnesses of the marital conflict. The boys got the sense of the loss of the father's authority. The former secure parental image had been almost destroyed, creating an enormous source of stress.

Both sat quietly and we had a one-hour meeting, talking about their experience, their emotions and the conflicts they were confronted with. . We discussed their feelings of shame and anger towards their parents, and I spoke of how wounded they felt.
They explained that they had been totally overwhelmed by their conflicting feelings regarding the terrorists' wish to destroy and to kill: as in a videogame, they had wanted to be the bad guy, and they felt guilty; but they had also wanted to become heroes, and they had been so disappointed by their fathers' fearful reaction. They didn't know what to do with their anger and tried to deny it.

Playing and talking with me, they got the sense of a container for their confused feelings. I tried to help them to figure out their emotion and to give a name to their affects. I was very precise in re-describing the dramatic events, and they were relieved to be creating a narrative with me. I never interpreted their conflicts or fantasies, but I tried to give them symbolic tools by which to organize their experience.
The way they both tried to deal with the conflict over their fears and their aggression, their guilt and their ambivalence towards their traumatized parents, made me think about the possibility that the challenge of the tragedy may also have a positive effect in their ongoing development by increasing their ability to withstand challenges in the future.

It took time for each of those children to agree to talk about their traumatic experience and to show their feelings. It was important for me to find the patience to wait and use transitional situations such as playing and telling stories. *Traumatized children need time to deal with the level of excitement and the contradictory emotions aroused by a tragedy.*

147

We can understand some symptoms as being a repetition of the fearful experience, and the frequent nightmares as being a signal of the distressed Ego, which has experienced an external danger, that was impossible to represent. The mind has been unable to figure out the event, to build a picture and give it a meaning. What may seem to be a denial of the traumatic event could be the sudden disappearing of the capacity for representation, and this would be the core of the trauma.

Furthermore, the 11th of September tragedy was not only destruction but also an attack. Thus the challenge for the psyche was then to integrate not just confronting the distress following the disaster but also the terrorists' wish to kill other human beings.

Terrorism – September 11th and its Aftermath

Earl Hopper *(London)*

On 11th September 2001 terrorists destroyed the Twin Towers of the World Trade Center and parts of the Pentagon, and murdered several thousand people. Since then, the 'Western Coalition' (a euphemism for the United States) has bombed Afghanistan; and the war between Israel and the Palestinians has escalated sharply. Military action against Iraq and various terrorist organisations is now imminent.

I have tried to think deeply about what it means to me to work in this context as a psychoanalyst, group analyst and sociologist, who is also an American and a Jew who lives in London, and who often visits and works in the United States and Israel. I admire many features of American society and culture and its political system. I also admire many features of Israeli society and culture, especially its democracy. However, I am appalled by Israel's policies towards the Arabs. I chose to make my home in London, because I love it here. I suppose that like many of us in the British Psychoanalytical Society, I regard myself as a citizen of the world's capital cities in which sociologists, psychoanalysts and group analysts eat, drink and argue (albeit that I often wish that in London and in the British Psychoanalytical Society in particular people argued more, not less).

I would like to describe a few aspects of my experience of the terrorist attacks. Like many others, I hardly believed the initial news reports. However, as I gradually accepted the veracity of the reports, I felt vulnerable and unsafe. I felt diffusely anxious about the dis-identifications with Americans by people close to me, combined with their sympathetic identifications with people who would soon be bombed. I was surprised to learn that many British people of my generation identified spontaneously with the helpless victims of the so-called collateral damage of American bombs on the basis of their own experience during infancy and childhood of being bombed, hiding in garden shelters or underneath reinforced kitchen tables – the fact that the bombs were dropped by Germans, and that their parents and older siblings were most likely to be fighting in co-operation with Americans against the Germans, made almost no difference to their spontaneous sympathies.

I began to use fairly primitive defences against my anxieties: not only dis-association, but also denial. I was surprised by my eventual realisation that I was capable of denial. Actually, I was relieved to realise that I was suffering from a form of post-traumatic stress disorder, partly directly and partly indirectly, sort of vicariously. I had trouble sleeping and began to have various anxiety dreams. Gradually I became convinced that I would have to make some creative use of this experience, and even entertained the hope that I might benefit from working through some of my anxieties about it.

Attempting to forge more mature modifications to my personal and professional identities has involved trying to make some intellectual sense of the experience of trauma and its aftermath. For example, since September 11th, I have been in the United States on two occasions helping to debrief colleagues who have been conducting support groups for those who were directly and indirectly affected by the attacks. I have also completed a couple of manuscripts that had been on my desk for a very long time. As it happens, one is about the social unconscious (2002a), and the other is about traumatised social systems (2002b).

I am pleased that during the last six months virtually all of my patients have been involved in their kaleidoscopic patterns of identifications and dis-identifications with terrorists, victims, perpetrators, bystanders, Americans, Jews, Arabs, Britons, Englishmen, patients, students, Afro-Caribbeans, Afro-Americans, Asians, parents, children, infants, etc., which cannot be understood only or even primarily in terms of the fragments of their infantile egos or their sense of what they have made of mine. I have not attempted to understand this material *only* in terms of the expression of psychotic anxieties within the transference and countertransference. I have also attempted to take up such communications in terms of the social unconscious. Most of the constraints of external realities are unconscious, and must be elucidated and interpreted sociologically.

Our most difficult patients are often too frightened to talk about external reality of this kind, and we often tend to collude with them in order to avoid these topics. Our most difficult patients perceive that many of us do not wish to hear about their social, cultural and political concerns, because our traditional, more classical theories and general ideas are inadequate for understanding what they are trying to tell us. They are aware that many of us defend ourselves against a sense of inadequacy by falling back on the interpretation of the transference only in terms of the biologically based unconscious mind of infancy.

I have become more engaged in attempts to communicate to colleagues and students a view of psychoanalysis that is based on the belief that:
1) both in the beginning and throughout life the ego is not only a body ego but also a society ego;

150

2) although social facts are completely intertwined with psychic facts, we still need to examine the relationships among these realms or levels or components of human reality, and not mix them together indiscriminately, because the 'person' is not the same thing as the 'organism', just as the mind is more than the brain.

A better understanding of terrorism and its aftermath will help us understand the forces of fundamentalism and idolatry within our own profession and its institutions. Such processes are typical of traumatised organisations. In fact, many organisations whose 'mission' is to train psychoanalysts and psychoanalytical psychotherapists within the context of a shrinking profession which faces competition from much improved drug therapies for disorders of affect, and from alternative psychotherapies, many of which we have inadvertently spawned, are traumatised organisations. Many of these traumatised organisations have elders who have themselves been refugees from social trauma of various kinds, for example, Europe, South-Africa, Latin America, and so on. On the basis of their own traumatic experience psychoanalysts from such backgrounds have contributed enormously to our profession, but this has not been without cost both to them and to us. Have they, in one way or another, repeated aspects of their own experience within our training systems and scientific life?

Fundamentalism and idolatry in our attitudes towards theories and techniques create intellectual terrorists who nevertheless would prefer to be loving participants in the development of their chosen profession. If we were able to recognise the necessity of the work of mourning our lost idealisations and our hegemony in the field of mental health care, we might also be better able to hold our creative members and students while initiating and maintaining authentic dialogue with them about psychoanalytical theories and matters of the interpretation of evidence.

References

Hopper, E. (2002a) *The Social Unconscious: Selected Papers*. London: Jessica Kingsley Publishers. (In Press).
Hopper, E. (2002b) *The Fourth Basic Assumption in the Unconscious Life of Groups and Group-like Social Systems*. London: Jessica Kingsley Publishers. (In Press).

In the same boat

Ilany Kogan *(Rehovot, Israel)*

When I accepted the offer to write about working as a psychoanalyst in Israel in the current political situation, I did not know that in a few days our plight would be shared worldwide.

Now that war is no longer just looming high on the horizon, but is an actual fact, the safety of the entire world appears to be threatened. What is the place of psychoanalysis in such a world? I will not deal with this question here. Instead, I wish to share some of my experiences of living and working in Israel during the *Intifadah*, the guerilla war of the past year.

A short while ago, at the start of the Jewish New Year, we 'celebrated' the anniversary of the *Intifadah*. When it broke out last year on the eve of the New Year, most of us were in shock. We were so close to peace, or so it had seemed to us. Apparently, while we felt that Barak was giving too much to the Palestinians, they felt it was too little. The *Intifadah* brought with it continuous shooting in Jerusalem, murder on the roads, suicide bombers blowing themselves up in public places, terrible destruction, and the deaths of children and youth, adults and the elderly, sometimes even entire families.

My initial reactions were depression and anger. I could not accept the fact that our hopes for peace were vanishing into thin air. In particular, such thoughts as – this region will always be subject to war and casualties, there is no solution to the conflict, there is no future for us and our children – weighed heavily on my mind.

My patients came regularly to their sessions. Many of them continued to discuss their lives, conflicts, dilemmas, wishes and fears as if nothing had happened. I listened to them silently, aware of their massive denial, thinking that one of us must be crazy but not sure who. In the end, I decided that the healthier individuals were the ones who were more affected by reality, a thought which conveniently placed me in the camp of the 'sane.'

Curiously enough, life went on, but it was far more strained and stressful. During the 5-10 minute breaks between patients, I would listen to the news broadcasts on the radio. There was no chance of not being aware of what was happening, because if I didn't hear the news for a couple of hours I would always be informed by some patient who, before tackling his own problem, would immediately tell me about the latest terrorist attack, numbers of casualties, and so on.

152

With the passing of time, I actually became numb. My anxiety vanished, and although I was occasionally upset or angry over of the tragic events, I went about my life as if nothing was happening. For my patients as well, life went on as usual, probably because we were all making a psychic effort to deny reality. I realised that I myself had developed certain 'pathological' defenses that characterised some of my patients at the start of the *Intifadah*. Sharing my observations with friends and colleagues, I discovered that many of them were reacting similarly. 'Is it possible,' I asked myself, 'that these 'pathological' defenses are adequate for coping with this situation? Apparently we all need these defenses. We are all traumatised, patients and therapists alike,' I answered myself.

It is difficult to describe the variety of human reactions to a state of constant danger, especially in a situation where the external reality becomes mixed with one's inner world in an inexplicable way. To offer a few examples:

- the hysterical patient who claims that his interchangeable somatic symptoms, his panic attacks, his fear of death, are solely the result of the reality we are living in (never mentioning the fragmented, persecutory mother whose image he carries in himself);

- the depressive patient, convinced that the dangerous reality is the source of his depression (from which he has been suffering for years);

- the passive-aggressive patient who talks about leaving Israel for a safer, quieter place because he cannot stand the dangerous state of affairs (never mentioning how much he wants to run away from analysis!)

Throughout this period I have tried to acknowledge my patients' fears, but not without pointing out to them their unconscious wishes and fantasies. Sometimes I acknowledge their fears by expressing my own feelings about the situation (consoling myself with the fact that Melita Schmideberg did likewise during the *blitzkrieg* in London). Some of my patients have affected me more than others. For example, I empathize with the anxiety of mothers over the lives of their sons who are serving in the army or the reserves; I willingly let a policewoman, who works late guarding dangerous places, come to analysis at unusual hours when I ordinarily do not work; I do not charge patients who miss sessions in analysis because of reserve army duty.

In spite of the difficult situation, or because of it, I feel there is no choice but to go on living, working and creating. One thing is abundantly clear to me: I listen to my patients with the ears and heart of an analyst, and also as someone who is living in Israel. We are all in the same boat.

Trauma and Retrauma: A Personal Voyage

Abigail Golomb *(Tel Aviv)*

Like many Israelis, and other people who grow up and live through crises and wars in their countries, my everyday life and professional choices are routinely influenced by external, traumatic events. In the years I have been working as a doctor, child psychiatrist and psychoanalyst, I can trace the early ideals, illusions and desires for quick and overall solutions to the disillusionment and acceptance of complex reality.

In medical school I remember the temptation of surgery, and the immediate, miraculous relief it could provide. I had a brief taste of the actuality of this during the Six Day War (1967). I had finished my internship and was sent to the Trauma and Burn Unit. The severe burns were quickly transferred to more specialised units. The lightly wounded soldiers and the staff were keyed up, excited and to a large degree oblivious of danger. I was later to learn to call this dissociation, but then it was part of the general adrenalin rush. The soldiers would describe how they got their injuries and flaunted their fearlessness - they panicked at only one thing: injections...

Years later, with more wars, more soldiers, more life-experience and more knowledge, I began to relate to the things I had sensed but not discussed: the complete denial of the existence of the soldiers transferred to the serious Burn Unit, the smell of their flesh, and their silence. They didn't joke, they didn't tell what happened to them, they were immersed in their pain, and there was a wall between them on the one hand and the less severely wounded soldiers and the staff on the other. At that time, this wall was hardly discussed in the professional literature. I recall the pictures and the smells and the silence as vividly as Post Traumatic sufferers describe, and remember my sense of guilt that I had so 'easily' erased them from my conscious memory.

I also went back to those pictures when I first tried to come to grips with transference and countertransference, projections and counter-projections.

The Yom Kippur War (1973) began three weeks before I was to start my analytic training. I took over a psychiatric day unit. There was no glamour in the air; fear was much greater; and we felt left out of the general war effort, caring for people who were more interested in their bodily fluids than in the external events. This was another lesson in dealing with countertransference and counter-projections.... When we finally began psychoanalytic seminars, we all felt distant and disengaged. Reading anything that didn't deal directly with the current situation or with helping the many victims seemed totally irrelevant, and we

154

approached early Freud and our teachers with anger and resistance. Learning to connect what we were reading with what we were experiencing took months.

I found myself being frustrated by colleagues who tried to separate totally between 'the analysis' and external events. I felt that trauma was a major part of our life, and that without understanding it and including that knowledge in every level of our work – we could not function as Mental Health professionals or as analysts. As helpers, a lot of the general frustrations, anger and fear were projected onto us; I longed again for a quick, easy surgical solution both to the general situation and in my psychotherapeutic work. I easily understood the desire for a quick, decisive military solution, a removal of a tumor/enemy or fixing a broken bone/border. It was difficult but necessary to learn to accept there was no easy solution but only complex, prolonged working through.

As I began working with children, the desire to fix things for them became even stronger. I saw the degree to which early traumas shaped their whole development and personality, and was amazed and confounded by the ease that society and the professional world denied these dangers. People wanted 'proof' of the damage, though every textbook explained that damage during the first years would often come out only in later years. I gradually realised that my main anger was at institutions, social systems, the legal system – anyone who had dealings with abused, traumatised or severely disabled children, and was not giving them the care they needed, at the crucial time they needed it. I treated abusing parents like patients – they had to be assessed, helped or even deprived of their children. But when removing a child from home took years, my anger was not at the parents fighting to keep them but at the various professionals who kept prolonging things. The retraumatisation by the system became my personal *bête noir*. And I realised that I had projected all my feelings of helplessness onto the system. I suddenly wondered how many of our war veterans, and how many of the traumatised children, did exactly the same: looking for that external, more anonymous all-powerful enemy.

Trauma came into its own over the years, and in fact began to be a catchall, thus making it a useless working term. There was (and is) a search for immediate, definitive treatment of trauma that would avoid longterm effects. Everything became trauma, including the use of trauma for political means. Small stories come to mind:
- Trying to form a professional group with Palestinian Child Mental Health professionals, to share expertise, and the group degenerating into a competition which trauma is worse: seeing your parents injured by a suicide bomber or seeing them beaten by soldiers.

155

- Seeing a severely disabled child put in a regular kindergarten, being retraumatised daily, because special classes were not 'politically correct' at the time.
- Talking with a group of Palestinian developmental health carers, who said that many families wouldn't bring in their disabled children, from shame, until many heroes of the Intifada lost limbs and came for treatment.

For years I was taught, when I took a case history, to ask people where they were during the Holocaust. Now I ask them about exposure to daily trauma, how they live through the daily events. How they talk to their children about them. I look for the denials and the dissociations, the general heightened sensitivity and anger and fear. Generations are growing up with trauma and retrauma as an integral part of their development.

As a result, we have not only the trauma itself, but the integration of the trauma/retrauma cycle into the fabric of our being. Perhaps this is the most dangerous trauma of them all.

This personal voyage leaves me wary of simplistic solutions, because they are so tempting; and wary of denying the projections and dissociations, because we cannot solve problems and treat traumas that are denied.

Children of Palestine – Heroes and Victims

Eyad El Sarraj *(Gaza City)*

Due to the current political situation, the author, a Palestinian Psychiatrist was unable to send his proposed contribution.. He is Director General of the Gaza Community Mental Health Programme and Secretary General of the Palestinian Independent Commission for Citizen's Rights and Winner of the Physicians for Human Rights Award in 1997 and the Martin Ennals Award for human rights' defenders in 1998.

In September 2001, along with Rafael Moses, Israeli psychoanalyst, and former Sigmund Freud Professor of Psychoanalysis, Hebrew University, Jerusalem, and an American and a European psychiatrist, he drew up a document addressed to Israeli and Palestinian leaders, denouncing violence and tracing the deleterious effects of

- the cycle of recurring traumatization involving violence, humiliation, retaliation and revenge
- the protracted exposure to conditions of uncertainty, anxiety and stress
- the personal and national impact of loss of family members and friends
- the dehumanization of the other side viewed as enemy
- the dehumanizing effects on young people of being involved in violence and killing and of participating in, or being a party to, oppression
- the distorted picture of the other side inculcated from a young age into future generations, perpetuating the conflict.

157

MULTIPLE DIMENSIONS

Ambition/ Jonty Leff

God bellowed, Let the first dimension be a dot!
And man conquered the first dimension
Putting dots everywhere like a used dart board.
God threw his dart to open the gate of his imagination.

Then God sat up in bed and announced,
Let the second dimension be a line.
Man got excited and used his lines and dots
In pictures and paintings.

God slumped in his slippers and grumbled,
Let the third dimension be a cube.
Man took his building blocks
And made cities and towns.

Then God, while brushing his teeth, became ambitious.
He roared, Let the fourth dimension be time!
Man looked at time and played with it
And death tapped him on the shoulder.

God blurted, with a mouth full of cornflakes,
Let the fifth dimension be the unexplainable.
And the ashes of man were put into a gridded box
And thrown through time.
Weaving in and out of light and sound
Like a needle going through felt without a thread.

[Thanks to W H Smith for permission to reprint Ambition (Young Words - award winning entries (age 11) from the 1988 W H Smith Young Writers' Competition, Macmillan Children's Books, 1989)].

158

Border Crossing: the Philosopher as Psychoanalyst

Marcia Cavell *(Berkeley)*

As a trained philosopher and a psychoanalyst in training, I am often asked, 'Why are you doing both? What do psychoanalysis and philosophy have in common?' I continue to find the question puzzling, since the disciplines so obviously share a large, common border, inhabited by questions about the nature of meaning, mind, thought, self, love, irrationality; about the relations between mind and body, between language and thought, between self-knowledge and knowledge of other minds; about the extent of self-knowledge, the realm of the intentional, how best to describe and explain human actions. These are merely some of the inhabitants. Across this border shots are sometimes fired, but also exchanges that are useful to both disciplines. Of such I hope there will be many more.

Let me give this common border a little detail more detail, suggesting as I go some differences between the ways in which philosopher and psychoanalyst make their explorations.

Discovering the meaning of a gesture, word, or action, is the central enterprise of psychoanalytic therapy. Analysis of the meaning of meaning has been a central enterprise of 20th century philosophy. An important assumption about meaning informs the work of the psychoanalyst, namely, that the meanings of a word or sentence are not self-contained, but spread out over a large network of other sentences, beliefs, and so on.

This is one of the assumptions — philosophers call it meaning holism — behind the psychoanalyst's insistence on the importance of so-called free association. Wittgenstein was perhaps the first philosopher who enunciated meaning holism, saying in only a slightly different context, "When light dawns, it dawns gradually over the whole." It is a view of meaning now shared and discussed by a great many philosophers in both the Anglo-American and the Continental traditions. It was not shared by such eighteenth century empiricists as Locke and Hume: they conceived of thoughts as little nuggets — data of sense, such as experiences of color, warmth, shape — that somehow get connected up with each other. With regard to infant phantasies, followers of Melanie Klein and Wilfred Bion, at least as I read them, still share this conception. Though I doubt that the psychoanalyst sees the implications of the Kleinian view in the way I suggest.

The psychoanalyst has more subtle methods for unearthing meaning than the philosopher does, but tends to take the notion of meaning itself for granted, whereas this is just what interests the philosopher. She notes that the senses in which thunder, the song of a bird, the movements of a flock of a geese, pointing, the cry of a baby, a shrug of the shoulders, music, words on a page, words said by a speaker, are meaningful, are very different from each other. The philosopher tries to formulate a theory of meaning that will distinguish among and comprehend these different senses. It must be a theory that also takes account of speech as action, of every speech act as a multiplicity of actions all at the same time: a statement may turn out to be also a warning, a plea for help, a complaint, a command, a question. Speech is communication. It is social. The psychoanalysts is intimately familiar with this fact. But she is perhaps less aware than the philosopher of its possible implication that thought, too, is social. And if this is so, the philosopher continues, what challenge might be posed to our assumption that thought — mind — itself, is inherently subjective? Perhaps our knowledge of other minds is not so impossible as philosophy itself had led us to think. Perhaps objectivity, so often disputed by psychoanalysts these days, is, in some sense, a condition of dialogue.

These matters bring us naturally to the psychoanalytic idea that meaning is often unconscious. Freud believed this was contested by philosophers. But what may look like a dispute has rather to do with ways in which philosophers are skeptical of the vast body of assumptions in which Freud embedded this idea; among them, that there is a realm of the mental which is guided by its own laws, and there is something to be called the unconscious that is temporally prior to the mind philosophers investigate. The empirical question of how and when mind develops from infant to older child interests the philosopher; but it is not a question she is professionally equipped to answer. She inquires instead about what we mean by thought, what its essential nature is, its prerequisites. Both psychoanalysis and philosophy draw on empirical evidence and theoretical reflection to develop a theory of the mind; this is another commonality between these disciplines. The philosopher insists, however, that conceptual analysis comes first; for how, she asks, can we design experiments to inform us about the genesis of thought without an idea to begin with of what we mean by it? The philosopher thinks that the assumptions the developmentalist makes and of which she may be unaware may call her conclusions into question. (Freud complained that philosophy is fond of airy speculation. This is not true of philosophy in the Anglo-American-American tradition. And I can't resist remarking that the complaint is odd from someone so given to such speculation himself.)

About action, philosopher and psychoanalyst both ask: Are explanations in the language of mind — beliefs, desires, longings, emotions — reducible to a language that is thoroughly physicalist in nature, as the early Freud held, and as some contemporary psychoanalysts who are influenced by work in neuro-physiology believe? Or is understanding human behavior in the language of mind, essential to the mind itself? About the self, both philosopher and psychoanalyst ask whether there is any such thing. Hume thought not, that all we can find is a vast succession of experiences, not 'owned' by anyone. Kant agreed, up to a point, but then went on to make a fancy distinction that granted a particular concept of self an honored place in human understanding. Like Hume, only with different phenomena in view — dissociation, splitting, intra-psychic conflict, repression — Freud too asks whether we can hold to the idea of a unified self.

Some years ago I wanted to learn to navigate the border between philosophy and psychoanalysis from both directions. I was interested in guilt as a phenomenon in ethics, and I thought I'd better learn what psychoanalysis had to say about it. It was the first step on a path that would turn out to be very long. I had no intention of giving up either philosophy or psychoanalysis. I still don't. Philosophy values clarity, as I do. But I also value the fine-grained texture that the psychoanalytic life — on the couch, behind the couch, in the study — brings to philosophical problems that can otherwise remain abstract. This is not a criticism of my first discipline: abstraction is necessary to its accomplishments. Every philosophical problem is so inherently complex and ambiguous that were we to begin by stirring the most clotted waters first, clarification would be impossible. Yet the philosopher has to be mindful of the ambiguities and

160

complexities that she may not directly address, and willing to encompass them when they are pointed out. She may have to modify her reflections substantially in light of the experiences with which the psychoanalyst is familiar. On her part, the psychoanalyst is not trained to discern, nor may she be temperamentally suited, to notice and examine her own assumptions. Psychoanalyst and philosopher need each other. Yet their differences make speaking across the common border difficult. To the psychoanalyst, the philosopher may seem to have her head in the clouds. To the philosopher, the psychoanalyst may seem hopelessly vague. The philosopher argues, for example, that our explanations of human action require us to use the concept of reason. The psychoanalyst responds: 'You philosophers speak of reason, as if irrationality were not the usual state of affairs'. The philosopher answers: 'By an irrational thought or action do you mean one in which there is no sense, no informing belief or desire? Or do you rather mean one in which the relevant beliefs and desires are appropriate not the present but to the past, the past as conceived by the 'irrational' agent?'

The philosopher argues that an analysis of meaning presumes a common reality with which we are all in touch. The psychoanalyst responds: 'There's no point talking about a common reality as something outside our minds, since all perceptions are filtered through subjective phantasy, defense, and desire'. The philosopher answers: 'To say that each of us experiences the world in a way unique to her, which is of course the case, is not to say there are as many worlds as there are minds. You and I cannot literally share our experiences of the overheated room, or the war, but we can share the room, and the war.'

The philosopher argues that in any account of meaning and interpretation, there is an essential connection between understanding the meaning of a sentence and grasping the conditions under which the sentence would be true. The psychoanalyst responds: 'We're interested in the meaning of a great many other things than sentences.' The philosopher answers: 'Let's see if we can formulate a reasonable theory of meaning where we have a pretty good idea of what we're talking about, namely, meaning in language. Then we can move beyond it.' The psychoanalyst says, 'Neither the psychoanalyst nor her patient need be interested in the truth of what is being said; in any case, it's psychic truth that counts.' The philosopher answers: 'You misunderstand me. I am not saying that every speaker is after truth; I am rather asking if some connection between meaning and truth must figure in a theory of meaning.' The psychoanalyst and philosopher share many concerns; but they are not always asking just the same questions about them. So there is, in Ferenczi's famous phrase, a confusion of tongues.

To develop a voice the psychoanalyst can trust, the philosopher has to loosen up, learn the psychoanalyst's language, find where and how translations are possible, get her hands a little messy, hold onto the virtue of her presumed clarity while yielding her chastity. The psychoanalyst who wants to convey her clinical knowledge to the philosopher has an equally rough time. Let's say that psychoanalyst and patient have been working for years on the latter's feeling that she is worthless. The pair gradually approaches what seems to be an early, false, unconscious belief of the patient's that her father left when she was very young because she was indeed worthless. The father's departure by itself need not have been so damaging without a mother who needed not to know that something important to the child had been lost; so that the child's false belief never got examined. Add to the story as well the mother's phantasies, as understood by the child, about the father who had left her, the mother, when she was a young child. When the patient finally comes to recognize that feeling worthless is not the same as being worthless, that the frequent rages that add to her sense of worthlessness themselves a defense against feelings of shame, and that her beliefs about why her father left are false, she recovers from her chronic insomnia, begins to enjoy her various successes, and stops acting out the worthlessness she has felt.

A familiar sort of story to the psychoanalyst, who also knows how absurdly abbreviated it is; she appreciates the vast complexity that such a quick telling must leave out. But the philosopher who lacks some considerable clinical knowledge cannot appreciate this. She will listen tothe tale with exasperation and disbelief: 'Why, for heaven's sake, would someone act out a feeling of worthlessness? How can a child have such a belief? How can the belief linger for so long? Why doesn't the adult know she has this belief? Once she does, why doesn't she realize immediately that it is false? What, for heaven's sake, is so difficult about seeing the difference between feeling that something is the case, and its being the case? Anyway, how do you know that the analysis of all this is right? How do you know that it has anything to do with the change in patient's state of mind?' Conveying the analytic work that is done over a number of years, four hours each week, to someone who has not had an analysis herself, or who does not have the patience to read some detailed case histories, is difficult. Even then the philosopher may of course remain skeptical. The patient's presumed discoveries will seem unlikely, and banal. — There is some truth in the familiar complaint against psychoanalysis that, on its own word, it can be evaluated only by those who are already believers. — But if she is willing to immerse herself in some clinical material, the philosopher can learn much about things that, as a philosopher, she may care about it; for example: the meaning and nature of self-discovery, the differences between knowing a truth and acknowledging it, the many faces of self-deception. I haven't yet mentioned about practice, about what a philosophy teacher who begins to occupy the chair behind the couch as well as the podium may experience. Socrates described the philosopher as midwife to the soul, delivering it from delusion. So there is a ready analogy between midwife and psychoanalyst. But it is deceptive. Socrates argued; he was not a particularly good listener; he had a quite specific idea of where he wanted his interlocutor to go; he was interested in intellectual rigor, uninterested in emotional weather; he initiated dialogues that took off from the remarks of his interlocutor, but his aim was the discovery of larger truths. The psychoanalyst who brings these attitudes to her patients has lost the game. She tries to avoid agreements; she listens; she tolerates the sort of passivity required for being led; she welcomes the multiplicity of meanings in the room; she is alert to what she and her patient are both communicating beneath and beyond their words. The psychoanalyst often fails at these tasks, but she tries. Like the psychoanalyst, all of us hear ambiguities and pick up feelings that are not articulated. We hear but we don't listen, and for a variety of reasons we usually aren't tuned to the best frequency. I have always loved teaching the large, introductory philosophy classes with their invitation to draw the big picture, point towards new horizons, sum up where we have been and where we are, dazzle with surprising references and allusions. These are just the activities I have been learning to resist. Our clinical training teaches us to be relatively silent, to be abstinent in certain ways, to wait.

These are extraordinary lessons.

From the Front of the Classroom to Behind the Couch and Back Again   Nancy J. Chodorow *(Berkeley)*

"Do you know," the student leaned forward over the small café table that separated us, "that we are reading and talking about what every one of us thinks about 24/7?" Having early in the semester read Horney, Freud, Chodorow, Benjamin and finally Irigaray's "The One Doesn't Stir without the Other," this brilliant Chicano undergraduate had become so anxious at the onslaught of described feminine anxieties, concluding with the visceral, sexually-tinged body-boundary diffusion described by Irigaray, that he had tried to drop the course. Now, further along, and having just read Person on sexual desire and men's fantasies about lesbian sex, Mayer on primary female genital anxiety, Rivière on gender as a masquerade, and Goldner on gender identity as a defense, he was mesmerized. These issues that we were reading about and discussing in an undergraduate seminar, 'Psychoanalysis and Feminism,' were, as he put it, what all undergraduates think about twenty-four hours a day.

The following year, as we are discussing in the same seminar Freud's *A Special Type of Object Choice Made by Men*, a Korean-American girl excitedly notes, "Freud says that the man wants to have a baby son so he can give the son to his mother. But that's <u>exactly</u> what a Korean man does! He marries a woman so he can bring her home to have a baby for his mother!" A Japanese-American girl and Vietnamese-American boy recognize the pattern from their family cultures as well. Students in a large lecture class eagerly discuss memories and family stories about their transitional objects. We all agree that the tacit Winnicottian contract, in which no one challenges whether it is created from within or given from without, is routinely broken – and with great joy -- by older siblings. They nod dreamily, talk animatedly to a neighbor, or look astonished, as we think about how we can be confused about dreams when we try to reconstruct them, and how there seem to be contradictory, impossible, or wavering identities in them. They are thrilled to learn about the primary process that can so easily make substitutions, condensations, and displacements.

In a graduate sociology seminar on interview methods, renamed by me 'Clinical Listening for Social Scientists,' we begin from the radical challenge to social science that, when you are interviewing, people don't say what they mean. The researcher's job, therefore, cannot be simply to record words. The researcher has to learn how to interpret, listen to listening, pay attention to affect, transference and countertransference, and use the self to understand the other. We read among others Casement, Faimberg, Schwaber, Jacobs, Poland, Loewald. They marvel at Poland's

163

writing style and at how Jacobs can possibly be so self-aware and so focused at the same time. They wonder how analysts can tolerate the anxiety of listening to the patient while theory is held in abeyance. One student discovers in his research on high-tech workers that two men whose behavior is exactly the same, and seems driven entirely by their company's incentive system in fact have entirely different underlying motivational systems, affects, and fantasies. These self-descriptions encompass relations to parents, different anxieties, and different fears – in the one case of feeling like a little boy at home with his wife, in the other of losing a primary identity as a craftsman and musician. Another student finds that the concept of countertransference transforms her understanding of difficult patterns of interaction and misunderstandings in her recent research in the former Soviet Union. Her identifications, resistances, and defenses shaped how she interacted, what she asked, and how she heard, as well as how and when interviewees became anxious, shut down, or defensive and when they seemed genuinely able to think.

When I undertook psychoanalytic training, I knew that I wanted to have a psychoanalytic practice and that my writing had gone as far as it could without clinical experience. But I was unprepared for the effects of this training on my career as a professor. I gained a much deeper understanding of the ways that affect and fantasy help shape cognition and perception and enable or prevent thinking – of the fact that students need not to be anxious in order to learn.

My primary professorial task now feels clinical as much as pedagogic - containing anxiety, helping students to be curious and to see the point of view of the other. Particularly, I have come to think that academic training, in which students are taught to read for faults and problems, and where discourse is adversarial (practices also found at our psychoanalytic meetings and in our journals), makes students (and psychoanalysts) unable to think. Such reading immediately redounds into unconscious worry about being criticized or into superego attacks on the self or. In the case of a teacher or class demolishing an assigned work (or when a discussant demolishes a presented paper), this generates anxiety about conflict between the parental couple, leading to an internal need to turn from one to the other rather than feeling contained by collaboration and therefore free to wonder and wander. I tell students that they had best assume, just as we do with patients (but often not with our colleagues), that writers and researchers are doing the best they can and that they are trying to solve problems with the data and theory available to them. We can learn much more from seeing how a thinker's mind works -even if her conclusions are completely contrary to our own beliefs - than we can from focusing on all the ways we disagree with that thinker.

164

As a result of becoming a psychoanalyst, I have come to see students, especially undergraduates, not as abstract learners but more in terms of their particular developmental place and its accompanying forms of relationship, with characteristic conflicts, tasks, and anxieties. Finally, my theoretical knowledge prior to training, that meaning and experience are created from within as much as from without, gained a clinically-based certainty that seems to have been communicated to students.

My graduate interviewing course and 'Freud and Beyond' graduate theory course, as well as my undergraduate courses, are in high demand, as social science students find that psychoanalysis meets their own sense that there is something missing in social and cultural determinism (or, in the case of psychology students, in hyper-scientism in research and theory). They welcome tacit recognition of the intense wonder and curiosity they also feel about the marvel of unique individuality, and they are particularly drawn to non-theory driven listening – to the idea that one can listen to rather than listen for. And, perhaps most affirming of the importance of psychoanalysis as both theory and practice, students of many backgrounds and ethnicities keep asking me how they can become psychoanalysts.

30 Years in the Credibility Gap: The Moans from Behind the Couch of a Psychoanalyst Trying to Survive in Academic Psychology Peter Fonagy *(London)*

There are too few academics who oppose progress in psychology. In fact psychological luddites are an endangered species. As a consequence of the lamentable absence of those who could succeed in holding back the wheels of advancement, psychology as a discipline has changed almost beyond recognition during the course of my professional life. I have had a remarkable opportunity to observe this 'evolution' having been in the same department of a leading UK university since 1971.

Thirty years ago things were very different. Learning theory and psychoanalysis were engaged in a heroic battle of the giants. In US academia at least, two intellectual traditions, both radical in their own way, both deeply reductionistic (not so obvious at the time but clear now with the hindsight that increased research expertise inevitably brings) were engaged in a life-or-death struggle for the supremacy of the study of the mind. Psychiatry, dominated by psychoanalytic ego psychology, and psychology, the almost exclusive dominion of Pavlov, Hull, Tolman, and Skinner.

Psychology was strong on method but poor on intellectual excitement. Who could take seriously a model of human behavior based on the lever presses of rats. Psychoanalysis, although relatively barren and mechanical compared to the present day, had Freud's rich and complex theory to draw on clinical experience had accumulated many hundreds of stories about people. Stories about individuals struggling with their social and biological heritage and talking about these battles to kind but serious professionals. Learning theory had little consolation to offer to the person suffering. So what if his painful reactions to sexual rejection were learned habits? There was a seemingly unbridgeable gap between the two traditions.

Yet, in those halcyon days, the status of psychoanalysis within psychology was actually remarkably high. There was disparagement of course, but the critics of psychoanalysis were, themselves evidently open to derision for their ludicrously narrow, profoundly biased and frankly self-promoting stance. Most intelligent psychologists were well aware of the limitations of their discipline and acknowledged this either overtly or covertly. Academic psychologists, when dissatisfied with their personal lives in the laboratory would go to a psychoanalyst to talk about their frustration each morning, before returning to their laboratory to gain further insight into the nature of anxiety by giving NIMH grant funded electric shocks to a variety of small mammals. While there was much talk of Popper and the need to verify psychoanalytic constructs empirically, these were considered attainable goals, a matter of time, rather than a matter of epistemic contradiction. Something that would have to be dealt with one day, like paying off one's credit card bills.

A number of developments destroyed the idyll of a genuinely divided subject that had an important even if second rank place for psychoanalytic ideas. These were in temporal order: (1) the rise of cognitive science and the fall from grace of learning theory, (2) the rapid advances in our understanding of brain-behavior relationship and the emergence of relatively effective pharmacotherapies, (3) the breadth of success of the talking cure and the proliferation of effective psychotherapeutic practices or schools of therapy. But these are external factors. If my years on the couch have taught me anything, it is that I should be suspicious of the wish to find solutions to my difficulties in others, beyond my mental boundaries.

Behind the couch in academe today, there has been a dramatic shift in attitudes. The psychoanalyst is widely regarded by psychologists in the same kind of terms as Hans-Christian Andersen's proverbial king, in the process of promoting 'Health and Efficiency' without knowing it. It is widely believed that time has run out for psychoanalysis. An explicitly psychoanalytic orientation more or less guarantees the failure of a job application in most psychology or psychiatry departments. It is well known that, in the US at least, many applicants for faculty positions remove their psychoanalytic training from their CV's to ensure that they will be seriously considered for a position. Psychoanalytic therapy teaching is rapidly disappearing from the syllabuses of major clinical psychiatric and psychological training programs. For me, personally most noticeable is the change of attitude from fellow academics. Where there had been perhaps somewhat grudging respect, now there can be overt hostility reserved for those colleagues who do not contribute to the department's 'academic standing', who ride on the coat-tails of those with genuine achievements. In most prominent universities these freeloader bring upon themselves the status of an 'untouchable'.

What factors might account for this change? Leaving aside broader social and cultural changes that lie outside of either psychoanalysis or other mental health subjects, there are problems for psychoanalysis that are specific to the study of mind. I will mention only the 5 central difficulties that I have personally struggled with 'behind the couch' again in order of perceived importance.

(1) The questions that psychoanalysis tends to ask have frequently been taken out of its domain and moved into other domains and re-cast in the language of modern sciences. These are cognitive science or neuroscience or an increasingly popular combination of the two, cognitive-neuroscience. When we appear to know so much about the specific neurobiology of OCD it is a hard sell to invoke the anal phase as an adequate alternative scientific account.

(2) Psychoanalysis never bothered to get its theoretical act together. After more than a hundred years there is still no generally accepted psychoanalytic theory of affect, memory, therapeutic action, defense mechanisms etc. These terms are widely used in explanations without ever being defined.

(3) Our claim to psychological knowledge rests on our ability to be neutral observers of the process of treatment – to discover as we heal. Yet, our increased sophistication about the analyst's involvement in the complex and intense interpersonal processes in the consulting room, deny the possibility of privileged access. Interpersonal interaction is governed by deeply unconscious processes that are so rapid that they must bypass conscious reflection. We have access to a small and undoubtedly highly selective segment of what happens between us and our patients: a selection too small to serve as the basis of our science.

(4) The clinical limitations of psychoanalysis in the face of severe disturbance have disappointed many. There is a chronic character to mental illness. Many problems, for example chronic depression, may not respond well to analytic treatment. Yet learning to live with a problem may be an appropriate aim for supportive therapy or cognitive behavior therapy, it is not consistent with the declared ambitions of a therapy that has the most profound levels of understanding as its core mission.

(5) Analysis may be the "impossible profession" but this surely does not excuse the ethically questionable and unprofessional behavior that periodically comes to light about significant figures in our professions which, even more disturbingly, also appear to be not infrequently, implicitly or explicitly, covered up by the psychoanalytic institution.

There are other problems but I think even these few, to the extent that they have reached public consciousness, account for the loss of interest in psychoanalysis by academics interested in the study of the mind. I naturally have a sense of profound injustice about this change. This is not purely a narcissistic reaction to the dramatic loss of respect. It is rooted in the sense of feeling that we (as analyst researchers) have done so well in meeting the Popperian objections to our theory only to find that (as it is often the case) the goal-post has been moved whilst we were busy preparing the shot.

There is more empirical irrefutable evidence for psychoanalytic ideas than ever before. In fact most of the discoveries of cognitive and social science over the last decades have confirmed Freud's ideas. Wonderful summaries of these have been published in both the psychological and the psychoanalytic literature (see for example Drew Westen's reviews). Here I only have space for the headlines, but take the physiological evidence that confirms that early developmental experience is formative biologically as well as behaviorally or the discoveries about the remarkable mental capacities of human infancy or the ubiquity of non-conscious complex thought processes or the many correspondences between neural structures as revealed by cognitive neuroscience and mental phenomena discussed by clinicians writing about dreaming, unconscious phantasy, or the transgenerational transmission of patterns of relationship representations and so on.

Some days, I ask myself, how is it that in the light of all these confirmations of psychoanalytic ideas we are not celebrated as the discipline that originated the notions of the unconscious, of meaningful dreams, of relationship representational structures, of biases in cognitive processing, of emotions being at the core of other information processing systems? Why are we not applauded as the originators of the talking cure, the idea that psychosocial intervention could address therapeutically the way people thought about themselves and others? Why is it cognitive behavior therapy that is getting the credit? It is not fair, I cry; I am being robbed of my past (discoveries) and being offered no shares in the (scientific) future. It is miserable that it is not sufficient for me to *have been* correct. I have to contribute to the discourse of the present and the future. I have to be the source of new insights rather than simply glory in the justification of the old by those who have traditionally been my worst critics. I have to go on proving my worth to my colleagues through the discovery of new facts, bringing new inspiration to empirical research from my clinical laboratory. The past has been written off and the challenge is survival in the future. Can I deliver using the same clinical sensibilities? Then I realize why I am once again in the 'credibility gap'!

Before the Couch Existed: Some Methodological Considerations on Non-Clinical Psychoanalytical Research

Moisés Lemlij *(Lima)*

In the beginning of the 1980's, with a group of friends of mine, Max Hernández and Alberto Péndola, psychoanalysts, Luis Millones, an anthropologist, and María Rostworowski, the grand old lady of Peruvian history, we founded a study group, the Interdisciplinary Seminar on Andean Studies (SIDEA), to attempt a multidisciplinary approach to the understanding of social and political contemporary phenomena in Peru by way of getting immersed in the historical and ethnohistorical roots of our country.

The Andean world represents at once a great difficulty and a kind of natural opening for the application of psychoanalytical method. Some of the difficulties presented by Inca history have been settled with a better definition of ethnohistorical method. We refer to those arising from documents which have been transcribed from the oral Quechua tradition and presented in terms of Spanish concepts and the lineal code of writing. These difficulties, this "resistance" stemming from the translation, means that a major portion of psychohistorical method, that which is integrally connected to psychoanalytical method, offers an interesting access to the Andean universe which underlies the Hispanic text.

The first task of SIDEA was to try to work according to the rules of historians and anthropologists. In our dialogue with the social scientists, the psychoanalysts attempted to interpret the material "by listening". A creative exchange gradually grew between text, circumstance and listeners, allowing us all to share a familiarity with the material and the method which developed. It was possible to "listen" analytically to the texts when approached with the demands of the methods of history and anthropology. In our case, this pre-supposed that documents had to be double filtered: the material only reports the point of view of the governors, and since there were European, the institutions and facts are expressed with a Western and Christian logic. We had to borrow from other disciplines to corroborate the facts and rectify the prejudices which bias the written documents. Without the support of archaeology, for example, it would have been impossible to determine the general trends of the process in which the facts described by the Spanish of the 16th and 17th centuries are buried. Similarly, the history of art and iconography helped us to reconstruct with greater accuracy the ideological perception of the Andean people who, after the Conquest, began using the European conceptual apparatus irrevocably. But on painting or sculpting images –

including the Christian-- the native artist took the original pattern and rewrought it, making it Andean.

Throughout the process we selected the texts and defined their contexts. Two stories, one regarding the formation and early development of the foundations of the Tawantinsuyu empire, and another regarding its apogee and splendour, constitute what could be called the official Cusco epic in the documentary sources we used. We then went on to the period of expansion and what was for the Andean world the catastrophe of the Spanish Conquest. The texts were written by Spanish, indigenous or mixed-race chroniclers and by civic religious officials about a non-writing society, whose concept of time was different from that of the West: it was cyclical and concentric, rather than lineal and irreversible.

We tried to gain access to the Andean way of thinking and its textual and contextual expressions so that we could see some of its particular structures, i.e. an interpretative reading of the mythical and legendary, and Andean historical discourse, bearing the socio-cultural dimension in mind. The mythical, the legendary and the ritual were interlaced in a complex weaving with a design which at times presented specific history deeply embedded within a myth, or in rites which reveal the insistence of ancient myths which reappeared at precise moments.

The attempt to understand the Andean world on its own terms involved a conceptual translation. Ethnohistory and psychoanalysis may be able to provide the bridges for reconstructing Inca conceptions and for understanding intuitively the categories through which they organized their vision of time and space, and the structures and unconcious conflicts underlying the actions of the men who wrought Inca History.

As psychoanalysts, we have an instrument which allows us to discover the structures at the basis of the discourse produced by the patient's psychic data, experienced or not. In exactly the same way, in the case of the Andean world we can follow the texts, their recurrence and subtle confusion to access underlying facts, assisted by the caution demanded by anthropology and history.

It is evident that to interpret a historical text is not the exact equivalent to the interpretation given to an analysand. In this field, the object of interpretation remains unchanged. What moves is not the objective text of the interpretation but the context from which it is interpreted. The text does not establish a transference relationship with the analyst and does not direct its feeling towards him. It is rather the analyst who forms a transference relationship with the material. The clarification and formation of the transference relationship of the analyst are important. It is not possible to evaluate the effects of the interpretations: the text remains immutable, and it is our understanding which vanes. Hence there is a danger that this should become simply tautology.

Having established an ethnohistorical syntax which clarified the structural aspects of the Inca past, we attempted to move into the field of semantics, the underlying aspects and their significant functions. It is here that analytical listening permitted the tentative formulation of an interpretative proposal which was returned to the ethnohistorians, and having been so produced a resonance among the whole interdisciplinary group and on occasions managed to produce a group insight. We are not saying that in each case we have achieved a substantial, modal and formal convergence, but we have attained a kind of mutual validation.

In summary, this was an interdisciplinary task in which psychoanalytical thought arranged the warp of the weaving, both in the discussion and the proposal we presented. For example, what we saw in the texts we examine was a change in kinship systems, a transformation in the relationship between rulers and ruled, the transition from a cyclical story of the origins to one which is a more dynamic and lineal description of historical time, a change in the codes which govern development and the passsage of an organization from narcissistic and diadic relations to a rough draft of the construction of a triangular structure. The atom of kinship, marital relations, kinship systems, unconscious structures, social organization, religious vision and concept of history all connect up, converge, diverge and are interwoven. From an attempt to construct an interpretation of Andean myths we have moved to a general theoretical proposal to be used in a broader way in social science and history.

My use of concepts from modern physics in psychoanalysis

Ofra Eshel *(Herzliya-on-Sea, Israel)*

As psychoanalysts, we struggle daily to grasp elusive facets of the human psyche and to be open to unknown experiences, ideas, feelings, connections and impacts, challenging fixed assumptions about what we are capable of experiencing and understanding. I have found that interdisciplinary correspondence – with literature, poetry, the Bible, films and science – enhance these inner possibilities. In this article, I describe my use of concepts and frameworks from modern physics and astrophysics to enrich and expand my understanding of psychoanalytic phenomena and the psychoanalytic process. In recent years, there has been a growing body of literature on the parallels and connections between concepts and theories of modern physics and psychoanalysis.[1] However, it is beyond the scope of this article to either review this interesting literature, or discuss the advantages and disadvantages of interdisciplinary correspondence in general, or of psychoanalysis and physics in particular. I shall therefore confine myself to my personal use of two enthralling ideas from modern physics in psychoanalysis: The astrophysical *'black hole'* (including 'singularity', 'event horizon' and 'wormhole') and Heisenberg's *uncertainty principle of quantum physics*.

1 'Black hole'

The term *'black hole'* has meaning in both psychoanalysis and astrophysics. In psychoanalysis, 'black hole' has been used to describe the nature of early infantile traumatizations of separateness from the primal mother, resulting in primitive mental disturbances. It was first applied clinically by Bion with reference to the 'infantile catastrophe' of the psychotic, and was developed and applied by Tustin to the psychogenic autism of children, and later by Grotstein (who added concepts from astrophysics) to psychotics and borderlines.

Yet, it was the astrophysical 'black hole' rather than the psychoanalytic 'black hole' that I came to apply to my analytic experiences, particularly in one analysis, to convey a different clinical phenomenon. I was grappling in analysis with massive, overwhelming, devouring deadness within the close intersubjective experiences of a person who otherwise seemed to function well in his social and professional life. It was not the 'black hole' used by Tustin and Grotstein to describe internal space in primitive mental disorders. Yet, I felt, it was a 'black hole' experience, and the astrophysical 'black hole' provided me with an apt and powerful name, way of expression, characterization and meaning for this quality of 'experiencing experience'.

Why the astrophysical 'black hole'?

The term 'black hole' in astrophysics – describing an idea about dark, invisible stars that was first speculated upon as early as 1783 – was coined by the American physicist John Wheeler[2] in 1968, stimulating excitement in astrophysical research and theory, as well as in science fiction.[3] A 'black hole' is caused by the massive collapse of a dying star. Eventually, when the star shrinks to a certain critical radius of infinitesimal size and infinite density ('singularity'), its gravitational field becomes so strong that nothing, not even light, can escape – hence its darkness. Everything is dragged back by the gravitational field, 'producing a region of space-time where infinitely strong gravitational forces literally squeeze matter and protons out of existence' (Penrose, 1973, cited in Gribbin, 1992, p. 142). The boundary of the black hole – the *'event horizon'* – is formed by the paths in space-time of light rays that just fail to escape from the black hole, hovering forever on its edge. *'Another way of seeing this is that the event horizon is like the edge of a shadow – the shadow of impending doom. ...The event horizon acts rather like a one-way membrane around the black hole: Objects, such as unwary astronauts, can fall through the event horizon into the black hole, but nothing can ever get out of the black hole through the event horizon. ... Anything or anyone that falls through the event horizon will soon reach the region of infinite density and the end of time'* (Hawking, 1988, pp. 98-99, p. 110). Falling into a 'black hole' has therefore become one of the great horrors of science fiction.

This compelling astrophysical description enabled me, in analysis, to capture the gripping presence connected to the psychically 'dead' parent, particularly 'the dead mother' (Green, 1986), in her child's psychic space of self-and-other. Using the astrophysical metaphor, it can be said that individuals under the impact of a 'dead', depressed mother exist in intersubjective psychic space dominated by a 'black hole'. They are either trapped in her sucking, devouring, deadening world – inside the 'black hole', unable to escape its destructive forces, or if successful in detaching themselves, remain 'hovering forever' on its edge, in the area of the 'event horizon', petrified of the imminent threat of being pulled into the 'black hole'. Consequently, they are unable to love and form close, intimate relationships. Furthermore, my use of the astrophysical description of the 'black hole' embodies and emphasizes the questions that I feel are crucial to the analysis of these patients: Can analysis provide the enormous counter-forces needed for extricating these patients from the powerful, gripping, destructive forces of the 'black hole', of the 'dead' mother? And can the analyst (when not a remote observer) survive and influence in this devouring, annihilating world of deadness?

In my paper *'Black holes,' deadness and existing analytically* (Eshel, 1998), I described an analysis in which I grappled arduously with these experiences and questions – how I struggled to hold, contain and remain analytically alive within these destructive processes, while experiencing annihilation and death along with the patient. I concluded with another term that astrophysicists and science fiction writers have speculated upon – the *'wormhole'*, an interior tunnel through the annihilating forces of the

174

'black hole', which makes it possible to pass through the 'black hole' and come out alive in another place in space. For me, this provides a further intriguing analogy between the inner journey through annihilating deadness in analysis – held, protected and contained by the sustaining analytic functioning, and the 'wormhole', which according to those astrophysicists, would require intense effort and perseverance to construct or keep open, stable and traversable.

II Heisenberg's uncertainty principle of quantum mechanics

The theory of quantum mechanics was developed during the first half of the 20th century from Planck's quantum principle and Heisenberg's uncertainty principle, bringing to modern physics inspiring-mystifying discoveries and puzzling questions about revolutionary effects, inseparability and indeterminacy. The key feature of Heisenberg's uncertainty principle (formulated in 1926) is that one cannot measure or observe both the position and the velocity (or several other pairs of variables) of a particle with great accuracy because *the process itself, the very act of observation, affects the observed phenomenon in crucial ways.* It does not depend on the way one tries to measure/observe or on the type of particle: Heisenberg's uncertainty principle is an essential, inescapable property of the world at its most fundamental levels. In quantum physics, particles no longer have *separate, well-defined* positions and velocities that can be observed. Instead, they have a *quantum state, which is a combination* of position and velocity (Hawking, 1988, 1993). This new worldview was completely contradictory to classical physics, which is based on the assumptions of determinism, continuity and sharp separation of observer and the object under observation. Has it led to similar changes, new possibilities and developments in psychoanalytic thinking? Mitchel (1993) and Spruiell (1993) believe it has. Sucharov (1992) connects the new framework of quantum physics to Kohut's introduction of the introspective-empathic mode of observation in psychoanalysis. 'There is finally the fundamental claim of modern physics that the means of observation and the target of observation *constitute a unit that, in certain aspects, is in principle indivisible.* This claim finds its counterpart in the equally fundamental claim of the psychology of the self...' (writes Kohut, 1977, pp.31-32, cited in Sucharov; my italics).

My own thinking in recent years about therapeutic action and the psychoanalytic process emphasizes *a profound 'quantum process'* – a combination of patient and analyst, and the crucial effect of the process itself. In my view, patient and analyst in the analytic process converge and form a deep state of experiential-emotional interconnectedness and impact upon each other. It is a conjoint, living, therapeutic entity that goes beyond the confines of their separate psychic existences, thus providing a new opportunity to get in touch, experience, know, contain and influence

175

hitherto unknown, dissociated, unthinkable aspects of being and relating. I therefore call it an *entity (or unit) of interconnectedness or 'twogetherness'* (Eshel, 2001, 2002). I will also mention, very briefly, another proposal of quantum physics – formulated as a 'sum over histories' by the American scientist Richard Feynman. According to this, a particle is not supposed to have a single history or path in space-time, as it would in classical non-quantum theory. Rather, it can have any possible history (Hawking, 1988, 1993). For me, this is connected in psychoanalysis to the intersubjective thinking that the analytic experience emerges and is shaped in one way, among many possible ways, within the singular combination of particular patient and particular analyst. But, more essentially, it is connected to the compelling possibility that the patient-analyst's experiencing of present 'history' in the treatment will become the new, real, most influential history for the patient.

In conclusion, I have attempted to describe some major ideas and concepts from modern physics that have enriched my understanding, experience and language and have reverberated and seeped into my thinking with regard to analytic phenomena and the psychoanalytic process.[4] I hope that this article will arouse interest, if not conviction (to paraphrase Spruiell, 1993), with regard to 'close encounters of the third kind' between psychoanalysis and modern physics. I further hope that it will evoke thoughts, experiencing and vocabulary which some people may be able to use.

References

Eshel, O. (1998). 'Black holes', Deadness and existing analytically. *International Journal of Psychoanalysis,* 79:1115-1130.
_____ (2001). Whose sleep is it, anyway? Or 'Night Moves'. *International Journal of Psychoanalysis,,* 82:545-562.
Gribbin, J. (1992). *In Search of the Edge of Time.* Penguin Books.
Hawkins, S. (1988). *A Brief History of Time.* Bantam Books.
_____ (1993). *Black Holes and Baby Universes, & Other Essays.* Bantam

---

[1] See: Rainer, 1933; Stone,1975; Rothenberg,1983; Epstein, 1987; Grossman, 1989; Grotstein, 1990; Zohar,1990; Moran, 1991; Sucharov, 1992; Mitchel, 1993; Spruiell, 1993; Galatzer-Levy,1995;Quinodoz,1997;Eshel,1998; Verhulst,1999; Gilead,1999; Hazan, 2000
[2] Tustin and her followers stress that Tustin's patient John, the little autistic boy from whom she learned about the 'black hole,' introduced this term some years before the physicist John Wheeler.
[3] The description of the astrophysical 'black hole' is based mainly on Hawking's (1988, 1993) and Gribbin's (1992) books.
[4] I have not entered into the argument of whether ideas from modern physics 'open up new perspectives, extending beyond mere metaphors ... [to] an analogy-type model' (Quinodoz, 1997, pp. 714-715), or whether they are inspiring, new metaphors that stimulate new ideas in psychoanalysis (Verhulst, 1999).

Part III: <u>BETWEEN SESSIONS</u>

ETHICS & PROFESSIONAL CONDUCT

There's no business like shrink business
(to the tune of 'No business like show business')

<u>Verse 1</u>
As doctors, psychologists, or teachers, or such,
We really felt unhappy just because
As doctors, psychologists, or teachers, or such,
Our pay was good but we could find no buzz.
We gladly bade our lowly jobs goodbye
For something analytical, and why?

<u>Chorus 1</u>
There's no business like shrink business,
Like no business we know.
With delusions of superiority,
You <u>know</u> just what the patient's all about.
Nowhere can you get such grandiosity
When you are turning patients inside out.
There's no people like shrink people,
Like no people we know.
Forget the patient's healthy side, pathologise!
Do not be real, don't sympathise,
Stay po-faced, and don't you dare apologise.
Let's go on with the show.

<u>Verse 2</u>
The couches, the grouches, the hopes and the fears,
The transference when it's really going great.
The violence, the silence, the acting-out, the tears,
The countertransference that we love to hate.
The patient's had a really awful time,
But interpretations make <u>us</u> feel just fine.

<u>Repeat of Chorus 1</u>

177

Verse 3

We verbalise and scrutinise, and analyse all sorts
Of phantasies, defences, conflicts, dreams.
We probe into secrets and fears and inner thoughts,
And nothing's ever quite the way it seems.
We rarely let the patient have a rest -
Resistance must be quelled to pass the test.

Chorus 2

There's no business like shrink business,
Like no business we know.
You get word before the day has started
That your favourite uncle died at dawn,
Top of that your analyst's departed,
You're broken-hearted, but you go on -
There's no people like shrink people,
Like no people we know.
A while ago they said that you would not go far,
But then you qualify, and there you are -
Only fifty papers more and you're a star.
Let's go on with the show.

Verse 4

Obsessing, regressing, confessing basic faults
To analysts who kick us into line.
We're meant to free-associate but hide our deepest
    thoughts,
A million sessions more and we'll be fine.
At last the training ground on to its end.
Thank God! 'cos we were going round the bend.

Repeat of Chorus 2.

[Words by British Psychoanalyst Marianne Parsons for the
'50 minute hour' cabaret, Mansfield House Farewell, July 1999]

178

On taking notes   Emanuel Berman *(Haifa)*

In my practicum in psychotherapy at Michigan State University no notes were expected: each session was either audio-taped or video-taped (with the cumbersome equipment existing c. 1970...) and then viewed or listened to jointly with the supervisor. This was both highly instructive and quite intrusive.

At the Albert Einstein Medical School in New York City, where I subsequently did my clinical psychology internship, notes were central. I felt no need for them; I was so invested in my 3-4 individual patients that I perfectly remembered every nuance of each session. One of my supervisors had to threaten to kick me out of supervision, in order to force me to take notes.

When in analytic training, first at the NYU Postdoctoral Program, later at the Israel Psychoanalytic Institute, I was already quite adjusted to taking lengthy process notes, and found them useful. But the conflict was there: when one of my supervisors took a longer vacation, my notes on that case immediately dwindled or disappeared. And once my training was over, it was a big relief to work with no supervision (alone with the analysand, at last!) and no notes.

But not for long. In a few years the celebration of autonomy was over, I started looking for supervision and consultation during various periods, and I started taking notes again - first only on analysands, gradually on all my patients. I should add parenthetically that the farther I am from my years in training, the lesser my differentiation between analysis and therapy.

I try to adjust the setting to the unique process evolving in each treatment. I may see some people once a week on the couch (usually long-term analysands who gradually reduced frequency over the years, or came back some years after termination for another chapter), and see others four times a week face-to-face (when we both reach the conclusion that the couch distances us, possibly encourages schizoid withdrawal).
My notes are shorter now, averaging a page per session: main issues raised, key associations or memories, dreams, central interventions I made, all in a nutshell. While today I write all papers or letters at the computer, I find myself sticking to handwritten notes when patients are concerned (each in his or her notebook, with a different cover), as I do in writing down my own dreams in the morning.

179

When the 10 minute interval in-between sessions is peaceful enough, I write my notes then. When internal or external reasons prevent it, I take notes on several patients at the end of my working day, before going home. At times I add on the margins thoughts that cross my mind, insights of my internal supervisor, just as - when in supervision - I often make notes of the supervisor's thoughts on the margins.

Shortly before a patient rings my bell, I usually read my notes from the session before, as a way of reconnecting. At crisis periods, or towards termination, or if I write about a patient (very rare for me, I take confidentiality most seriously) I attempt to read all notes from that analysis or therapy. This may require many hours, but is always most intriguing ("how could I forget this point from three years ago, which relates to..." etc.).

Let me turn now to my supervisees, and particularly those who are analytic candidates. For many of them, I discover, note taking is conflictual: it represents the intrusion of supervision or of the institute (Berman, 2000); reduces the intimacy of the analytic dyad; encourages a verbal factual focus at the expense of attention to non-verbal experiences, subtle countertransference feelings, reverie; and brings forth an evaluative super-ego viewpoint inhibiting spontaneity. At times this conflictuality leads to reluctance to write, or even to amnesia as to what went on in the sessions.

In attempting to deal with such difficulties, my emphasis is on sharing and understanding them, not on a fast solution. Unlike the supervisor I mentioned, I make it clear that note-taking is not an essential element or a condition for supervision. Honestly, I also had the experience of supervising conscientious note-writers whose emotional experiences in analysis were blurred behind their thorough notes, and a meaningful progress in supervision became possible on a rare occasion when the notebook was forgotten and the supervisee came 'naked'.

One of the questions I raise when a difficulty in writing comes up, is whether this is a general difficulty (possibly related to broader conflictual aspects of the supervisee's professional identity or experience of training), or a unique phenomenon in our joint work. In the latter case, it may be related to transference towards me (e.g., a particular sensitivity to being evaluated by me?), to countertransference towards the patient (e.g., something in the work with this analysand which makes writing it up more burdensome?), or - maybe most likely - to a complication in the total intersubjective field of our triadic system (e.g., a way in which presenting the sessions to me is experienced as disloyal, in the context of an exclusive alliance formed unconsciously between patient and analyst?). These questions, in my experience, may lead to valuable insights promoting both the treatment and the candidate's training, much beyond the specific issue of taking notes.

At times, the difficulty with remembering and writing after sessions leads to another solution: taking notes during sessions. This poses a dilemma for me. On the one hand, I deeply object to this solution, for the reasons Freud raised. (I go farther than him, and never write down dreams during the session, not wanting to cloud my spontaneous contact with my own free-floating attention when listening). On the other hand, I don't believe the authoritative expression of my views will help the supervisee much, if the underlying anxiety is not resolved. I know of candidates who, feeling overwhelmed by the task and by the supervisor's position, took notes in sessions for years while hiding this fact from their supervisor, therefore never exploring its possible impact on the analysand and on the analytic/supervisory process.

My solution is to explain my concerns, but not to turn them into an absolute rule, and to pay more attention to dynamics that may be involved, hoping for their gradual resolution in supervision and in the candidate's analysis. I try to make it clear that while remembering, writing and reporting in supervision are all valuable, they are less important in my view than what transpires in the sessions between analyst and analysand.

Paradoxically, an intense session forgotten a minute after the analysand left may prove eventually to have been more effective than a session well-remembered, and conscientiously written down and reported, in which the effort to remember and to make the supervisor happy prevented deeper affective contact between analysand and analyst.

Reference

Berman, E. (2000). Psychoanalytic supervision: The intersubjective development. *International Journal of Psycho-Analysis,* 81:273-290.

The illusion of confidentiality Penelope Garvey *(London)*

The International Psychoanalytic Association makes the following statement on confidentiality; *'Psychoanalysts shall respect the confidentiality of their patient's information and documents'.* A clause contained in an earlier statement, 'within the contours of applicable legal and professional standards', has been deleted. This now enables the IPA to support members, who choose to resist, when ordered by law to disclose information on their patients.

In his introduction to a book on Confidentiality, Fulford quotes a Chinese proverb 'put a frog in hot water and it will immediately jump out; but put a frog in warm water and gently bring it to the boil and your frog will not try to jump out until it is too late'. The gradual erosion of clinical confidentiality in this country has become a cause for concern to those working in the public sector; those working in the private sector may wrongly consider themselves immune. With little or no consultation of those professionally involved, legislation was passed this year (2001) formalising the right of the Secretary of State for Health to access and to make public identifiable clinical notes for justifiable medical purposes, to collect all personal health information from the NHS and the private sector and to do so without the consent or knowledge of the patient. Further proposed legislation, to make disclosure of information by health professionals mandatory in certain cases (probably threats to life and child sexual abuse), has been withdrawn and, due to pressure from both public and professional bodies, some consultation will take place before its reintroduction. Such legislation would eliminate professional discretion. It would be an enormous change from the long held tradition of professionals using their clinical judgement in the matter of disclosure and of arguing their position in Court.

In Great Britain, the law is the only profession to have a legal privilege of confidentiality, for the rest of us confidentiality is a common law principle but not a legal right. Patients can sue us if we breach confidentiality, but Courts have unfettered discretion to order anyone to produce documents in the interests of justice; those who fail to comply are in contempt of Court and risk a prison sentence until they 'purge their Contempt'.

Since 1990, when patients gained the right to see their notes, only those parts of the notes containing references to third parties can be held back from them or from the Court; but it is possible to request a restriction on who sees the notes. If a patient consents to the release of their notes it can be argued that disclosure will cause them serious mental or physical harm but it is not an easy point to win; particularly as lawyers themselves are released from their duty of confidentiality if requested to do so by their clients. Most insurance policies provide no cover to fight such a case.

Other professions face similar problems; the 1997 Police Act gave police officers the power to record clergy conversations with parishioners; so long as they were not taking part in the specific act of confession. Journalists who refuse to disclose their sources have been sent to gaol. They do, however, have the possibility of pleading a Public Interest Defence under the Contempt of Court Act. For us, it would seem that the prevailing governmental, and possibly public view, is that it is in the public interest for us to disclose information. Bollas has written about the situation in the USA with its disclosure legislation and has warned of the danger of our being turned into agents of social control. While legislation here continues towards the increased sharing of information, in the States the tide seems to have turned. The American Psychoanalytic Association, in alliance with a number of psychotherapy and other groups, backed a psychotherapist who refused to disclose her notes; ultimately winning the case in a landmark victory in the Supreme Court (Jaffee v Redmond 1996). This wide alliance continues to influence both public opinion and new legislation. Its militancy is such that one Senator likened the American Psychoanalytic Association to the Oklahoma City Bombers.

There is considerable variation in the law on confidentiality across Europe, both in the law itself and in the precision with which it is defined. German law is the most precise; doctors, psychologists and psychoanalysts must maintain confidentiality, they have the right not to disclose information in criminal or civil proceedings and the confiscation of notes or correspondence by the police is forbidden. Breaking confidentiality is a criminal offence unless requested to do so by the patient, in which case the psychoanalyst cannot refuse. However, there is a duty to disclose in cases concerning Aids and child sexual abuse. A similar duty to disclose exists in Spain and Sweden. Only in Italy are health practitioners never required to report on their patients.

Many professional relationships require confidentiality, but in most cases, if the client requests that confidentiality be broken, the essential relationship remains undamaged. This is not the case in psychoanalysis or psychoanalytic psychotherapy. The patient's communication has to be understood in the context of the relationship and cannot be separated from its intended effect on the psychoanalyst. The main aim of psychoanalysis is to increase the patient's understanding of themselves and thus to increase their autonomy and capacity to be responsible for themselves. To do this the psychoanalyst tries to remain neutral and to describe, but not play a part, in the patient's drama other than in the consulting room.

Courts may unwittingly provide support for patients who, frustrated by this process, wish to force their analyst into their world or to intrude themselves into the analyst's world.

In this country we have so far failed to convey that confidentiality is an essential ingredient of psychoanalysis and psychoanalytic ways of working. Our best hope may be to wait for rulings on privacy and the build up of case law under the Human Rights Act 1998, such as that in favour of Catherine Zeta Jones and Michael Douglas on the matter of their wedding photos and Hello and OK Magazines. Alternatively or additionally we could follow the American example, explain our case and take a stand.

References

Bollas, C. & Sundelson, D. (1995) *The New Informants: Betrayal of Confidentiality in Psychoanalysis and Psychotherapy.* London: Karnac

Friel, J. (1998) In the matter of the British Association for Counselling, the Association for Student Counselling and the Association of Colleges.Unpublished legal opinion obtained by the British Association for Counselling in Bond,D.(1999)*Confidentiality Counselling and the Law.* British Association for Counselling information sheet. London

Fulford, K.W.M. (2001) The Paradoxes of Confidentiality in Cordess, C. (ed)*Confidentiality and Mental Health.* Jessica Kingsley: London

Jaffee v Redmond(1996) see Mosher http://psa-uny.org/jr/articles/mosher.htm

The Public Face: The media, justice and cutting edge client groups
Valerie Sinason (London)

How do we as psychoanalysts and psychoanalytic psychotherapists deal with the media? There is genuine public interest as well as fear over the communication difficulties that are part of human existence and the wish to make sense of them. In England, some analysts have spoken on radio on aspects of child development, violence and sexual disturbance in children, motherhood, fatherhood, perversion.. Others have been intervied or written newspaper columns on various family problems. *The media can reach more people and offer more chance of encouraging the idea of treatment than many books.* However, against this there is the use of distortion and misquoting to attack crucial analytic concepts and ideas and the fears this evokes.

As a professional practice ours is private and confidential. This is very much in contrast to psychoanalysis as a public body of knowledge open to attack, debate and multi-disciplinary dissemination. Holding this dichotomy is difficult. Within the UK there has been a longstanding tension concerning the correct interface between the individual psychoanalyst or psychotherapist and the media - including whether there should even be one. Whilst the serious newspapers and journals have filled their pages with regular attacks on psychoanalysis as personified by Freud or as a body of knowledge or treatment, the biggest professional response until very recently has been a "no comment". Behind this was awareness that no rational answer would really aid a certain level of phobia round the subject. However, there were less rational reasons for the lack of response too. Starting a House Journal at the Tavistock Clinic while a child psychotherapy trainee in the late 1970's was to prove a formidable task but allowed a lot of us to see at the level of a local protected in-house journal what the wider fears might be. Concerns about patients learning more about their therapists, therapists learning more about their (professional) patients and their colleagues and fears that the whole profession could be brought into disrepute by the irrevocability of the written as opposed to spoken word. One week I was aware that several senior members of staff were avoiding me after I conducted an interview critical of Bion. I learned there was concern his patients might object. Howwever, later that day Dr Bob Gosling entered the Tavistock and beamed at me. "Wonderful interview with Malcolm Pines - and I really liked his comments on Bion!"

I was learning, as a trainee, that with a secure attachment honest criticism is not experienced as frightening. However, just as individuals can need to have delusional attachments to their therapists, so can their

185

therapists to their institutions or to their own past analysts or therapists. It was child psychotherapist Dilys Daws through the Child Psychotherapy Trust and psychoanalyst Anton Obholzer as Chair of the Tavistock who lessened the fear of liaison with the media. As staff members we were asked to respond to media enquiries helpfully and were assured that distorted responses by the media would be understood as an inevitable by-product and not as our own error.

Gradually, it felt not only safer but also useful to provide journalists with comments on my own key areas of work - learning disability and sexual abuse. When working with subjects that have almost attained critical mass understanding the press can bring about change quicker than any single professional group. Indeed, the White Paper on Valuing People with learning disability is a result of professionals, parents and Press all combining together in a useful way. Without professionals liaising with the press it would have taken longer for vulnerable witnesses with learning disabilities to be accepted as witnesses in court. Indeed, twenty years ago there were more insightful journalists than therapists prepared to consider that learning disabled people were being sexually abused and could make use of a verbal therapy!

Ten years ago, as a result of supervision work concerning a learning disabled survivor of ritual abuse my range of work topics broadened. Ritual abuse and dissociative identity disorder are very difficult experiences to contend with. Here, unlike learning disability, the subject was not even close to being a critical mass area of knowledge and therefore acceptance. This is why books and papers and intelligent media liaison are so important.

Where a subject breaks through a societal shield, for whatever reason, it is useful to try to turn sentences into irreducible 'sound-bites' so that they cannot be put through a 'cut and paste' method of semi-distortion. However, with all the care in the world, such distorting is not possible to avoid. Even deciding to not speak to a particular tabloid does not end the problem as distorted quotes are made or created from past interviews. Colleagues can be as affected or more affected by media distortion than other members of the public.For example, a BBC religious programme wanted a short interview when a book I had edited *Treating Survivors of Satanist Abuse* was launched in the House of Lords in 1994. Although the subject was very controversial at that point I considered that a BBC religious programme would maintain a high level of reporting and agreed. A taxi was sent to pick me up and I enjoyed a discussion on ritual abuse with the driver who was also booked to wait for me. A thoughtful interviewer asked me some questions and I answered them. Without my knowledge and to my later shock the programme was then completely re-arranged. To my surprise, instead of the one interviewer who had actually interviewed me there was now interposed a second one. My careful

186

sentences had been cut and stuck into different sections as if in answer to the new fabricated questions put by the fake interviewer.

Even more serious was the introduction to the programme. "First it was Reds under the beds, then it was abduction by aliens and now it is thousands of microwaved babies but Valerie Sinason stands by her book". Microwaved babies? Where had that come from? The taxi-driver, who was listening with me on the way to the Tavistock Clinic, instantly understood. "Boy - they really stitched you up didn't they? I expect these religious bods don't want to be linked with the implications of religion!"

At the Tavistock Clinic I was assailed by a Psychotherapist who began, "Valerie, are you mad? Do you really believe thousands of babies are being microwaved each year?" It was then that I learned that capacity to deal with and understand certain kinds of media distortion has nothing to do with professional training. The Taxi-driver had won on every level! I found cognitive methods very useful in demanding an apology from the programme and a correction in their next programme, which happened.

Time has moved on and organised abuse has been understood as a concept together with the links between it and domestic abuse, changing the nature of some media and professional responses. However, where major media distortion exists it can be hard to affect change without considering the implications of libel laws. A legal letter is expensive and major papers can largely ignore the contents knowing that they are under no compulsion to respond in the absence of an actual lawsuit.

Moving from the media to the problems of subjects that are not yet historically at the critical mass level, one is adequately protected by ethical rulings. For instance regarding patients with dissociative identity disorder. Who is the named patient? If in a given patient personality wishes their communications destroyed and another wants all of them kept what is to be done? Secondly, where critical mass levels have not been achieved and patients are as disbelieved over major crimes they wish to confess to as to their victim experiences what can be done? The Clinic for Dissociative Studies has answered this by having a special link to The Metropolitan Police, to consider how to deal with major allegations made by vulnerable witnesses so that therapy can then have a chance to proceed.

As with psychotherapy with learning disabled survivors, which I helped to pioneer twenty years ago, therapy can be a place where courageous survivors land in the absence of justice. Where patients are not receiving basic civil rights the meaning of a treatment alliance is different Now thanks to the greater understanding by the media our psychoanalytic work is free to address itself to the internal world and its representations of the external world in the peace of a consulting room. With an edited book on *Attachment, Trauma and Dissociation* we traust we have the stamina to last the next ten years or so for critical mass breakthrough. to have the freedom to stay with psychic processes, not through collusion or cowardice, but because the wider social arena has taken on the subject.

A Psychoanalyst at the NGO Forum of the World Conference Against Racism, Racial Discrimination, Xenophobia and Related Intolerance   Isaac Tylim *(New York)*

On the way to JFK International Airport, the taxi driver turned his head towards me in the back seat, and expressed the usual curiosity for his passenger's destination. He was surprised when I told him that I was going to South Africa. "South Africa, South Africa!" he exclaimed "how much things have changed there since Mandela...what are you going to do there?" Indeed,I replied, "I'll be attending a conference on racism". With an almost confrontational tone, the driver demanded a description of my occupation. He was astounded to hear that I was nothing less than a psychoanalyst interested in the subject of hatred and prejudice. Seemingly provoked by the answer, the driver solicited a brief explanation of what a psychoanalyst might wish to accomplish in such remote territory. It took me a few moments to gather my thoughts and offer a simple and honest response to a very important question. Deep within I felt insecure and somewhat puzzled as to the role I was to play at the event. I knew that psychoanalysis has a lot to say on the subject, but I was fully aware that it lacked the means to translate technical or abstract terms into a language capable of conveying meaning to people from all over the world and from all walks of life. While I was reflecting on this serious matter, the driver's silence managed to create a safe space for what was being stirred up in my mind. Meanwhile the back seat became, for a 45 minute ride/session, an analytic couch on wheels in the middle of rush hour traffic on the Long Island Expressway. After the Queens Boulevard exit, unable to keep the front seat inquisitor further on hold, I reverted to what is familiar to my profession, replying with the most neutral tone I could sustain in bumper-to -bumper traffic: "I am going to do something that I do well: listen" I finally declared.

The driver's inquiry has been a common one among people I've encountered on the way to and from the NGO Forum on the 2001 World Conference on Racism. The Forum met in Durban, South Africa from August 28th to September 1st which overlapped two days with the United Nations World Conference Against Racism (WCAR). What does a psychoanalyst, accustomed to the safety of the private domain of his office, have to contribute to pressing public issues? How can psychoanalytic insight related to hate, aggression, and violence fare on the global scene? After attending presentations, listening to protesters, victims of one or another form of racial discrimination, I found myself reflecting on how much things have change in South Africa over the last decade. Holding the WCAR in Durban was certainly a testimony to the fall of Apartheid. But a lot has also changed in the psychoanalytic profession which allowed me to leave the safety of my consultation room. In South Africa I learned to listen to those racist discourses which more often than not are silenced in a private encounter for want of symbolic paths of expression of our most distressing racist feelings.

Attending the conference, and listening with what in my field is referred to as the 'third ear', convinced me of psychoanalysis' special position among the social disciplines in understanding the phenomenon of racism. Racism is ubiquitous because hatred of the 'other' or 'different' is present inside every human being regardless of race, color, or creed. Psychoanalytic theory offers a comprehensive account of how, in human development, the discovery of the other as other has the potential to inflict major narcissistic wounds which are not easily overcome. Differences between self and others, between the sexes, and between the generations may be regarded as springboards towards racist attitudes that emerge in all cultures. In other words, if we look carefully within ourselves we are bound to discover the hidden racist lurking in the background. The difficulty lies in recognizing and accepting that which we tend to attribute — or in psychoanalytic jargon — project onto the other, the threatening 'not me'. After Durban, I felt more that we must own that part rather than seek an external container for the racist attitudes that reside in all of us.

The WCAR aimed at giving voice to neglected victims, and to let the oppressed talk — seems to have been the motto of the conference. The latter coincides with the bread and butter of my occupation: assisting individuals to find words for their experiences so they may be expressed and understood. Only by creating a space for people of all groups to engage in dialogue, can desirable change be attained. Moreover, to my surprise, large parts of the discussions at the conference were devoted to what is often the subject in my private sessions with analysands. The frame created in order to facilitate the encounter between people must provide safety and be reliable. In parallel with the analytic hour in which violations to the frame from within or without often occur, at the WCAR the frame devised by its organizers was often attacked by internal or external forces leading to modifications of pre-established agendas, bringing to the fore a form of intolerance that tended to proclaim itself as the most neglected or silenced. The force of its representatives often cascaded into a violent language which not only overshadowed other people's ply, but which also became a form of discrimination in its own right. Under these circumstances the conference itself became a theater of racism and intolerance, reenacting the very same issues it was supposed to overcome. The accusation that it was a racist conference was raised by many delegates who felt excluded and cheated from the possibility of

189

engaging in a real, adult, and constructive dialogue.

Witnessing UN Secretary Kofi Annan handling an open discussion at one of the forums, substantiated the issues I am stressing here. Mr. Annan clearly stressed the need to speak against racial stereotypes. He invited all parties to talk (again putting words onto experiences). During the question and answer period, Mr. Annan, with poise and determination asked a yelling audience member to "calm down...you are to listen, not to behave that way... there is no need for you to scream...talk like a mature person".

Mary Robinson, the UN Commissioner on Human Rights, in her opening remarks stated that a conference on racism is a conference about relationships of neighbor to neighbor, nation to nation. As a psychoanalyst, I couldn't agree more. In the privacy of my consultation room, or in the heated debates that took place in Durban the importance of relating to each other and listening to what the other has to say, may bring us together. In talking about our inner selves, the racist that lives inside may be owned. Without ownership, eradication may never turn be realized.

Working as Editor Between the Sessions

Jean Arundale *(London)*

Since January 1994 when I took up the post as Editor of the *British Journal of Psychotherapy,* my spare time between sessions has been earmarked for the Journal, not to say watermarked, postmarked and pencilmarked. Editing is quite a change of pace from clinical work, requiring a shift out of the predominately receptive mode. It is absorbing, rewarding, sometimes quite busy and occasionally exasperating. The Journal had been running for ten years when I began, founded and edited by the psychoanalyst Bob Hinshelwood, already well-organised and well-established as a leading journal in the field. Having recently finished my PhD when I began, I knew a little bit about academic papers but as for the publishing world of copy dates, production, proofs etc., I was a neophyte. Fortunately Ann Scott, the deputy editor had worked extensively in publishing and knew the score. Initially, I doubted the efficiency of my admin skills (I tended to lose bits of paper and forget to write letters) and I wasn't at all sure I could fit everything into a busy clinical and professional life – but the only thing to do was to plunge in, learn how and see.

A high point of the editor's job for me is going to my NHS job at Guy's Hospital every week and collecting the post at the editorial address in the York Clinic. Before opening the big brown envelopes containing submissions from the UK and around the world there is an intense moment of anticipation while I imagine the brilliant papers within, the definitive article on a new theory, a dynamic clinical report, exciting reviews of the literature and stimulating ideas that will inspire psychotherapists and guide us all toward new procedures and refreshed interest in our work. Often I am not disappointed. I take the papers home, send a letter of acknowledgement to the author, and choose two readers from the panel of peer reviewers who will be interested in the paper and/or give the paper a fair review. Then I bundle up three copies and send them to a member of the Editorial Board who will take care they are sent out and then receive the written reports that are prepared for discussion in the editorial meeting.

The editorial meetings take place six times per year. Before each meeting a sense of drama builds up as I wonder whether I and the Editorial Board and the peer reviewers will agree during the evening of discussion on whether or not to publish a paper, or will disagree and have to argue it out. I place a bet with myself on the outcome – as a wry game. There is often a lively and intense discussion as we debate the pros and cons of particular papers. The Journal has a wide remit, representing a broad spectrum of psychotherapies, mainly psychoanalytically based but

191

including CBT, CAT, group, family, child, marital, empirical research and theoretical papers. The Board consists of representatives of nine psychoanalytic psychotherapy training organizations in London and although there are theoretical biases, politics as such plays no real part. We go for quality, relevance and usefulness to practitioners and these issues form the lines of debate. When there is a deadlock, I break the tie using the editor's prerogative

After the editorial meeting I am faced with the task of writing to the authors, informing them of the outcome of the editorial process. The most uncomfortable part of the job is having to disappoint the authors whose papers we have decided not to publish and letting them know why. Many of the accepted articles will need rewriting, often a number of times, so my letters to those authors include guidelines for required changes. At one point I dreamed that I posted myself and was crouching inside a pillar box, letters cascading onto my head!

Four issues of the Journal appear each year. Before the copy date for each issue, I gather together seven or eight papers that I think will be an interesting combination, plus the book reviews and clinical commentaries garnered by the section editors. After this I write the editorial, sweating a bit over getting it right, and then give the precious bundle to the Production Manager for copy editing and sending off to the printer. Proofs come back two months later for checking, then there is the delightful *frisson* when the new issue arrives in the post, sparkling in its three dimensional reality, furthered by the knowledge that it will go out to nearly three thousand subscribers for, hopefully, an educational and pleasurable read. There is a sense of satisfaction in this periodic cycle, particularly when there are no disgruntled authors or readers to deal with.

Besides these set activities I do other things to drum up business. I occasionally commission articles and attend conferences to scout out good papers, asking speakers for publication rights. One of the most stimulating parts of the job is when each year the Journal works together with the Freud Museum to put on a day conference. Thinking up an interesting topic each year, and then inviting speakers for the day, is a challenge I enjoy. The papers from the conference are published in the Journal and many excellent articles have been obtained in this way.

Although I have always considered my work as a clinician practicing intensive psychoanalytic psychotherapy a first priority, editorial work offers a fascinating view of the wider world of psychoanalysis and psychotherapy, an opportunity to think about overall trends in the field, new movements, political struggles, research, etc. Working with authors, editorial board members, reviewers and colleagues and being involved in the purpose and mechanics of a learned journal is a privilege that adds a dimension of richness and depth to clinical work.

192

On Retirement
Abe Brafman *(London)*

I want to write about 'retirement', that point in time when you, supposedly, stop 'work'. 'Retirement' and 'work' mean different things to each person and I will describe what they mean to me.

I am considered a hard worker. This must be linked to my fascination for challenges. They trigger off some compulsion to find plausible answers for problems, serious or otherwise. But I have also learnt that I have a need to help others. I can recognize the childhood roots for this trait that led me to medicine and later to psychoanalysis.

I am always struck by how some colleagues define their role vis-à-vis their patients. There is an element of devotion, a notion of impartiality and purity of motives, a statement of total involvement with the patient that gradually builds an image of mystical proportions. Rightly or wrongly, I do not see myself like this. Seeing a patient has remained 'a job of work'. I am alert to whatever images they make of my person, but I still feel no more than a professional trying to discharge his duties. However intense my concentration on what the patient says and does, I find there are continuous inpingements that other facets of my private life make on my attention. I believe that patients can distinguish between competent professionalism and genuine tenderness. However much patients may desire affection, they value professional expertise more highly. I aim at being competent, rather than at offering a replacement 'good object'.

Sadly, however, unwelcome signs of ageing now challenge this self-image. Attention, memory and concentration do not operate at that optimal level that guarantees ideal self-confidence and self-esteem. Family and personal matters introduce pressures that meet increasingly lower levels of tolerance and resilience. Equally disturbing is the changing view of the problems brought by patients. Ordinarily, it is easy to ignore personal opinions and opt for an 'objective' view of a patient: we focus on his psychopathology, rather than considering what kind of person he appears to be. I refer to that unorthodox classification of people into those who are likeable *('simpáticos')* and those who are not. When younger we do not mind taking on patients seen as 'objectionable' or 'unpleasant', convincing ourselves that such impressions do not result from our personal prejudices and preferences, but from a counter-transferential reaction to the patient. This is not so easy to do as we get older. An obvious consequence of such selection is that we reduce the number of patients we are prepared to take on and we soon find ourselves questioning our motives when accepting each patient. The distinction between 'I like' and 'I need' can be quite difficult to establish. Essentially, 'need' is a factor linked to money and self-esteem issues. Are we now choosing the 'easier' patients? Or those who can pay higher fees?

Ageing and/or infirmity represent serious threats for those analysts who depend on active clinical work to obtain sufficient income. At the same time, patients can also represent a needed source of self-esteem, if not of a sense of purpose (a 'raison d'être'). Professional success is always an important source of self-worth. This may be closely related to ambition or perfectionism and success here benefits not only the professional, but also his patients. There is, however, danger when the therapist cannot bear any development other than success, since this raises the possibility of patients being abused if they cannot produce the results needed by the professional. At this point, we are no longer considering a search for excellence, but a desperate need for sustenance of a precarious self-image. If this is regrettable at all times, it is plainly worrying in old age. Frustration can be the key for self-scrutiny and personal development, but at a time when one's body, brain and mind are no longer functioning at optimal levels, frustration can often lead to despair.

What gives a person a sense of purpose in life? Predictably, this question tends to come up when we feel lost, depressed, disenchanted with life and people, or isolated and lonely. When this painful question hits us, we look around and search for the presence of people – friends, relations, colleagues - who might comfort and reassure us. If these are not available, we seek proof that there are still people who need us, who make us feel that our presence is valued and desired. And... yes, sadly and regrettably, it can happen that patients remain the only antidotes to total isolation. This can lead to a reversal of roles, where, instead of obtaining help, the patient comes to nurse his therapist.

I now find that some of my colleagues have decided to stop seeing patients. There are others who, in spite of being older than we are, continue with their work. Some of them have been through serious illnesses. We begin to hear stories of colleagues falling asleep during sessions and we know others whose social presence is far from optimal. Considering how difficult it is for a patient to have enough self-confidence and courage to stop his analysis or therapy with a faltering analyst, perhaps it is incumbent upon us to take these matters in hand – in practice, however, this is unlikely to happen.

At the end of the day, each of us is really left with his own conscience. I stopped my NHS work at 65, the statutory age for retirement and this was a major trauma for me. I write these lines more than five years later and I am aware that my physical stamina is lower than it used to be. I

194

hold on to the belief that my cognitive faculties remain at an acceptable level, even if lower than I used to know them. I am lucky to be in a position where I do not depend on my work income to preserve my standard of living. But I often ask myself whether my patients are fulfilling some need of mine. I can only acknowledge my awareness of a lifelong need to help others. This is inextricably linked to the experience of an enormous sense of regret at the thought that there are children 'out there' whom I would be able to help. However grandiose or presumptuous this may sound, it is the main reason that makes me regret the eventual arrival of that day when I will not be able to work any more.

We all know that the analyst's work is a solitary one. This work will often attract people who have discovered that the caring professions can offer solace for an otherwise lonely life. I have always thought of myself as something of a maverick, but I am privileged to have built a large and rewarding family life and I hope they will satisfy any unconscious need to help others. In spite of this, I still find myself hoping that I can continue practising my work for a few years!

A Natural Experiment in Abstinence

Pirkko Niemelä *(Turku, Finland)*

In order to apply for psychoanalytic training, you have to be in analysis with a training analyst. In the beginning of the 80's there were only two training analysts in Turku, my hometown, and both had long waiting lists. So I first worked in analysis with a younger analyst and after four years changed over to a training analyst. Both my analysts were men, psychiatrists, wise and well trained. The younger one obeyed the rules of abstinence to the point of frequent silence while the older and more experienced training analyst was freer in his style. I give you an example.

When in my first analysis, I applied for a family therapy training program, my analyst was one of the training committee. The Monday after the test I came into my analysis. I told to my analyst that I knew the training committee had had their meeting on the Sunday, and that he knew whether I was accepted into the program or not. As usual, he did not comment, which was all I also expected and was accustomed to. Later I received the letter of acceptance from the training committee.

Some years later I was in my training analysis. I had applied for the psychoanalytic training and had had the three selection interviews. I came into my analytic session on a Monday, and told to my analyst that I knew that the training committee had had their meeting on Sunday, and that he knew whether I was accepted into the program or not. I said also that I knew he would not tell me now if I was chosen but I had to wait for the letter. He laughed and said: "You came in, my congratulations".

When in the analysis with the younger analyst, I did not resent too much that he did not answer me or that he did not say very much. I expected an analyst to be very strict and stingy in his responses. When I did not get a response, I said to myself, and probably to him too: "Here we go and train my ego again, not to expect anything". But did his strict abstinence bring me closer to my own thought, fantasies and feelings. Did it open to me, or to us, my unconsciousness?

When I then later was being supervised for my first psychoanalytic patient, my supervisor taught me to test my responses through what would happen afterwards: Did my response open or close the patient's mind at that moment. In my own work I often find that my responses about what comes to my mind, e.g. when I tell my patient what I remember s/he has said earlier, dreamt earlier etc, opens the work more than my silence. In the above Monday responses neither response opened me my mind very much at that moment as we did not stop to examine how I felt about the response, but certainly I felt my training analyst's congratulations as welcoming to the psychoanalytic training and group.

I bring these examples as food for thought.

196

SINGING/DANCING IN THE RAIN

BRUSH UP YOUR SIGMUND*
Words by Don Campbell

VERSE 1

 The goils today in society
 Go for classical therapy.
 So, to win their hearts,
 One must quote each line
 Abraham and Melanie Klein.
 One must know Hoffer, and believe me, son,
 Winnicott also Erikson.
 Unless you know Glover and Jones and Sacks,
 Dainty birdies will give you the axe.
 But the analyst of them all,
 Who has got 'em all a flutter,
 Is the doctor people call
 The shrink of nineteen Bergasse.
 Brush up your Sigmund.
 Start quoting him now.
 Brush up your Sigmund,
 And the women you will wow.

VERSE 2

 If you can't be a shrink or a patient
 All the goils'll think ya queer or delinquent,
 But just give an Oedipal 'terpretation
 And she'll make the weekend reservation.
 If she rejects your romantic bid,
 Just say where would be ego without id.
 Brush up your Sigmund,
 And they'll all kow-tow!
 Brush up your Sigmund.
 Start quoting him now.
 Brush up your Sigmund,
 And the women you will wow.

VERSE 3

If you don't have a couch or a high fee,
You will never get beyond her right knee.
If your blonde won't respond to your suntan,
Tell her 'bout Dora and the Wolf Man.
When your broad is about to say, 'Cheerio',
Just remind her of Breuer and Anna O.
Brush up your Sigmund,
and they'll all kow tow.
Brush up your Sigmund.
Start quoting him now.
Brush up your Sigmund,
And the women you will wow.

VERSE 4

When your advances yield no concession,
Just suggest that she lift her repression.
If when you whisper sweet woids she can't hear ya,
Just enlighten her about hysteria.
When you worry you'll lose your sweet treasure,
Let her sample your Principle Pleasure.
Brush up your Sigmund,
And they'll all kow-tow,
And they'll all kow-tow.

To be sung to the music of Brush Up Your Shakespeare from Kiss Me Kate (Original Words and Music by Cole Porter).

198

Browsing Psychoanalytic Journals

Alex Tarnopolsky *(Toronto)*

'Books showed me the world, but I learned to live through women'. This statement, once found in Arthur Koestler's diaries, now prompt~s two contradictory thoughts. The first is about its possible political incorrectness; the second is about its truth. First: will we ever be able to talk without blushing? The peculiar fascism called 'political correctness', seems familiar from my years of university politics in Argentina. In the 60's in Buenos Aires, political correctness was more properly labelled 'ideological terrorism'. Shall we ever recover intellectual autonomy?

The second thought is about the truth and the truism captured by Koestler, that we learn to live, to grow, to heal through relationships and through love. Love in its many forms from companionship to passion, from curiosity to affinity to ideological enthralment. Browsing psychoanalytic journals, I found again a paper by Christopher Bollas*. There, Bollas gave academic form - or idiom, as he would say - to Koestler's idea about learning to live and learning to be, with his notion of the 'transformational object', an object that alters self experience. He means, the mother at a stage when she is experienced less as an object than as a process of transformation, a stage where there is no delusion for she actually transforms the baby's world. Bollas goes on to say that:

> '..this feature of early existence lives on in certain forms of object-seeking in adult life, when the object is sought for its function as a signifier of transformation. Thus in adult life the quest is not to possess the object; rather the object is pursued in order to surrender to it as a medium that alters the self The memory of this early object relation manifests itself in the person's search for an object (a person, place, event, ideology) that promises to transform the self'

And here Bollas may prove Koestler wrong, because we also seek books to transform ourselves. I have always thought that Bollas's writings make sense as a result and a development of his dialogue with Winnicott, Klein and Bion, a dialogue I understand and also extend in my mind: how does the transformational object relate to Kohut's self-objects -or to Bion's reverie? These questions illustrate one of the reasons why I read: to follow the development of some ideas, to see how through generations of analysts, themes repeat themselves and appear not to change, to be always the same -and yet they change so much. Their apparent immobility (was not projective identification present in Tausk's influencing machine?) satisfies the sceptic in me, the presumptuous scholar that sniffs 'just old wine in new bottles'. But the concepts are different because they are inscribed in a different context and acquire a new twist and a new glow. This satisfies the child in me, my need to be surprised and excited again by an unexpected penumbra of the meaning, or even by a new turn of phrase. Using again an example from Bollas (for the reason of friendship that shall become clear below), isn't it wonderful that after decades of projective identification he could have referred to it without naming it, saying something like 'those patients who hyperbolise their presence through the others'?

But in truth I do not read psychoanalytic journals. I buy them, browse through them. I shelve them, then, I sigh at them. The *International Journal* I look at more attentively because I find there many friends, teachers and mentors, and bigger and lesser domestic gods and idols of psychoanalysis. *Free Associations* makes me feel homesick for England. *The American Journal* is unfortunately piled and reserved for reference, a confession that does not make me feel too bad because, probably, many American colleagues will pile the *International* and read the *American*. Like many of us I buy journals and some books for collection, as one buys objects of art; and for reference, just in case. Usually the case comes up, and I congratulate myself for having found, usually on a weekend, that necessary reference or unexpected review that allows me to pursue my work. When I read, I follow a line of thought in a research-like manner with the hunter's rather than the fisherman's urge. But then, in the course of browsing through the new journal, I also stop and read: frequently I read my friends. This is both a deficit and a virtue, for concepts are meaningless in a vacuum, they become bowdlerized and insignificant. Lacanian, Kleinian or Kohutian ideas only make sense -deep sense, not just dictionary sense - when you are steeped in its sources, and have struggled with them, worked with them, made them somehow yours. You cannot read out of context - which is another way of saying that you cannot read out of intellectual friendship -the idea that we can read and write in another quest for some type of love. This explains the necessary parochialism of most papers -the fact that reference lists contain mostly one school of thinking. The *International Journal* is an excellent and not very common example of universalism in its editorial policy. In contrast, recently I saw a paper rejected by another journal with a most candid letter. The authors, the reviewers said, have excellent ideas which are very useful indeed, but they are too tied to their frame of reference – (how couldn't they be?) .The reviewers ended most frankly; 'Perhaps we are prejudiced, but we do not like the approach'!

Perhaps browsing through journals is the most we can do, given the plethora of publications, obligations and the strictness of time. So, I browse frequently, read sometimes, collect always; and when I read, I talk, argue, admire and scorn. From time to time I also write. For what we write is also the shadow of old relationships, and stretching to new ones.

* Bollas.C (1979) The transformational Object, *International Journal of Psycho-Analysis* 6O:97

200

The Presence of Winnicott in Me Saúl Peña K.*(Lima)*

"Oh, my God may I live when I die" [D.W.Winnicott]

I would like to share some of what I have learned through my personal bond with Winnicott as his supervisee when I lived in England as a trainee, and from my own subjective reading of Winnicott's works with which I already had an affinity before our work began It is a difficult task to define Winnicott's technique because he was different with every patient. He emphasized the fundamental importance of authenticity as an indispensable condition to get closer to the truth. However, what is authentic in one analyst may not be so in another – as became apparent in our work together. Within the conceptualization of his technique, more important than following a precise recommendation, that could be wrong, is choice based on what one is. To be oneself is fundamental and what makes a relationship therapeutic, because it highlights the importance of spontaneous gesture, not licentiousness or lack of boundaries, on the contrary, and here we enter into the area of paradox.

The analyst's attitude of listening and his unconscious are the essential aspects of his theory. All this leads to recognizing in our science an anti-dogmatic attitude and redemption of an objective subjectivity. Paradoxically this is the road we choose to reach most objectivity. Its more accomplished manifestation would be a lucid passion, accompanied by rapport, empathy, intuition, creativity, originality, and intimacy, giving each a place in every specific patient-analyst bond, within the frame of a good enough facilitating environment that contains potential *play space.*

To Winnicott playing between analyst and patient consists in learning how to live, experiencing and discovering whatever factors are involved in mutuality and creativity. It is there that the potential space, cultural experience and symbolization are located. The epistemophilic enigma is vital: the desire to know, the possibility of feeling and thinking.Analysis then is the result of superimposition of two zones of play: that of the patient and that of the analyst, provided that both play together. When playing is not possible, the analyst's role is to make this possible: 'To transform into a playing field the worst of the deserts'. Winnicott said that playing is universal and related to mental health. Playing uses a particular space situated between what is inside and what is outside, stimulating creativity and health and enriching the self and the environment. Playing means recreation, entertainment and even craziness. It is an illusion, and it is an offering.

While experiencing such basic trust the problem of separation is relegated to a second level. Creative playing with illusion and the sense of reality has meaning and enhances self-discovery and the capacity to be alone. The space between analyst and patient is also expanded to involve family, society and the world at large.

Winnicott believed that as when the child plays it comes into contact with itself in an atmosphere of freedom, and with intensity seeks some unity and continuity in his external and internal life, so the patient creates the analyst and the analyst creates the patient, marking a guidepost for the process of separation, differentiation and individuation, realizing the existence of contrast. Learning and subjectivity cannot be separated from the symbol and the symbolized. For Winnicott growth happens not only through interpretation but through anything that permits realization of something not perceived before. The patient has to participate not only in the search for his own interpretation, but in the utilization of it.

Winnicott's dialectic of paradox is seen in presence-absence, illusion-disillusion, me not-me, good enough-perturbation, trust-mistrust, satisfaction-dissatisfaction, encounter-disencounter, dependence-independence, receptive-intrusive, feminine-masculine, spontaneity-rigidity, truth-falsehood, being-acting, life-death. A paradox as the beginning of an idea of contradiction, persons that live as if they were others. Winnicott emphasized that it is equally important that the analyst goes on acknowledging and discovering his own capacity to express aspects of his personality as well as the essence of his self, the communicative and the isolated. It is this way that he discovers the paradox of being human and the nature of the bond; his ambivalence about creativity and destructivity inherent to life itself. At moments of enormous impact in the relationship something surprises the therapist and the therapist does not respond, moments such as coldness, indifference, lack of pity and rage which makes the analyst dark and impotent.

The way Winnicott dealt with paradoxes told us more than his words. I learnt about paradoxes and the dialectics of life and death - even though I disagreed theoretically about the origin of the death instinct- by watching Winnicott in his work, his living, his emotions and his thoughts. Where I found differences between us was in the fact that Winnicott favoured 'being' but disagreed that feeling of annihilation and emptiness are related to the death instinct. Winnicott accepted aggression, aggressiveness, hate, rage and anger. He did not care if they come from the death instinct, but I believe that the death instinct exists. Winnicott's psychoanalysis appraises primary creativity and moral values in humans with which I completely agree. I just wanted to add the

202

instinctive roots of being, erotic and thanatical. I perceived a monistic attitude in Winnicott's thinking, to him instinct did not have priority. I am in complete agreement about questioning the existence of innate envy, but throughout all my clinical experience I have found the death instinct present. In my culture it is an inevitable reality and part of human existence at a concrete and symbolic level, in health, and illness. For Winnicott, development, maturation, creativity and integration of the being in time and space are the only innate activities. For him painful experiences or environmental failures, and instincts are affected by experience and translated as disillusion, hopelessness and the will to die.

He himself was capable of being receptive and welcoming and at times he permitted himself to firmly confront, taking timing into account. In our contact he allowed me to differ. His listening attitude was contemplative, reflective and meditative. I found his contribution in the conceptualization and treatment of borderline and psychotic patients indispensable. This kind of psychopathology results from serious, enduring and early developmental failures which the analyst tries to rectify by creating a maternal bond of primary identification at the level in which the patient was beginning to be when this was cut, breaking his psychosomatic unit. Empathy involves non-verbal communication, as well as body language, the simple recognition of a twitch as well as the mutuality of the therapeutic experience.

Communication with psychotic aspects of the patient inevitably awakes similar aspects in the analyst's unconscious. If analyst and patient develop a basic trust allowing the feared madness and that lived in the past to be lived as such in transference, then the patient will be the owner of this experience, achieving recuperation and a new beginning, thus recreating his identity. But the analyst who treats severely disturbed patients has to face his own anxieties related to existence, survival and his identity. This is what transference psychosis is all about. In some situations the analyst has to face his own regression in which his intimacy, privacy and discretion are threatened, and certain aspects of himself are exposed. The revision of clinical material is indispensable to development and to understand metapsychology.

For Winnicott, transference is not reduced to libidinal impulses, rather it is an integrative experience of being held throughout time, continuity and maturation. He often talked about recognizing his own mistakes and failures. He had patience but did not have ready made answers "I will let the patient know when the appropriate time comes, if I remember". He did not hide his fallibility and believed that when the analyst succeeds he is able to become a good substitute mother and other. When he fails he recreates the past in the present.

203

What I learned with Winnicott is to be prepared for the unexpected. Every experience is unique, distinct and has a particular value, free and totally contrary to all dogmas. The analyst makes mistakes but does his best to correct them. Mistakes are useful because these show the analyst's imperfections and help the patient to correct over-idealizations. Whoever hides recognizing hate towards the patient cannot work with his own hatred and might get into a collusion, thus failing to alleviate his own and the patient's suffering.

I would like to conclude with something I fully share with that great master, from whom I had the privilege of learning: "The only company I have when I enter into that unknown territory which is each new case, is that theory which is always with me, which constitutes part of my being and which I do not even have to appeal to deliberately."

I would like to express my gratitude to my colleague Dr. Efrain Gomez, Professor of Psychiatry of Baylor College and Texas University, and Jean Evans for translating this English version from the Spanish and to my assistant Mabel Sarco for her permanent help.

Reflections on a Blank Screen   Carol Topolski *(London)*

It's the twenty first century and our familiars are no longer acts, but screens. We write on screens, talk on screens, buy, sell, swap on screens and assume the ubiquity of screens when we go about our business in public. And then we go to the pictures. We settle down in a darkened room with hundreds of strangers to experience a collective hallucination, from which we recover two hours later. The film has its story to tell, but each of us in the audience makes our own film as it flits and fits round our own internal narrative. The heroine sobs as her lover returns to his wife and the man in row C dabs his eyes: his brother was killed when he was ten. The hero strides into a room where we know a crazed Vietnam vet is hiding and the woman in row F bows her head: her mother remarried when she was six. Unlike any theatrical production, film has no truck with 'as if' and invites us directly into the illusion that what we see and hear is real. Real and immediate. No need to suspend disbelief, no laborious pretence that painted polystyrene is a granite boulder - cinematic seas and skies are briny and blue and we can swoop with the camera through one to the other.

Like Mapplethorpe's photographs, we can practically smell the skin as the camera moves slowly over its surface and round its angles. If the director chooses, we can linger longer over an experience than ordinary living permits: moving in slo-mo round the tousled lover wrapped in sheets; watching as orchid blooms pop on the stem as it flowers over days. Intellect is left at the door of the cinema; we gratefully put our emotional selves in the hands of the director to be excited for the next couple of hours: take me, take me, I'm yours.

Like a dream, film is to be believed over the course of its playing, and like a dream it toys with rationality. Film time, like dream time, flows, stops, retreats, hiccoughs; film characters, like dream characters, live, die, merge and disappear as the familiar techniques of dreaming move us through the narrative with its displacement, condensation and abbreviation. Film is a temporary psychotic state of mind, a "turning away from reality" as Freud, who famously refused to contribute to film-making, regarded the dreaming experience. It insinuates itself into a mind temporarily emptied of defenses and provokes responses from the unconscious with a directness unlike any other art form. Goebbels, after all, had the mad genius to harness Leni Riefenstahl to the Nazi caravan, and her films plugged seamlessly into a nation's desire for perfectibility and triumph.

205

And it is film, more than any other art form, that comes into the consulting room on a patient's coattails. Film refracted through the patient's internal prism: their own film. Their account of the experience is often preceded by "have you seen....?" based in the assumption that both analyst and patient inhabit a world where film is at the heart of a common cultural vernacular. If dreams are the royal road to the unconscious, then films may be the royal road to dream; like the recounting of a dream, the telling of the internal film a patient has made while watching an external film is an account of her interior landscape and a wish to map it. A patient of mine brought in the film "Breaking the Waves" with a strong identification with the bruised and used heroine. Then she saw it again and brought it in again. And again. And again. This was powerful film, a desperate, grueling film about a young woman lost in the grip of her paralyzed husband's perverse fantasies, and my patient's compulsion to repeat the viewing experience told me something of the way in which she found herself in the ineluctable grip of her own perverse internal world.

This was the film she chose to put between us as a way of representing an historical scene from her life: a difficult, jerky art house film of some considerable cultural weight. Another patient will bring in a foreign language movie, another a tiny budget British film about small town mores: films whose text the patient believes the analyst will understand and which may in turn be the kind of film she would select in her own life. The kind of film a patient brings might be a clue, then, to a process of identification with the analyst, a wish to be coterminous with a mind that is conceived of as vast and learned. Or it may be evidence of a wish for approval - "Look how clever I am, mummy, I can understand these difficult things." A patient may struggle with the foreign language of the analyst and bring a film that seems to speak the same tongue, uses the same syntactical structures. But perhaps the analyst needs to cherchez Bruce Willis, to trouvez Sylvester Stallone.

Where is the big budget actioner with money and special effects splatted all over the screen? What forbidden or unspeakable aspects of a patient's inner world does such a film represent and why can she not lay it on the analytic table for consumption? Perhaps they represent for the patient a moral decadence, or a punishable wish for surfeit; or angry, violent, mindless wishes to collapse authority and revel in triumph. Perhaps confessing to a weekend Stallone fix might result in a catastrophic separation from the analyst and her world; the patient fears the loss of her place in the inner sanctum where the analytic couple speak their shared language.

In saying "have you seen.....?" the patient imagines that the analyst has had the same experience as her of tripping over reality into fantasy, that

206

the analyst knows something, from her own interior, of the loss of self in the dreamed experience of film. The patient must imagine that the analyst has emerged from the experience intact, can distinguish the real from the imaginary and can hold her as she slips around in her own confusions between the two. Patient and analyst collaborate in the spooling of the patient's internal film; the work shares film's characteristics as it jump cuts from one location to another, as it freeze frames endlessly on one detail, as it flashes back and fast forwards through the patient's history, as it moves between close up and long shot. The analyst is audience and director as she experiences what goes on between the two of them at the same time as analyzing the material, noticing the editing and the sudden dark screen.

The analyst is a screen herself, of course, though perhaps no longer the blank screen of classical technique. Just as film is projected onto a featureless surface, so the patient's internal film is projected onto the analyst who, like the screen, reflects it back through understanding so that it may become in the next instant, a new memory. A new genre.

What exactly do you *do?*

Jeremy Holmes *(Devon, UK)*

Like many people in our profession, I have learned, rather painfully, to be reticent when asked in social situations about what I 'do'. I usually start by saying I work in a hospital, move on, but only if encouraged, to explain that I am a doctor, and then wait for further expression of interest before confessing that I am a psychiatrist. This then tends to produce a variety of responses, including embarrassed/nonplussed laughter, an instant change of conversation, a long inquiry about how to deal with a anorexic daughter or alcoholic husband, or probes about what species of psychiatrist I might be – the pills or a psychoanalytic variety. If I am incautious enough to confess to being psychoanalytically minded (but not, as it happens, a psychoanalyst, of which more later) the conversation usually then tries to clear up the inevitable confusion between psychiatrist, psychologist, clinical psychologist, psychotherapist and psychoanalyst. Finally, my interlocutor (if not by now beating a hasty retreat) ends up asking questions such as "does that mean you are especially perceptive, see things that ordinary people don't notice?", "doesn't that mean you have to be analysed yourself?", "don't you find it depressing listening to people's problems all day long?", "do people like you ever actually *cure* anybody?", or "aren't your patients just bored housewives with nothing better to do than come and talk to people like you?".

Faced with all this I find it difficult not to be defensive. Recently, in answer to the perceptiveness question I found myself replying, tongue-in-cheek but also in mock-portentous deadly earnest, "yes, isn't amazing that, although we have only just met, I can see into the innermost recesses of your soul, instantly knowing everything about you, your sexual hang-ups are all laid bare before me without you having to utter a word…".

What is going on here? Do psycho-people in Paris or New York or Tel Aviv have the same difficulties, or is it just we repressed Brits who cannot cope with our inner world and the sexual innuendo it inevitably appears to entail? Does the unconscious evoke the same combination of fascination and fear the world over or is it just in Northern Europe that we have to mind our psychic P's and Q's? Or is it my own ambivalence about our subject which prevents me from being more unabashed about promoting the vital importance of a psychological perspective not just to individuals but to society at large?

Curiously, a similar suspicion of psychotherapy has prevailed, at lest until recently, within British psychiatry itself. When I explain to psychiatric colleagues that I am a psychotherapist the response may be an ironic "oh so you are a *believer...*?", or I may be made to feel that I am letting the biomedical side down in some way by associating with people like psychologists, or worse still, the implication is that we are all psychotherapists and who I am to suggest that there could be any sort of special expertise in a field that is, at bottom, not much more that good bedside manners.

Working as I do in a district general hospital, in which all medical specialties are represented, prejudice can be even more naked. When the hospital's chief surgeon first came to my quiet, comfortably furnished, yet essentially modest office, he was visibly envious at the thought that such a lowly specialty as psychiatry should be better off than his cramped space shared with a secretary. I had to explain to him that my consulting room was the equivalent of his operating theatre, and that exploring the psyche can be in its own way as delicate a task as his most tricky operations. He remains unconvinced, although a grudging respect and surprising friendship seems to exist between us. The idea that psychiatry is something of an medical interloper, suitable only for doctors who are dim and/or disturbed, and that psychiatric work does not really equate to the life-and-death of 'real' medicine, dies hard.

How to respond to all this? – representing as it no doubt does aspects of my own inner world as well as a valid reflection of the reality of the stigma which besets our patients even more than ourselves. I tend to adopt two main strategies. The first is to try to outplay my opponents at their own game. I emphasize the scientific basis of psychological therapies, citing the evidence for example that antidepressants are no more effective in treating depression than psychotherapy, not to mention poor tolerance and side-effects. I quote effect sizes and go on to discuss some of the mechanisms of action of therapy — nonspecific factors such as remoralisation, creating a secure base, the importance of enhanced reflexive function for intimate social animals such as ourselves, mastery and play as vital ingredients in psychological health. At the same time I suggest that so-called evidence-based medicine can be a lot less scientific than it purports to be, and that many of the apparently physical problems that it deals with are psychological in origin.

My second tack is held in reserve for a particular kind of sceptic whose objection to psychotherapy is more political than scientific – those who suggest that it is a new form of opiate which diverts people from tackling material deprivation and the social causes of distress. Here, rather than trying to outflank, I tend to try to join with them in the idea that psychotherapy is, at best, a form of humanism that recognizes the essential value of the individual, and helps people to realize their true

209

potential – an existential therapy that enables its subjects take responsibility for themselves and their lives, facing up to the destructive as well as creative possibilities of the human condition.

It would be good to end on this upbeat note. But I have already hinted at a part of me that identifies with psychotherapy's critics. Perhaps it is linked with my father's proud claim that, unlike his Jewish wife and son, *he* had no unconscious, and what was more, had no intention of ever developing one! When, some thirty years ago, I considered applying for training at the Institute of Psychoanalysis, in the end I did not go ahead, consciously at least because I did not wish to become part of what I perceived as an esoteric cult. Today I am stuck with the consequences of that rather arrogant and ill-informed opinion. But at least as a psychiatrist I am reasonably clear what my skills consist of – they boil down to being unfazed by madness and knowing roughly what to do when someone becomes disturbed. Alongside that unglamorous but practical work lies the elusive, fascinating, priestly, envy-provoking role of the psychotherapist, a professional who can legitimately claim expertise in the field of the inner world and of interpersonal relationships. If my original perception that analysts tend to dine exclusively with other analysts is correct perhaps that is because no such revelations are necessary. But will someone (perhaps one of the contributors to this book) tell me how to slip their job description into non-analytic dinner party talk without it becoming a conversation stopper?

Not His Master's Voice
Barbie Antonis *(London)*

This book offers the rare opportunity to share some thoughts and feelings that have been brewing for some time now. They stem from an idea which came to me while at an International Psychoanalytic Conference in Barcelona some years back and even then represented a problem that I had played with, and tugged at, long before, probably since my initial training as a psychotherapist, while living in Cambridge. In a nutshell, the problem is this: with who's voice do we speak to our patients? And the question behind this is, of course, how do we discover our own voice in our therapeutic and psychoanalytic work? (This is the theme of a future book of edited papers).

These questions may sound as if they are intended to echo Paula Heimann's seminal observation (1956) that in considering transference and counter-transference phenomena we inquire 'Who is talking to whom about what?' and a later development of this in Pearl King's work on Role Responsiveness (1978). But I want to approach the question of one's own voice in relation to the analyst's identification , not with the patient's internal figures , who may be actualised in the transference, but with his or her own training figures - analyst, supervisors and consultants. Also implicated is identification with a 'group' voice, a 'voice' thought to represent a particular, if fantasised, way of thinking about experience with patients in the consulting room. This identification may happen at the cost of personal authenticity and authority.

While thinking about these problems of 'voice' and 'identity'as a psychoanalyst I realised that my personal link to these issues exists in what I like doing outside the setting of the consulting room. Sometimes between sessions but more often outside my professional hours. This activity, or pastime-cum-self-expression brings me to the heart of this piece. Namely singing-which is certainly a direct way of using my voice. To be not-analyst in the service of finding my own voice as analyst. Though I sang here and there during my childhood, only in my twenties did I get into my stride and join a rock/blues band. As the vocalist for Camden Goods (!) we gigged from Hampstead via Upper Street to the Marquee. Some material was our own, but we played Ellington tunes, Joplin numbers (Janice not Scott) and Chuck Berry was well represented. Later on, with Bedrock, in Cambridge, no May Ball was too much trouble, and the Alma pub gave us a regular and friendly venue. We played similar material, though leaning more to the blues, thanks to a fine physicist guitarist and a biologist who loved the drums. And singing has become a necessary counter-balance, a respite and even a restorative, to the difficulties of analytic work . However, like good analytic work, it is also enormously satisfying. Singing represents a channel for emotional expression, the mood and tone of which can encompass anything from joy to sorrow through jazz, blues, rock, slowhand and songs from musicals. There is a dilemma and paradox here too. If I sing a song written and sung by Peggy Lee am I doing no more than copying her voice? I'm not interested in pastiche or imitation though singing along and trying out her phrasing is good practice and a valid learning experience. When I sing a Cole Porter number it will always be his song but the way I sing it, I hope, is with my own voice and not simply a facsimile or imitation.

I am using this metaphor to clarify my own thinking and argument since it concerns me that being a psycho-analyst obviously entails becoming a psycho-analyst. Within the 'becoming' process there are pressures to conform, to comply, to copy as well as encouragement to learn, to discover, to wait, to find out more and essentially to listen and reflect. Identification can serve ego development well, but over-identification is a danger when it obscures anxieties about acceptance into the fraternity and this is surely a dis-service to personal growth and thus no credit to the profession. Moreover the pressures within the analytic process itself yield their own anxieties and resistances, so adding to the wish for a solid theoretical framework and theory of technique, and may foster a desire to hide behind someone else's voice. What worries me here is, I think, something like the issue which Ken Wright addresses so helpfully in his 2001 paper where he proposes a thesis that the infant's need to resort to projective identification is inversely related to the mother's attunement to her baby. The parallel I want to draw concerns the availability of a training environment that is open to one's own creative discovery within psychoanalytic work and hence the provision of a climate that is likely to enable independence of mind, rather than adherence to proscribed formulaic method and the attendant dangers of clone-analysis.....and not finding one's own voice. Without this what is it that the patient gets ?

Whether it's a jazzy song or a mellow blues, or even a raunchy Nina Simone or Bonnie Raitt number that I choose to sing it's going to become my song only when I find my own voice to sing it. This is the metaphor in my mind for genuine psychoanalytic work, and the one I find helpful to describe the necessary, if difficult, goal of psychoanalytic education. *It's the singer, and it's the song.*

References

Heimann, P. (1956) Dynamics of transference interpretations, *International Journal of Psycho-Analysis*. 37: 303-310.
King, P.(1978) Affective responses of the analyst to the patient's communication *International Journal of Psycho-Analysis* 59:329-334.
Wright, K. (2001)Bion and beyond, Enid Balint Memorial Lecture. Bulletin of the British Psycho-Analytical Society. 37/7:36-45.

Melodious Interpretations   Marianne Parsons *(London)*

Hitting the right note that will be bearable for patients to hear - be they children, adolescents or adults – can be very difficult, but it can be even harder when working with the young child. Unlike adults, children are usually brought to therapy because their parents are worried about them. They don't have the adult's 'work ethic' on their side to help them to struggle with their resistances and are more likely to shut their ears and their minds to anything that feels uncomfortable. Little children tend to act on how they feel more impulsively and concretely than adults. Child Psychotherapists are well used to little children putting their hands over their ears to stop the words reaching them when the words feel dangerous, or talking or singing loudly to drown out the therapist. But the defensive need not to listen can also be expressed very playfully. One of my child analytic patients, Sally, who felt unable to hear me say anything about her feelings of sadness, asked me one day to act the role of a fairy. I was to meet a witch (acted by Sally) who could do magic and make wishes come true. When I said the fairy's first wish was not to feel sad ever again, the witch (Sally) quickly interrupted me by turning me into a frog who could only croak. What a wonderful way of shutting me up!

Patients of any age need to have a good-enough experience of safety in the relationship with the analyst or therapist if they are going to risk facing difficult feelings. With children this need for safety is sometimes more immediate, and their therapists have to find creative ways of communicating in a displaced way that allows the communication to be heard. With Charles, an 8 year old atypical boy full of horrendous panic and almost phobic of words, I drew cartoon stories on the blackboard, keeping them purposely hidden from view. This didn't fail to arouse his curiosity to see what I was doing and allowed him to risk becoming engaged.

Jamie, aged 5, struggled with shame and anxiety about not being a big boy, and was terrified of losing face and couldn't bear the idea that I might have anything to offer. He couldn't let me talk. I found myself making up songs, singing softly as if to myself, about the monkey puppet he was fond of. At first the songs were simply about Monkey's adventures in the games, but gradually they were about how Monkey was frightened of feeling little, how he wanted to be big and how he wanted to stamp and yell at the big people etc. I used the melody of Schubert's Trout Quintet for these bits of rhyming doggerel and I sometimes wonder if this patient, now grown up, has any special feelings (positive or negative) about that piece! Here's an example:

Our friend the blue-tailed Monkey
Just hated feeling small.
He didn't want to wait till
He grew up strong and tall.
The nasty older monkeys
Just laughed and called him names,
"You're just a little baby,
Go home, play baby games."

So the little blue-tailed Monkey
Felt really hurt and sad,
But that made him feel more little
And so he got real mad.
He yelled at the bigger monkeys,
"I'm just as good as you!
Just wait until I'm bigger
Then I'll look down on you!"

He was able to listen to these 'interpretations' not only because they were displaced onto the puppet, but also because they were further displaced from talking into song.

Although one wouldn't sing or draw interpretative offerings with an adult patient, it is just as important to be creative in finding ways that will help the adult to experience a sense of safety in the analytic setting. Without a background experience of harmony (safety and attunement), it is quite understandable that the patient will not be able to bear to face the inevitable discords that will arise within him and also in the relationship between him and the analyst as the transference unfolds. To follow the musical theme a bit further in relation to analysis, the analogy of the piano accompanist is a useful one. An accompanist worth his salt does not set the pace, direct the musical dynamics of the singer or instrumentalist, or play like a soloist. Instead, the accompanist attunes himself to the other's style and follows his lead whilst providing a reliable and sensitive setting for him to express himself through the music. Gerald Moore, one of Britain's foremost piano accompanists, entitled his autobiography, "Am I too loud?" Maybe we would do well to ask ourselves this question more often when we work with our patients!

214

Shuffle Ball Change

Alan Kindler *(Toronto)*

There I was, just a few moments before going on stage, one sunny Spring afternoon in the square in front of City Hall in Toronto. I was performing with a tap dance troupe led by my recently acquired tap dance teacher, Heather, who knew no shame. unlike myself and a few other erstwhile 'tappers' in the group. We were billed as 'Heather's Hoofers' and this was to be our 'coming out'. I knew that I was there because I have always wanted to be Donald O'Connor, Gene Kelly and all of those slim hipped, agile, beautiful men who tap out miraculous rhythms with their feet and because I have always wanted to be in a show. But now I was suddenly struck with the dreadful thought, "What if, by some strange coincidence, one of my patients were to be in the square today? Worse still, what if it were one of the patients whose appointment I had cancelled (abstinently, of course) so that I could be here? As a well analyzed tap dancer, I had to confront the next question that flapped into my head. "Was it possible that I really wanted my analysands to see me tap dance up here on the stage, like Donald and Gene? Is this the me that I needed them to know instead of the passive one who sits, motionless, cerebral and invisible?" Why is the exposure of this part of me so forbidden anyway? You can see where I'm heading as I think about my moment in the sun.

Why are we so hidden? Was Freud really so fatigued by the pressures of relentless face to face work that he had to seek solitude and anonymity behind the couch, free of the conflicting demands of personal display and neutrality? Or was he actually 'Freud Astaire' but deathly afraid of exposing his tap dancing self to waltzing Vienna for fear that it would not be regarded as scientific? Should we be bound by Freud's need to hide his tapping self by introducing the couch and so many other rituals of invisibility? Is that always, or even often, a good thing for psychoanalytic treatment?

The good news is that things are changing. Analysts are emerging as authentic participants who have spontaneous responses and reveal themselves in ways never dreamed of in the last century. Technique is passe and creative improvisation is acceptable, even desirable these days. But so far, no one has included tap dancing in the training curriculum.

CHASING DREAMS

The Rags of my Dreams* Jehane Markham

The rags of my dreams
Decorate the bare walls
With blisters of colour;
I will have cried that day
I will have swept the floor then.
Sometimes things fall into place
With an unimagined sweetness,
My goodbye keys on the chair
The copper waterfall of the beech tree falling outside
And the feelings inside
Growing like fibres in the woven cloth.
The postman slithers the letters through the letterbox,
They fall like a hand of cards upon the mat.
The cat licks herself patiently,
All wait for the dreams to come,
To be sewn with brilliant thread,
To lie around me
Like a cloak of love,
To keep me from the dead.

*This was written half way through my second therapeutic analysis,
a few months after I had moved from one session a week to four.
This poem first appeared in Ambit literary magazine, U.K. 2001

Brief encounters of the Borges kind

Gregorio Kohon *(Buenos Aires/ London)*

Sergio had met him a couple of times before. Once, at the National Library: he just requested to see him at the front reception, and to his own surprise, *el Maestro* obliged. They talked about The War of the Roses, the state of Israel, the emerging poets of Buenos Aires. The old man, without shame nor pride, confessed his ignorance about the *porteño* young writers of the 60s. He was too busy to read anything contemporary, he said; the little time he had was spent studying yet another dead language.

Then, a few months later, they met again. Sergio had thought of editing a volume of Jules Vernes' *From the Earth to the Moon*, which would have included comments by different authors; whatever came to their minds while re-reading it, each of them would write it down on the margins of the text. Besides Borges, Sergio had invited Marie Langer, Julio Cortázar, and Raúl González Tuñon. This time, Borges described his feelings about man's incredible achievement of landing on the moon. He was at home that day, looking at a gray square of light in one corner of the room, unable to see the pictures on television because of his blindness. Listening to the description given by his mother of the events taking place on the moon, profoundly moved and shaken, he could do nothing else - he said - but cry. Nevertheless, in spite of his intense feeling of wonder, he was also sad and somehow disappointed; perhaps the romantic side of the moon, he thought, so many times sung to by so many poets across so many centuries, was going to disappear.

Then, the last encounter. It was midnight, the threat of rain was in the air. He prepared the paste for the posters; with a wide brush, he laboriously mixed the powdered glue with water in a five-litre paint can. His hands were becoming stiff, the water was freezing, his fingers hurt. He was hoping the police wouldn't hassle him; sometimes they stopped their unmarked cars and checked on him; they were unpredictable, anything could provoke them. In Argentina, even to kiss a girl on the streets was a transgression of the law. A few years earlier, Sergio had been reprimanded by two uniformed policemen for kissing his girl-friend just outside the Teachers' Union Library. "It's illegal to do this in public, you know," they had warned the young lovers. Sons of bitches.

That night's posters announced an exhibition by Carlos Alonso, one of Sergio' favourite painters. Sergio was day-dreaming, picturing himself being invited to the opening with those attractive daughters of the upper classes, full of stories about their trips to Europe, the prizes at the latest Venice Biennale, the Cannes Film Festival, the Opera season in Milan, all the beautiful people that attended those events, wanting to be seduced by successful artists. Sergio knew he was envious of their money, of their casual French expressions, of their Earl Grey and Lapsang Souchong teas, of their malt whiskies and Harrods underwear. He despised himself, but he couldn't help it. They had all that money, while he had to work his butt off so he could just about survive: during the day, doing

217

market research; at night, sticking up posters for the art galleries. He felt sorry for himself, but managed to tell himself off: *Tough shit, you fool!*

When Sergio looked up the street, there he was, hurriedly passing in front of the heavy iron doors of the *Centro Naval*. The old man was walking alone, moving his stick from left to right, seeking a security that his eyes couldn't offer him. Looking from a distance at the fragile figure of the old genius whose political sympathies had caused him to be insulted and abused, Sergio felt an unconditional admiration for him.

Sergio stood still. He let the brush stand in the horrible sticky compound and dried his hands as best he could on his dirty jeans. The old man, after walking rapidly towards Paraguay, suddenly stopped. He looked around a couple of times and slowly moved closer to the window of a shoe-shop. He knocked with the top of his walking stick on the big glass pane and listened attentively to the sound of his tapping. He looked to the left and then to the right, and repeated the procedure one more time. After this second attempt, Borges moved on. He seemed particularly happy. It had begun to drizzle.

Sergio coughed on purpose, to give the blind man notice that there was someone there; then he walked towards him: *Hola, Don Jorge, cómo le va? Soy Sergio Goldstein.*
- Oh yes, Sergio Goldstein, it's been a long time, what a surprise! I see you persist in being, like Spinoza.
- I try my best, *Don Jorge* -Sergio said- The young writer never knew if calling him 'Don Jorge' was the proper form of address, but he wanted to show the old man respect: 'Borges' was too familiar, 'Jorge' was impertinent.
- Your friend Miguel told me about your father's death, I'm so sorry - News traveled fast. Borges continued: - Death is painful only for those who survive the dead; otherwise, the idea that one is to die is quite pleasant, comforting. Can you imagine if one persisted in being forever and ever? That would be all right for the stones, the mountains and the oceans, but not for human beings. For example, I'm completely fed up with Borges: *Yo que soy el que ahora está cantando/ Seré mañana el misterioso, el muerto...* - he recited, quoting himself -You know, my mother recently said to me: "Jorge, what a shame! I don't think I'm going to make it to a hundred." I told her: "Mother, you shouldn't take the decimal system so seriously..."
They both laughed, and started to stroll towards Retiro.
- I smell glue, don't you? -Borges asked. Sergio explained briefly what he was doing.
- Extraordinary, what writers must do to earn a living - Borges remarked.
- I would hardly call myself a writer, Don Jorge - Sergio said. He also meant it.
- I was also forced by circumstances to do some peculiar jobs, I've been employed in strange places -Borges commented.
Sergio asked him about the time when Perón became President, when Borges was removed as director of a small library in the *barrio de Almagro* and relocated as inspector of domestic fowl for distribution to the municipal markets.

- No, that was different - Borges explained - At the time, I sought an explanation from a friend who was working for the Government: "Why," I asked him, "if I am a writer, was I worthy of such a generous offer?" He said: "You supported the Allies during the war, didn't you?" "Well, yes, of course I did," I agreed somewhat disingenuously. His answer was: "Well, what did you expect then?" That, of course, put an end to our friendship.

- Nowadays, you've upset quite a few people with your political views - Sergio reminded him.

- What else can one do in a country like this? People are very ignorant, there is a sick admiration for the criminals who have chronically succeeded in stealing from us. I only express my scepticism, I hate politics anyway. I think politicians are in the game only for the money they make out of dirty deals; they're all swindlers and charlatans, what kind of a country is this, that wants Perón back in power? Can you make any sense of that? - Borges had become agitated.

- Don't you think we have some redeeming qualities? After all, we can't be *all* bad - Sergio said.

Borges thought for a minute.

- Argentineans do have one redeeming feature, the only one -And after clearing his throat, he added: - It's the cult of friendship!

And then Borges returned to politics:

- You know, I dream of a system of government that could be kept to a minimum - he continued - One shouldn't have to take notice of who is in power, or what such and such a minister said today, what kind of dress their wives prefer. Not that I know much about those things, they're completely irrelevant pieces of information. For me the really important things in the world are the movements of the planets or the daily changes of the tides. In Switzerland - for example, where I lived for five years - nobody knows the President's name.

- Maybe that's true, but the only thing they've ever done is to invent the cuckoo-clock and chocolate. Have you ever seen *The Third Man*, with Orson Welles?

- No, I haven't actually, let me just say that cuckoo-clocks are better than *dulce de leche*, or even better than that appalling sport, soccer - And after a short pause, he added: -Soccer, as you know, was invented by the British.

The drizzle had stopped but the temperature was still dropping steadily.

- This idea of a minimal state, Don Jorge, would turn you into a political anarchist.

- Really? I don't know, I'm a pacifist, I don't support any form of violence. Anarchism seems too close to terrorism; what I value the most is freedom, for example the freedom to write whatever one likes.

- Don Jorge, some of your friends in power right now are not very keen on freedom.

- Oh, really? Since I don't read the newspapers...

It was always difficult to tell when the great writer was serious, when he was playing to an audience or being ironic. Sergio thought that he should go back to his can of paste and his posters.

-Yes, the freedom to write... - murmured Borges -Anyone who wants to live has to rely on the illusion of a story.

- It's the first time I've heard you quoting a contemporary French writer, - said Sergio.

219

- Who do you mean? - Borges was genuinely surprised.

- Maurice Blanchot, you just quoted him, I remember well, it's from *Au Moment voulu*: "Anyone who wants to live has to rely on the illusion of a story."

- Well, it's extraordinary, isn't it? I don't know who Maurice Blanchot is, let alone being acquainted with any of his books. It's uncanny, a nightmare come true. I've been aware I had been stealing from Borges, now you're telling me that I might have been borrowing from somebody else, from a real writer. I knew I wasn't a genius, you know, that was one of many false charges that others always brought against me. Maurice Blanchot? All my life I had to live with the possibility of discovering one day that I might be a copy of somebody else, that all my writings were one form of plagiarism. Are you sure, Sergio, that that was Blanchot's?

- One hundred per cent.

- I wonder, if I am an invention of Maurice Blanchot's mind, he might have imagined me, and I am his dream and his creation; it wouldn't be that bad, except that I wish he had made me invisible. There is nothing I wanted more in life than to be invisible.

It was time to say goodbye; Sergio should have finished sticking up the posters by now. And the next day he had to get up early to do his surveys. Besides, the posters might get stolen.

They had been walking around the Plaza San Martín, one of the nicest parks in the city, with ancient magnolias, palms, *tipuanas*, cedars, rubber trees and *palos borrachos*.

- I've been told that there is a new sculpture in this plaza, a fountain in fact - said Borges.

- Yes, it's *La Fuente de la Doncella*, - Sergio confirmed. - It had to be removed from Plaza Lezica, where it stood since 1931, to this location; the local residents objected to the nudity of *la Doncella* - the Maiden…

- A bit extreme, don't you think? Not that I care that much about nudity, I forget what the body of a woman looks like -This unusually intimate confession embarrassed Borges, and he quickly changed the subject: - Don't you agree that few cities in the world are as ugly as Buenos Aires?

- For once, I have to disagree with you, Don Jorge, Buenos Aires is quite beautiful.

- Do you really think so? Oh well, I believe the *Obelisco* spoiled it forever.

Sergio smiled, and said nothing. He wasn't sure, but suspected that that absurd monument had been built at the beginning of the century, a long time ago.

They bade each other good-bye.

Everything was still there, exactly as Sergio had left it. He picked up all the stuff and started making his way down Florida, sticking up posters on every space available, mostly covering up previous announcements. The newspaper headlines were to announce the following morning: *Borges joins the Conservative Party*.

In the in-between dreamtime /Jim Rose *(london)*

The fifty minute reaper across
Tides of affects and cathects
Roughly disconnects.

No mistake for whom this bell tolls
She says rising from couch
Making with outwards slouch

In negative after image
Her absence creates a presence
Of her very being-essence

Outward footsteps ..... and shutting door
Complex unwinding psychic tangle
I...a-jangle-dingle-dangle

My room re-adjusts as well it might
A pillow plumped in silent time
Pieces of being in re-align sublime

Vital in that needed step-down
Can there be in re-align sublime
A very own dreamtime ?

Finding bearings, setting moorings
Re-align in dreamtime dwell.......
Ah..............there's the doorbell.

221

Pulling up stakes   Harriet Kimble Wrye *(Pacific Palisades)*

Pulling up stakes takes on new iridescence, possibly transcrudescence today. It is the weekend before my last two weeks as a practicing psychoanalyst before leaving to take a two year travel and writing sabbatical around the world. After my last session today, Jim and I set out on one of what will be several fully loaded trips moving household gear from LA to the Sierras, readying for the lease of house I've lived in for twenty-seven years.

The Explorer is loaded to the gunwales, listing slightly, sea kayak lashed on top and towing our llama trailer, commandeered as a moving van, to transport all our essentials, as well as items for sacred practice for our move to the woods. Inside the TwinBrooks Timber Llamas' trailer are Jim's recumbent bike and my mountain bike, backpacks, kayak paddles, snowshoes, skis, boxes of books and CDs. Topping it off are a few arcane items such as the fully outfitted scarecrow from our vegetable garden, wearing cast off bits of favorite old clothing from everybody in the family, too familiar and comical to leave to just any tenant inhabiting our house during the sabbatical.

Lately, every day of with patients has been intensely poignant, as we contemplate finishing analytic relationships ranging from a few to sixteen years in history. It's a wild roller coaster ride. It is quite an extraordinary experience to have your whole practice, all patients I've seen for a number of years, in what in psychoanalysis we ominously call "termination". While one patient plans to transfer to a colleague, the others (along with me, I emphatically add) are all in termination on some form of emotional roller coaster ride of partings and impartings.

For the past five months since I returned from the Middle East, therapy sessions have been poignantly inscribed with tenderness, anger, resentment, tears, gratitude, bittersweet sadness, nostalgic reminiscing, attempted Shanghais, alternately brave and fearful anticipation, and occasional bursts of liberating exhilaration. More than once I have quoted from *I Never Promised You a Rose Garden*, as we ruefully acknowledge limits---my own, my patient's and the limits of analysis. The sessions have also been marked by negotiating these shifting sands in an effort to ultimately weave this ending chapter into a good good-bye, in contrast to so many earlier ragged ones that have left scars, feelings of rejection or abandonment.

I hate the word termination—it sounds so traumatically terminal, evoking the Terminator, or being terminated or having a terminal illness—or the least malignant association I can think of, to something like "departing from terminal A." It is the beginning of the voyage of "real life" after analysis, and that's a good thing, but on the whole, I think we'll have to come up with a better word, evoking thresholds, transitions, embarkation, launching, births, or imparting.

I have been fascinated as I'm invited to partner each of my patients in this concluding analytic dance, marked by the theme and variations of their analyses and therapies, replete with recitatives and codas and their evocative impact on me. Themes I hear them talking about are their identifications with the child left behind, with me and the father in me, and sometimes with the shadow figure of my husband, as well as emerging conscious efforts to non-defensively discover the "real" me and my outside interests. At the same time I sense them absorbing my voice and my bodily presence as well as details of the consulting room. As a way of tolerating our upcoming separation, while they are drinking me in, I am doing the same with them, savoring the uniqueness of each one whom I know I will miss terribly.

All this reminds me of reading the story of *Frederick* to Gabriel and Ariel when they were little. Frederick was a mouse-poet who lived in an ethereal world of poetry and illusion. While the other mice were busily gathering bits of wool and feathers to make nests in the stone wall for winter and nuts and seeds to eat during the snowy season when food would be scarce, Frederick was out gathering impressions. He gathered memories of flowers, birds and rainbows, colors, images of light and dark and textures. The other mice chided him mercilessly for his foolishness, but of course neither man nor mouse can live by bread alone, so during the long dreary siege of winter, Frederick's poetry brought vitality and warmth to the little colony in the wall. I can identify with Frederick, getting ready for a long figurative winter in the woods and on the road, relying primarily on the company of one person, my husband, after having been so intensely and richly related to so many.

We're both anxious about that. How much strain will there be on our marriage to be each other's all and everything? We're so different. Jim is straightforward and practical, like the other mice in Frederick's colony, he's busy loading the trailer, securing a post office box and arranging mail forwarding, paying the taxes. He is action, a man of few words. While he is busy taking care of all that business of moving, I am sitting in my office on the verge of weeping with the poignancy of it all. I comfort myself thinking that Frederick the poet and his brethren the action-mice in the mouse colony needed each other, and each provided the other vital sustenance. En Sh'Allah. God willing. Let's hope!

223

So today, Dr. Frederick gathered poetry from several sessions. One patient has just convincingly finally shaken off her own depression and the oppressive residue of her parents and grandparents' depression. She feels ready to fly on her own wings in a solid way, not like the occasional manic flights she's gone on in the past. She gazes around the office, carefully storing her own visual memories of this small room where such momentous changes have taken place.

Someone else who has long struggled with a pattern of the controlling behavior, distrustful cynicism, attendant sarcasm and distancing characteristic of his own parents, is now deeply aware of what was once anathema, his vulnerability and dependency. He has been letting both of us into the secret as well as his shame of never feeling really loveable. As it dawns on him more and more that over time in our relationship, he has been experiencing something quite different, he has become much more in touch with valuing his analysis and our time together. Today he cried openly in a good way he was never really able to do before. Instead of a hard-edged "I can do it by myself, thank you very much," he can value and appreciate others in a way that is surely more likely to make him more accessible to intimacy and romance.

Another has just finished writing a book, finding her own voice and transforming a life of too much forfeiting of herself and her talents, turning to others for completion and affirmation. She is home from a highly successful national book tour which concluded in her own hometown with an extraordinary reading from her book, which inspires me in my own writing project. Visiting her once commanding but now frail father and his compatriots in a rest home, she read to them from her book. We both know what this means for her, coming into the authority of her voice, while her aged father, her childhood idol wanes dramatically but gracefully. Both knowing his death will come soon, and our ending sooner, I quietly relive the dying of my own father who was my hero and my enemy. Well, in that sense, pulling up stakes is iridescent, luminous with shared meaning.

Another woman for the first time spent her session lying down on the couch. It was a breakthrough for her, here "on the clubhouse turn" to thus relinquish control and outward focus, and to be finally able to enter into meaningful discourse with her inner life. She has long been trapped in tortuous performance anxieties and the concrete pressures of a demanding profession. She brought two dreams that were richly evocative; thoughtfully associating to them, playing comfortably in the land of metaphor and illusion that is dream work.

Then there was the hour with the young man who has the makings of a poet, but who has been in the throes of an unfinished separation from his parents. We have been enjoying the kind of juicy and potent therapeutic contact that at times makes me feel I should not be accepting fees for the privilege.

Another relative newcomer has overcome some rather impressively crusty layers of his own cynicism and resistance to his wife's insistence that he "see a shrink." Surmounting his own cynicism and much to his own amazement, he has actually found our sessions quite valuable to him in his family life as well as professionally. After a weekend ski trip, one of the first purely pleasure-seeking outings he has taken with his family, he told me with new-found pleasure of teaching his small son the rudiments of skiing.

Well, it's really going to be hard to leave this swiveling chair in this little monastic cell of a consulting room. Every bit as much as my patients are going through the throes of the long goodbye, I certainly feel I too, am doing the same. I'm hoping that in their own lives they can also take in the notion of 'westering' as it has been called, when it is time to pull up stakes, take risks, take the leap and follow a dream. I feel deeply grateful to them all for the privilege of accompanying them on their journeys toward psychological growth, and fortunate to be in conflict between leaving one extraordinary experience for another.

Anyway, the horn is honking, Jim has the sagging car loaded, and after all this suchness and muchness, I am ready to join him to pick up the last of the shopping list for the weekend and then hit the road. In our case, that is Highway 5 heading north in the afternoon out of LA toward the San Joaquin Valley and the Sierras, and, unfortunately, the other side of iridescence. I think I'll enjoy calling it transcrudescence. I think you'll know what I mean.

Giving up Chase
Lynn Spouse (*Kenya, UK, USA*)

Years of passionate overwork as a Child Psychotherapist, difficult work with survivors in Macedonia and Rwanda and despite becoming a University Lecturer, i.e. fulfillment were all thrown out of the window when a friend from 30 years previously turned up. Without much thought, other than 'oh! Wow – am I really allowed to love and have fun!' I got married. This meant a lot of travel and the shocking realization that the cost (for a few years anyway) was to give up my old life around the couch.

Travel meant America, Canada and many months on our boat *'Chase'* with Harry the Golden Retriever 'damn deck dog'.
British Colombia in the Spring meant looking out on snow-covered mountains - rapidly melting – and watching deer, moose, coyotes and bears in the wild garden. Once I saw a little baby bear, chomping the dandelions. Harry the dog got really excited. Well Harry has two excitements – one, which sends him forth and the other, which keeps him back. Coyotes, wolves and bears frighten him and he stays inside. But baby bear excited him. So I knew Mummy bear was not around. Mummy bears are very dangerous! Then Harry escaped and went bounding over to baby bear that shone up a tree with astonishing speed. Harry was most upset, as he wanted to play.

I throw sticks into the raging river for Harry who cannot quite swim against the current. He is so funny trying. But he swims out to the side into the slack water where he finds a face-saving stick and trots, bounces, wheelies and shakes his way back to us. This is even funnier when we throw from the log bridge as he goes hurtling underneath us bewildered as to where his stick is. I am training him up to be a very strong swimmer and super fit, just in case he ever falls off Chase, our boat.
Oh! I forgot to mention the birds. There are lots. Robins are obscene – very large and with a juicy orange colour. We have humming birds, wood-peckers, bald eagles and others. But I need to buy a book. We also have butterflies - because there is a lot of grass to cut!

We also have lots of weather and the most amazing cloud formations. This is gliding paradise as, there are so many hill and cloud thermals, and waves. But I have a lot to learn before I will be allowed to go soaring. I am learning to glide tho' and have gone solo and fly with John who has his licence. Well, over the summers we sailed Chase from the UK to Mallorca where we prepared her for a Transatlantic Crossing. Unfortunately, in a moment of tiredness, we wrecked Chase on a reef on the beautiful island of Graciosa in the Canaries. It was a great shock. We are both safe and unhurt and so is Harry. We are doing fine but are sad. Unfortunately she was only insured for third party as it is impossible to insure ferro-cement yachts.

We had sailed from Spain, which took six days. Chase sailed like a dream with her new sails. As we were going across the Straights of Gibraltar she did 10 knots with the wind reaching 40 knots at times (rather than the 20 kts forecast). Then after four days of gray weather and a day without wind, things cheered up. Day five was perfect. We had sun, warm air, and swimming for Harry, and he saw lots of dolphins, which he gets very excited about. In fact he spent most of the days at sea looking out for sea life. I lay out on the deck cushions and thought that this was indeed the life. John opened a bottle of Champagne for lunch (about the only time we met) and we celebrated: 'being in the Trade Winds with a tropical destination'. The next day I put all the food and drink away in lockers I had painted. Everything was sorted out at last and all the containers were labeled and we were organized. We arrived at the first island, Graciosa, at around 4a.m. and craving sleep decided to anchor in Francesca Bay. Anyway something went wrong with the autopilot and in the pitch dark of the moonless night we overshot the third out of four 'waypoints'. John corrected this manually but a mixture of currents, tide, wind funnel effect etc. meant that we hit the reef at low tide.

Chase rolled onto sharp rocks and was holed. In half an hour I was waist deep in water and we spent the next two hours rescuing stuff in the dingy and taking it ashore (we could just stand). The ground was lava rock and very sharp. There were strong waves, undertows and sea urchins. We very quickly got cold but at dawn a wonderful couple, came with a Land Rover (the island doesn't have tarmac roads) and took me to their home for coffee and dry clothes. A Spanish doctor, did the same for John. A German yachtsman was very helpful in the initial attempts by fishermen to pull her off the rock, as he knew all about yachts. But on a second attempt they sadly pulled the main mast off, snapping it in two. We watched in horror and knew then that Chase was doomed.

We went back on the next half tides and continued to rescue things. We now had more helpers. A Dutch single-handed sailor and a Dutch sailing couple were there at our sides for two weeks. They helped John and the German sailor to anchor her away from the shore to stop her being pushed farther up at high tide. We also rescued things at half tide, including some of the sails, winches, bits of navigation equipment, etc. etc. with the help of our new Dutch friends.

Then we went every day to scour the beach. It is extraordinary how quickly the boat broke up. She was soon just a quarter of a boat, rubble,

227

and wood all broken and pushed by the waves to the stern. She had almost turned right over, the doghouse and deck were gone and the bow and stern breaking up.I lost were my books, my telephone book and most of my clothes. John has lost his new sails, mast steps, anchors, new bread maker, masses of expensive boat equipment, his charts and his dream to sail the Atlantic...

We should have stayed at sea until dawn although John has done many a night 'anchoring'. It was a mixture of tiredness, euphoria at having arrived, a very low tide, a new and untested auto-pilot and a strong current. We had also spent two long in the Mediterranean.

But, we have found a special place in the world and some special people who will remain friends. The most important thing is that we are safe and so is Harry the dog who thought this island was paradise. I think we have captured the hearts of the people here because of Harry!

Lets hope that we can 'learn from experience' and 'do better next time'. I learned to really respect the power of the sea and how quickly one tires and gets cold. Had we been anywhere where there had not been a village, we'd have been in a bad way. As it was we didn't really stop feeling cold for three days, shivering at night. John had trouble breathing. I had nightmares about the crash for the first four nights, which were followed by a rescue dream. I then didn't dream until I was at my parents in France when I dreamed that the remains of Chase sailed off, the front end at least, into a harbour. Jolly good bit of resilience, hope and optimism. So that is the saga. We are beginning to see the funny side of it and of the life we lead – just a bit of retired flotsam and jetsam – exciting but confusing. We then went to France with deckless dog, the fearless Harry, to my parents –seeking sanctuary...

But, what does the future hold? I expect we will be in Canada for part of the year and in Africa for the other part. Neither of us has ever found anything to beat it. I was born there and John lived there for 12 years. He has a plan for training Africans to be computer programmers and doing distance work. But that is a very ambitious thing to do - we'll see. I would love it as there as there are loads I could do in Africa with children. I really miss my contact with those rude, snotty, swearing, angry, violent, aggressive, sad, cut-off, imaginative, affectionate brats I used to field in Child Psychotherapy!!! Not that there is life 'beyond the couch' as I have been 'found' and 'borrowed' to help wherever I have been.

So why are we off to South Africa and America to look at bargain yachts now the Rand and the American economic climate are so favorable?

Go on and dream: A mission to be a psychoanalyst

Natalia Indrasari *(Indonsesia/Hawai)*

I have lived in various places in Indonesia all my life, as we followed my father who served in the Indonesian army. I think I started to be fascinated by people's behaviors observing these as we travelled. I was probably still too small to understand the concept of cultural relativity and ethnic differences, but I could tell that people differed geographically and also in each place, from each other. I became even more aware of difference when I moved back to Jakarta. I started to notice that residents of the capital were less easy to understand and found many inconsistencies in people around me. They had double standards about some things or said one thing when they meant another. I remember telling my mother about my confusion and she said that it meant that I was a big girl already aware that there are more things about people than I could know. What I learned from my surrounding was that as a little kid, you could be honest and people would not mind whatever you said or did. Once you started to grow up, you learned to conceal your intentions and speak in a different way to people based on who you are talking to, their age and their social status.

As people around me started to be more interesting, I found myself observing a girl who worked as a maid in our house. She was normal in her everyday being, but when startled she would burst out with obscene words and made gestures at the same time. When she stopped she seemed all exhausted and sometimes cried, begging my brothers to stop startling her. She was young, probably early twenties at that time. From that day I began noting this condition, I now know to be called *'latah'*. Although I found these people interesting to watch, I really didn't know how to feel for them – whether sorry or amused. As I met more and more people with latah, and realised that their characteristics are so different from each other, I started to learn to ignore it. As I could not find any similarities between the people who had it, I just supposed that everybody could be latah. Latah started to be as common for me as seeing people sneeze. It started to catch my attention again when I was studying Psychology at the university. I was in my first year and noted that younger people had latah, even some high school students and men. It convinced me that if latah did not only happen to middle aged women like the textbook said, there may be other inaccuracies and unanswered questions.

As I advanced in my studies, I learnt about psychoanalysis. The first course was the psychoanalytic view on personality. Honestly, I could not help but noticing that my instructors and professors also had dual standards about psychoanalysis. On one hand they made it sound like a very good theory to explain people, and I personally felt that this could be a tool that I could use to answer my questions about latah. On the other hand, they made it sound like something dangerous and somehow I picked up indirect warnings not to use it in my course papers. I read a lot of the students' theses that suggested the possible use of psychoanalytic theory to explain their research problem, but I didn't see any follow up.

My suspicion was confirmed when I decided to learn more about psychoanalysis after graduating from the university. I received a lot of clear warnings from my professors. The faculty people that I talked to were divided into two. One block really supported my desire to study more about it and from them I found out that there is not even one trained psychoanalyst in Indonesia, although there are a lot of psychiatrists or psychologists who use psychoanalytic theories to explain their clients' problems. The reason, according to my professors, is the length of training and having to stay abroad to do it. It is so expensive they only could afford it if they got scholarships, but unfortunately, according to my Vice Dean, no organization would give a grant to do this training. The other block was just against the idea. They tried to convince me that psychoanalysis is difficult, not in fashion anymore and based on western culture, thus it could not be used in explaining Indonesian people. I obviously don't agree with the last one because I then took up psychoanalytic studies for my master degree anyway.

Doing an MA at the Centre for Psychoanalytic studies at the University of Essex, I discovered that there is so much more than Freud in Psychoanalysis, that Libido is not the only answer to people's behavior as I'd been taught, but it is often about complicated interactions between at least two factors - mother and child, good and bad, love and hatred, internal drives and external pressures and how people cope with these matters. Using my new tools I went back and did some empirical research on latah for my final dissertation, seeking some of the answers to my early questions. I found its aetiology more complex than just repressed sexuality as commonly supposed, but an interaction of insecure attachment, traumatic neurosis, compensation and projective identification. I learned from the participants in my study that avoidant and ambivalently attached people have different patterns in their latah behavior. The similarity between the two types is that both have some kind of love and hate relationship with the latah and the people who startle them. They said they hate it because it is embarrassing and tiring. However, they have a secondary gain after they become latah. The difference is that 'ambivalent' people project their hatred of latah towards themselves, while the 'avoidant' project their hatred towards other people that they perceived as 'weaker' than they are. They tend to see the latah they have as 'karma' because they made fun of people with latah in the past. Therefore, when they started to copy people's words when they were

230

startled, they completely stopped making fun of the others. They believe that they can never be cured and were very anxious about it, which in turn made them more susceptible to extreme physical stimuli.

The avoidant people use latah to be accepted in a peer group. They admit to feeling more accepted after they have latah. However, sometimes this type of person goes too far in embarrassing themselves. A point may come when they feel the need to retaliate to the people that embarrass them but are afraid they will leave them. Therefore they displace this need onto other people who they regard as having high susceptibility and make them hyper sensitive to shock. In this way, they can maintain a 'good' balance between being a 'victim' and a persecutor, which gives them false sense of being liked and accepted in a certain group of people.

Latah is indeed a product of society. For the society like Indonesia where obscenity is frowned upon, the saying of obscene words when latah-startled is totally excused. Therefore, these people became the tools of people's 'need' to hear someone say 'dirty words' without putting him or herself in trouble. Once a relationship is established between the latah and their startlers, they start to use each other to fulfill their goals and needs. The collusive relationship becomes so intense that sometimes it is hard to help the latah people without breaking their 'friendship'. What made me glad about this research was my increased understanding of Indonesian culture. It convinced me that we do need to build our own psychoanalysis of Indonesian people whose characteristics are both similar to, and different from, people from other countries.

I have a dream of training as a psychoanalyst and eventually helping establish a Psychoanalytic Institute so it could facilitate people who have interest to be trained locally and utilise this institute to explore questions about us Indonesian. There is still a long way for me, though. I am currently taking an MSc degree in Counseling Psychology at Chaminade University of Honolulu, Hawaii, and hope to be accepted in a PhD program somewhere with a psychoanalytic orientation, do my internships and complete further research. Hopefully by the time I am done I will meet the psychological as well as academic requirements to be accepted in psychoanalytic training somewhere in the world. But I don't have to worry about that now. I just need to concentrate on what I am doing and try to get the best out of it. Wish me luck...

Where Mind Meets Matter: how the unconscious continues to surprise us

Elizabeth Lloyd Mayer *(Berkeley)*

Sometimes a personal experience turns one's world upside-down. This is a story about an experience like that. It's also a story about the ways that experience started me re-thinking my relationship to psychoanalysis.

I have a daughter who fell in love with the harp at age 6. In 1991, when she was 11, she had begun performing a bit. In December of that year, her harp – not a classical pedal harp, but a small, levered, extremely valuable instrument built by a master harpmaker – was stolen from the theater where she was playing. For two months we went through every conceivable channel trying to get it back. Nothing worked: police, instrument dealers across the country, American Harp Society Newsletters - even a CBS TV news story.

Finally, I acted on what amounted to a dare: "If," said a wise and devoted friend (not, I hasten to add, an analyst), "if you *really* want that harp back, you should be willing to try anything. Try calling a dowser." Dowsers are that strange breed who locate underground water with forked sticks. But some dowsers, said my friend – the really good ones – can locate not just water but lost objects as well. Right, you heard it – *lost objects* . . . with *forked sticks*.

Well, nothing was happening on the police front and there I was with the dare my friend had issued, and my daughter, spoiled by several years of playing an extraordinary instrument, had found the series of commercial harps we'd rented simply unplayable. So, half-embarrassed by the act but desperate, I asked my friend if she could locate a really good dowser – the *best* , I said. (Shades of looking for a good analyst.) She promptly called the American Dowsing Society (an organization just larger than our American Psychoanalytic Society, but with a far more heterogeneous membership: well-diggers, plumbers, oil mavens, farmhands, and an assortment of New Age seekers). My friend came back with the phone number of the Society's current president: Harold McCoy, in Fayetteville, Arkansas.

I called him that day. Harold picked up the phone – friendly, cheerful, heavy Arkansas accent. I told him I'd heard he could dowse for lost objects and that I'd had a valuable harp stolen in Oakland, California. Could he help locate it?

232

"Give me a second," he said. "I'll tell you if it's still in Oakland." He paused – then: "Well, it's still in Oakland. Send me a street map of Oakland and I'll locate that harp for you." Skeptical, but recalling the dare – what, after all, *did* I have to lose? – I promptly Fed-Ex'd him a map. And waited. Two days later, he called back. "Well, I got that harp located," he said. "It's in the second house on the right on D_____ Street, just off L_____ Avenue."

I'd never heard of either street. But I did like the sound of the man's voice – whoever he was. And I don't like backing down on a dare. Why not drive to the house he'd identified? At least I'd get the address. I looked on an Oakland map and found the neighborhood. It was miles from anywhere I'd ever been. I got in my car, drove into Oakland, located the house, wrote down the number, called the police, and told them I'd gotten a tip that the harp might be at that house. Not enough information, they said. Not good enough for a search warrant.

But here's where things began to get interesting. I found I couldn't quite let it go. Was it the dare? Was it my admiration for the friend who'd instigated the whole thing? Was it that conventional avenues to retrieving the harp were getting us nowhere? Was it that the police were closing the case – claiming that the one place a unique, portable and highly marketable item would not remain was the city where it had been stolen? Or was it just that I had genuinely liked the sound of that voice on the other end of the line, and meantime had a devastated daughter on my hands?

Whatever it was, I got an idea. I could post flyers in a two-block area around the house, offering a reward for the harp's return. It was a crazy idea, but why not? As my friend said, what could I possibly lose? So, I did just that. I posted flyers in those two blocks. And only those two blocks. I was embarrassed enough about what I was doing to tell just a couple of close friends about it. (Believe me, I didn't include my psychoanalytic friends at that point; I was having enough trouble with my own internal warnings about magical thinking and the irrational lengths to which the mind can go, especially the mind of a mother wanting to save her child from distress.)

Three days later, my phone rang. A man's voice asked if this was the number for the harp. He tells me he saw a flyer outside his house and it described a stolen harp. He tells me it's exactly the harp his next-door neighbor recently obtained and showed him. He won't give me his name or number, but he offers to get the harp returned to me. And two weeks later, after a series of circuitous exchanges with the same male voice on the other end of the line, he tells me to meet a teenage boy at 10:00 PM, in the rear parking lot of an all-night Safeway. I arrive, a young man loitering in the lot looks at me and says, "The harp?" I nod. Within minutes, the harp is in the back of my station wagon and I drive off.

Twenty-five minutes later, as I turned into my driveway, I have the thought: *this changes everything*.

One of the ways it changed everything was that I began wondering about all kinds of things I'd never questioned much before. And eventually I realized I had a choice. Either I had to re-think everything – all my views of space, time, reality, and the nature of the human mind – or I had to say the whole thing simply hadn't happened. Meantime, there was the harp, back in my living room.

One of the things about getting interested in something is that you begin seeing things related to that something all over the place. You notice new things. But you also pick up on new things and question old things – and suddenly you have what amounts to an array of evidence in front of you which turns out collectively to represent information you've never looked at before. As analysts, we have that experience all the time.

That began happening as I started discovering a vast, strange new territory of research regarding anomalous mind-matter interactions. First I looked into the scientific evidence for dowsing (needless to say, it was research about finding water, not lost objects). But very soon I began encountering reports from some very respectable scientific minds about all kinds of other, possibly related anomalous phenomena.

In addition, as psychoanalytic colleagues began hearing I was interested in anomalies, I was inundated by accounts of their anomalous experiences – personal as well as clinical. Often they were experiences those colleagues had never revealed to another professional associate. Their accounts – by e-mail, snail mail, in Institute corridors, at parties, in a Discussion Group on "Intuition, Unconscious Communication and 'Thought Transference'," which I have now been leading for several years with Carol Gilligan at the APA – came at a rate which kept me wedded to the project of sifting through the huge domain of research on anomalous mind-matter interactions. I was certainly struck by the stories, but I was equally struck by the apparent relief my colleagues felt at telling them. Both seemed to me to represent evidence of conflict, conflict that goes way beyond psychoanalysts and what psychoanalysts do or don't comfortably talk about in how they know what they know.

The fact is, we live in a culture which leads most rational people to feel uncomfortable having the odd experience they view as anomalous. The

234

crunch comes when people have those experiences anyway. Then there's a conflict – one which can corrode the most personal and private corners of how people experience themselves in the world. It's conflict about what to do when an anomalous experience comes your way and you can't allow yourself publically to acknowledge it. It's not about getting it to make sense. It's about admitting to it at all.

As analysts know better than anyone, there's a sense of helplessness that ensues when people need to deny their experience of what's real. Worse, the sense of self-betrayal can become a slippery slope, as honest people start to feel dishonest and thoughtful people stop themselves from thinking. The fear of appearing credulous or crazy leads to daily, subtle disavowals that end up paralyzing people's creativity, conscience, and – ultimately – their freedom to be themselves in the world.

The harp's return forced a question on me. Certainly, it wasn't a new question, but suddenly it had new weight. *How do we know what we know?* Especially, how do we know what we know in the dim realm dominated by what we call intuition?

I'm beginning to think that efforts to understand anomalous events like the harp's return may teach us something about psychoanalytic knowing as well as intuitive knowing in general – most of all, may teach us something about a peculiar quality of deep connectedness that undergirds both. What if we as psychoanalysts were to take on the challenge of truly comprehending such events, treating them as possible avenues into exploring the human mind and its relation to reality as filled with fundamental impact for our world as Freud's extraordinary discoveries were for his generation? Is it conceivable that, in this day and age, psychoanalysis could galvanize our grasp – a genuinely systematic and non-superstitious grasp – of a radical connectedness and its relationship to knowledge that could help take us towards just those new levels of healing, societal adaptation and human capacity we're desperately needing? Maybe – even – turn us into better, more helpful psychoanalysts?

It's an exciting possibility.

(from a more extended account of the same events in Elizabeth Lloyd Mayer's forthcoming book about anomalous experience and its relation to unconscious mental processing)

The Vampire   Luis Rodríguez de la Sierra *(Madrid/London)*

'He possessed to the ultimate degree that demonic instinct and allure that influenced others, independently of reason . . .'

[Goethe, Conversations with Eckermann]

'He believed in nothing, save for vice itself and a living God who existed for the sole purpose of making possible the enjoyment of evil.'

[Flaubert, Portrait of Lord Byron]

The Vampire, one of the most enduring, popular myths of all time, has innumerable links to other legends and superstitions. The image is also entwined in a multitude of diverse perversions. In addition it is a universal myth not confined within any one specific cultural tradition. All this would indicate the existence of a psychic representation of the myth, necessary for its projection and dissemination; a representation that has been in existence since a remote past and which can be considered as one of the most archaic images we know.

A mere glance at the various mythologies of the ancients reveals vampiric tendencies in many of man's gods. We find these in the legends and mythology of the Greeks (the Lamiae) and Romans (the Strigas), as well as the rest of Europe, Asia (Biblical Lilith) and parts of Africa. These gods were all given to sucking or drinking blood. We encounter a whole group of deities in Tibetan Lamaism, the Vajra, who drink blood to achieve control over life and death. In one of the oldest tales ever recorded, the legend of Gilgamesh, hero of a Babylonic epic, the theme of the Vampire appears already with characteristics described in so precise and gory a fashion as to be just like those Vampires of medieval and more recent times. The oldest depiction of a Vampire appears in a prehistoric Assyrian bowl. It shows a man, copulating with a headless Vampire. In pre-Colombian Mexico Vampires appear, known as 'sihuateteo', women who have died in childbirth. The Chinese Vampire, Ching Shih, cited frequently in the stories of the T'ang dynasty, originates in a much more distant past and bears a great resemblance to his Western counterparts. Possibly the myth of the Vampire came to Western Europe from India, via Turkey and the Balkans.

It is in a work of Lord Byron that the Vampire first makes his full triumphal entrance in European literature. Lord Byron, himself an ideal prototype for all the Vampires that ever have been or ever will be; an aristocrat by birth, handsome and seductive, the cultured and cynical libertine of the Ancient Régime lived on in him. He anticipated the decadent and narcissistic dandy of the Fin de Siècle. In his eternal quest for new sensations, Byron turned transgression into a positive value. At the famous gathering, which saw the birth of Frankenstein, in Villa Diodati, Lord Byron's mansion by the shores of Lake Leman, the poet

236

conceived his famous essay *'Fragment of a Story'* (June 17th 1816) which was published as a postscript to *'Mazeppa'* in 1819. It was his retort to a story, *'The Vampyre',* by John William Polidori (London 1819). Taking advantage of Byron's absence, Polidori had set about developing a concept outlined by Byron, plagiarising the idea and thus becoming the first literary Vampire. Later contributors include Goethe (1797), Baudelaire (1857), Le Fanu (1872) and Bram Stoker (1897) who were all to write about the Vampire as did the Marquis de Sade (1791)*. However, with rare exceptions, the Vampire theme is absent from psychoanalytic literature. Two authors immediately come to mind though: Ernest Jones and Fenichel. In his book, *'On the Nightmare',* Ernest Jones (1931) dedicates an entire chapter to the theme. Fenichel (1945), in *'The Psychoanalytic Theory of Neurosis',* discusses infantile sexuality, noting the frequency with which 'we can observe suction fantasies of an oral-sadistic type directed against the objects', and uses the word 'Vampire' in this respect.

The Vampire myth is extremely complex and would seem to represent the condensation of a broad range of psychopathological conditions. If it is certain that in the delirious fantasies of psychotic and severe borderline cases, the figure of a voracious, relentless persecutor – the Vampire – features prominently and frequently, my attention has always been drawn by the fact that this same fantasy is to be found in patients who are far less disturbed, and whose psychopathology would originate at a later developmental stage, closer to neurosis than to psychosis. Actual cases of vampirism are fairly rare, but the Vampiric content of many desires and fantasies can often be seen as reaction-formations, as sublimations and in dreams. Similar fantasies of drawing blood or biting someone until they bleed are often encountered in the analysis of neurotics. Although they may feel the desire to bite, for example during sexual intercourse, it remains a thought never actually acted out. I would also like to mention two examples of Vampire-like activities not considered pathological: the Eucharist in which the blood of Christ is drunk, and sucking on a cut finger.

The Vampire myth can be understood as a fantasy at various levels of development. We can situate it in the oedipal phase, with the Vampire seen as an abductor of women, killing or enslaving any remaining men that cross his path. The Vampire portrayed in "Nosferatu", the film by Herzog, is a depressed Vampire who regresses to an earlier level of sexual development, the sado-masochism of the Oral-Sadistic and the Anal-Sadistic stages. The richness of psychopathological nuances in the Vampire is limitless. Just ponder over the parallels with the psychopathology of the neurotic, the addict and of some sexual perversions, above all homosexuality, male as well as female. Oddly enough these latter themes barely rate a mention in the psychoanalytic literature, whereas contemporary fiction is full of references and allusions

237

to the intimate connections between vampirism and sexual perversion. It is no accident that the Vampire is frequently presented on screen and in novels as a figure of the ultimate seductiveness.

The fantasy of joining the dead, seen now from the perspective of hatred, may be clarified: the mechanism is identical to the substance of childhood terrors, that is to say, the fear of reprisals for having done bad things or for having had evil thoughts. Anyone who has repressed feelings of hatred is much more likely to encounter bad dreams, nightmares or the fear of encountering evil spirits, thus revealing his fear of being punished by the person towards whom he has had these malicious intentions. Generally speaking, one could say that the great abundance of these unconscious murderous wishes explains the attitude that is held towards the supernatural, an attitude that is a mixture of fascination and terror and explains the intertwined feelings of love and hate in our relationship with the Vampire myth.

Freud (1905 – 1916/1917) tells us that all emotions that reach a certain level of intensity, including the feeling of horror, have an effect upon sexuality. The sexual connotations attributed to the Vampire would be nothing more than the projection of suppressed sexual desires. Ernest Jones, in his book *"On the Nightmare"*, thus explains the idea that the Vampire can transform himself at will into various animals, for example bats, eagles, wolves, cats, etc. The seductive and mental character of the Vampire takes perfect form in Lord Ruthven, the satanic lord of Polidori and of Lady Caroline Lamb, in her novel *"Glenarvon"* (1816), a character clearly inspired by Lord Byron, her lover.

Ernest Jones related the fantasy of sucking blood to cannibalistic ideas on the one hand and sexuality on the other. According to him, the Vampire's nocturnal visits and the drawing of blood can be connected to wet dreams, as is confirmed in many of the legends of folklore the world over. He continues by telling us that the mixture of sadism and hatred also forms a part of the explanation for those fantasies in which a spirit that visits us by night can overwhelm our willpower and being through loving embraces that end up taking away our life. When the more normal aspects of sexuality are repressed, there is a tendency to regress to earlier stages of development. Sadism is one of the principal types and oral sadism, one of the initial forms of sadism, plays an important rôle in the myth of the Vampire. The earliest stage, which is that of sucking and precedes the biting stage, would be that with the greatest connection to the love side of the relationship, while sadism would be closely connected with the element of biting in the vampiric ritual.

Is it perhaps a mere fascination for the macabre that has assured the survival and the present importance of this myth? Can it simply be explained away as mere atavism? Is it the instincts of death and destruction that have given substance to the universal extension of the Vampire myth? Or perhaps we can just say that man's perverse nature is

238

capable of conjuring up the image of the Vampire in whatever phase of his development, as an incarnation of evil and the antithesis of good. Possibly so, but there are many and various means of expressing this, usually tied to a specific culture, whereas the image of the Vampire transcends these boundaries with a rare universality. It would not be illogical to suppose that this myth has much greater implications than are at first obvious, or to suppose that its significance and universal persistence suggest roots that penetrate deeply into the evolution of the very core of our psychic essence. The image of the Vampire seems to symbolise the dichotomy between our animal nature and the social essence of the human being and represents the desire to conquer the secret of life using the methods of a wild animal. The Vampire symbolises the omnipresent desire to conquer the secret of life, at the same time containing elements of the renewal of life itself. On the other hand, the negative side of the same coin is symbolised by the terrible desire for survival, which would bring him to destroy a human being in order to maintain his own existence. If the fear of death can be compared with the fear of the unconscious and if life has its parallels in the lukewarm blood that flows through the human being, the Vampire could be seen as a projection of the struggle for life. After all, in one of the most sacred rituals in our western culture, the Eucharist, we drink the wine that represents the blood of Christ to renew ourselves and show symbolically the triumph of the forces of life over death, of the forces of good over the forces of evil.

Finally I wish to evoke the Byronesque Vampire: the fascinating seducer, magical and supernatural. The Vampire whose allure certain people try to resist but to which others frequently succumb. We are thus left with the image of the fascination of evil. Vampirism, as a mortal sin, is contained by the image that most often comes to mind: that of the perverse nature or essence of the vampiric act, in which the bite and the sucking of blood produce an orgasmic sensation, which supersedes the normal act of coitus.

References

Byron, Lord (1819) *Fragment of a Novel,* in *Mazeppa.*

Fenichel, O. (1945) *The Psychoanalytical Theory of Neurosis.* New York: W.W. Norton & Company, Inc.

Freud, S. (1905) *Three Essays on the Theory of Sexuality.* S.E.7.

       (1916-1917) *Introductory Lectures on Psychoanalysis.* Part III. General Theory of The neurosis. S.E. 16.

Jones, E. (1931) *On the Nightmare.* London: Hogarth Press

Polidori, J.W. (1819) *The Vampyre.*

* Detailed references to these and other writings appear in the author's paper on the subject 'Treatment Report on the First Eighteen Months of the Analysis of a 13-Year Old Boy', *The Bulletin of the Anna Freud Centre,* London, 1986.

THE CREATIVE URGE

'Noah Releasing the Dove'

'The artist has many tasks to perform if he is to function creatively. These concern essentially the facing and working through, of areas of conflict, inside and outside himself, which must then be integrated and made meaningful through his art work[...] It is the very mysteriousness of the powers of integration that constitutes art. The area of the human personality that does the integrating is also the source of art...

Clinical psycho-analysis and art-work share one major task: to make the unconscious conscious.[...] The artist in company with us all, is concerned to exteriorize his inner awareness. This is done in bodily activity but also by means of a psychical projection, whereby one sends forth from the self, attributes to an external object...

Freud has shown that in human life there is the need to respond to a series of losses that occur... Adult creativity may occur after the controlled regression to such points of incomplete integration or fixation, and their working through which provides a release of energy previously used in maintaining the painful experience out of awareness in some degree, while the coming together of the self as enhanced self-awareness gives an additional boost to confidence and drive. This is the basis of much inspiration and of the burning need to go into action and render the mental images in some real medium' *[Genesis exhibition notes, 1974]*

Sculpture and writing by British Psychoanalyst Ismond Rosen
[Reproduced here by kind permission of his widow, Ruth Rosen]

240

Noah and the Dove* Valerie Sinason *(London)*

Fearful of deluge
winged heart drenched
I enter his house alone
I enter his tree land

Where the oxygen flows
and the copy of my soul
is carved in cedar wood

He holds me
as only sky can hold bird
knows me as sea knows fish
I home in him
and find my element

I nest on the ark of his palm
watching his God face
rise above the leaping waters

And as I mend
I look out and see the dark ring of water
and my warm breath is a small God
that feathers and shivers
the wings of waves

And to move
to want to move
is when the water inside you
leaps for longing to meet the water outside

And "Dove?" He asks
His voice holding
the body of my soul
He placing me as look-out
from under the Ark of his neck
He re-membering my wingspan
Letting the rolling air
take me for call of mate
"There is land"

* Poem about my psychoanalysis with the late Dr Mervin Glasser
inspired by Psychoanalyst Ismond Rosen's Sculpture of Noah

241

Creative Writing; Sublimation Or Exploitation?

John Woods *(London)*

Writing a play about psychotherapy, about adolescence, abuse, drug addiction, suicide, and failed treatment may well have seemed an unpromising prospect, perhaps more a recipe for disaster! But I started writing with no clear aim in mind. Instead I was giving vent to feelings and thoughts about cases (people whom I was trying to help), and staff group dynamics (situations involving people I was supposed to be working with). In fact the background experiences were a general mix of therapeutic 'failures' and professional (near) disasters. Because they were 'impossible' situations, full of unknowns, and subject to any number of interpretations, I felt free to imagine stories and the characters. The fictional form of letters appealed to me because I felt I could give free rein to my imagination, and say things that would otherwise be unacceptable.

The play opens with Mary addressing the audience, reading out the long suicide letter that she has just written to the social worker who has taken away her children. Trting to justify her actions, she complains about the lack of help, and the inept treatment she has received... 15 years later, Mary's son Sylvan fails to attend his sessions with an inexperienced therapist , but writes to her. She replies, but gets into difficulties with her seniors...

At the time of writing I vaguely thought that this series of letters might tie together well enough to make something like a novel. But when I showed some early drafts to one or two people, they thought it could work dramatically. And so I shaped the piece in that direction. I was well supported by my fellow professionals. Sally Willis, a group analyst with a background in the theatre, felt that the piece could work on the stage, and so she set about recruiting a cast. This consisted first of amateurs, who gradually, as performances proceeded, gave way to trained actors. I feel particularly indebted to Bryan Boswood for fostering that first stage, and to Ann Alvarez who promoted the first public airing at a Conference on Trauma at the Tavistock Centre in November 1999. Since then five further performances have ensued, and more are planned. But despite the confidence of others, each time the event drew nearer I have been almost overwhelmed by anxieties approaching the level of sheer terror. My worries about disapproval, ridicule, embarrassment, rejection, have turned into a rising panic as I realised how much of myself I might have exposed, unintentionally, in these stories. But now, as I see the piece again and marvel at its being brought to life, and see different aspects, connections I had not exactly planned, I wonder also at how it all came from somewhere that was both *me* and *not me*, from something that cannot really be called *my* unconscious. As I have been reassured, (as well as amazed), at the positive responses it has received, I have also begun to feel somewhat detached, and separate. It is as though the story has a life of its own, becoming a sort of magic formula which calls up those characters, people who are perhaps like old friends, from another part of my life.

Who is Who?

I did not set out to produce a play, so it is not surprising that the text is not exactly a drama. The characters do not speak to each other, but are trying to find their own voice. The process started with the adolescent, Sylvan who wanted to be heard, but could not bear anyone to listen. He came to represent not only the young people I may have failed, but also the failed young man I could have been. Poems came to mind that seemed from him, not me. Here was a different version of myself. Since I was not really that self-destructive young person, I had to think what would have happened to have made me so. What would his mother have been? As she too became real her voice became clearer and I knew then that she was still consumed with rage. That was the anger and the protest that echoed down the years and was burning up this boy. For a time I found myself dreaming what seemed to be her dreams. Thus she in turn became another inner voice, another self-possibility. She was not my mother, but (again) could have been. I have been asked whether *John*, the group therapist, is actually *me*, or is *Sylvan* really *Woods?* *Helen*, the junior therapist undergoes an initiation into malignant staff group dynamics which is very similar to my own experiences a few years ago, (in a team that shall remain nameless.), and pays the *Price*. But I also had great sympathy with her boss *Dr Hermann,* who takes the role of villain. He has the courage to say the necessary 'No'. So when Nancy Brenner of the Anna Freud Centre said that she could hear my voice in all the characters, even though each was believably different, I felt I had received the greatest compliment. But if they are all aspects of myself, what am I doing using my patients' material , their lives, in this way?

The Use of Art and the Use of Patients

After a recent performance I looked at Joyce McDougall's *Many Faces of Eros*. She says that 'there is always a risk that a creative act will be experienced unconsciously as a crime against the parents'... because... 'one must assume the right to be both fertile womb, and the fertilizing penis,' (McDougall, 1977: 101). *Sylvan*, my adolescent character proclaims art as 'the only important thing'. He is using his creativity as an alternative to reality. Poetry is an area of omnipotence for him, and he rejoices that he does not know what it means, i.e. that he has no responsibility to relate it to the reality of the rest of his life. Coming from a family of artists, I know that art is far from automatically good and

243

healthy. It is characteristic of adolescence to try things out, to test limits, to seek outlandish experiences, and then after a while, to work them through, in something like psychotherapy. In my story, however, *Sylvan's* creativity draws upon his hatred of the parents, and his self hatred, and he is left without a safe haven. In this scenario both therapist and patient are exploited.

As a psychotherapist I feel in awe of both Science and Art. A practitioner is expected to work within the limits of observable phenomena, but I also believe that there are certain problems of psychotherapy that are only accessible through creative means. The effectiveness of treatment may depend on unmeasurable qualities, like the capacity for empathy, or the ability of therapists to be guided by their own internal process. This brings us up against subjectivity, wishful thinking, and omnipotent solutions to the clash between fantasy and reality. But art too cannot exist in a solipsistic universe. If it is to communicate (and is it worth anything if it does not communicate?), it has to be about a struggle with reality.

In a discussion of my play, a Portman Clinic colleague Dr Estela Welldon associated to an experience coincidentally similar to an episode from *The End of Abuse*. She had been agonising over a difficult case, an assessment report of a young mother for the Court. She visited an art gallery and saw a Giacometti that perfectly expressed the emptiness at the core of a maternal relationship. Then, said Estela, she knew what it was she was seeing in the clinical work. In my story *Helen*, a junior therapist, preoccupied with her feelings about *Sylvan*, sees Rodin's statue of The Prodigal Son and her hopes are sustained, that in some way her patient, will, after all, find salvation. In these events there seems to have been a moment when the therapist steps back emotionally, detaches herself somewhat and looks at her own experience from a new angle. In this way she finds a communication which is both from outside and within her own world, a perception of art that makes sense of both the separation and the involvement. In the aesthetic experience, so it seems to me, therapist and the patient are the same, even though they are also different; the privileged self of 'therapist' gives way momentarily, to an inner experience for the therapist of the underprivileged self we call 'patient'.

Individual & Group; the Psychic and the Social

In the final episode of the play we hear from Ruth, Mary's daughter, and a child no longer, ranting against her group therapist. She rages that he does not, and cannot, understand her history of loss and abuse. But then her therapist talks about his work with her, in relation to other group members.

244

At last it seemed that the protests could be heard, in the arena of a group. I do not think I was saying here, as some have thought, that I believe only in group therapy. No, like much else in the text, it just seemed right in that context. I felt at that time that to write about individual therapy was going to be more difficult and I was putting it off to some other time. But the group also came to mind I think because it represented, as it does now, my own need of the family, friends, colleagues, and our 'therapeutic' community of other therapists, who have sustained me. No psychotherapist can go on indefinitely with 'individual' work without regular recourse to his, or her, own group, of whatever description. In this play an organised depiction of my inner chaos has been made real and comprehensible by a group, a complexity of several groups, too numerous to mention here. These real groups seem to have nurtured the neglected children of my imagination. What emerges at the end in her final letter to her therapist, is an acceptance by Ruth that she cannot have him to herself, and so she is released from the traumatic loss of her mother. What I felt I was witnessing as it came to me in this story, was that which had been so difficult, a healthy separation and growth, a completion and a new beginning.

The End of Abuse by John Woods is published by Open Gate Press

Notes on Sublimation, Psychoanalysis and the Sublime Or 'Fate can do nothing against one'

Helen Taylor Robinson *(London)*

In *Civilisation and its Discontents* Freud writes

> *'Another technique for fending off suffering is the employment of the displacements of libido which our mental apparatus permits of and through which its function gains so much in flexibility. The task here is that of shifting the instinctual aims in such a way that they cannot come up against frustration from the external world. In this, sublimation of the instincts lends its assistance. One gains the most if one can sufficiently heighten the yield of pleasure from the sources of psychical and intellectual work. When that is so, fate can do little against one. A satisfaction of this kind, such as an artist's joy in creating, in giving his phantasies body, or a scientist's in solving problems or discovering truths, has a special quality which we shall certainly **one day** be able to characterise in metapsychological terms. At present we can only say figuratively that such satisfactions seem 'finer and higher'. But their intensity is mild as compared with that derived from the sating of crude and primary instinctual impulses; **it does not convulse our physical being**. And the weak point of this method is that it is not applicable generally: it is accessible to only a few people. It presupposes the possession of special dispositions and gifts which are far from being common to any practicable degree. And even to the few who possess them, **this method cannot give complete protection from suffering.** It creates no impenetrable armour against the arrows of fortune, and it habitually fails when the source of suffering is the person's own body'* [S.E.21:80. Italics added].

I want to use this brief extract from Freud on his understanding of sublimation, with reference to how, as analysts, we might take up experience 'behind the couch and between sessions' such that the civilisation of 'psychoanalysis' in which we have all been reared, and some of its veritable discontents, can be approached with Freud in mind, but **without Freud's mind** (i.e. his way of using his mind and my discontent with it). In this little extract (and there is more here on 'work' as not entirely sublimation, pleasure in art as but a mild narcotic, and all kinds of other illusory ways Man has for keeping suffering, most unsuccessfully at bay), I want to look at the difference between Freud's wishes for psychoanalysis and its capacity for sublimation and what he feels is a necessarily disappointing reality, psychoanalysis' limitations, as against its potential, and particularly, the emphasis he gives to each. For it is part of my discontent with him and has a bearing on how we, as his analytic offspring, proceed.

Firstly Freud abandons 'the sublime' for 'sublimation' as the aim in the human struggle. And here is my prime discontent.
The metaphoric meaning of sublimation 'elevation to a higher state or plane of existence; transmutation into something higher, purer, or more sublime'(O.E.D.) and the psychoanalytic meaning 'the action of directing an obstructed impulse away from its primitive aim to activities of a higher order' (O.E.D.) are linked but different. The chemical process from which the metaphoric image arises is the process of chemical action by which a solid substance is subjected to heat and the vapour that arises when cooled down and solidified again seen as refined or purified, certainly improved if not highly so. Putting our aim as sublimation then for Freud is redirecting our obstructed impulse into a higher form. And this is leaving aside the question of the aim as conscious and/or unconscious.
But if we challenge Freud here then we might ask why the human psyche's aim is set on sublimation and not upon that which is sublime. We might ask why we need to be agents, and active verbs express us, as in 'to sublimate', to carry out the process of sublimation in the scientific sense of the original, why we are denied by Freud's account the adjectival form of 'sublime' which describes or informs us as to a given noun, or indeed why we are denied the substantive noun form itself' **the** sublime'. For it is this restriction of use that I view as leading Freud away from the contents and towards the discontents in his exploratory thinking here.
The sublime' may be defined as 'of ideas, truths ,subjects etc; Belonging to the highest regions of thought, reality or human activity (O.E.D.) As the noun substantive, 'the sublime', as against sublimation 'is'. It is not something to be **created** by the more or less healthy psyche, for it pre-exists us and in relation to it we come second. Here 'the sublime' is Prime as in 'the- already- created to which we also give the name god or godhead, and it is all that is good **without us and our strivings**. In so doing, we leave Ourselves, the whole psychoanalytic exploration of the Self, out of the picture as godhead, and come in second place to what already exists. This second place might be called the everlasting condition of human suffering immutable, to which Freud also refers, and with which I express my second discontent.
For if we suppose an existence in which we came First, we would have to assume that for us, such a primacy provided all as desired and all would be Well. Suffering is, however, the knowledge of coming second in the world-as-is, the sublime as created, the given universe that has no thought for us as godheads, us as Prime, our primacy. Which is why the work of poets who contemplate the divine and praise it (all poetry is prayer, all poems for Rilke 'praisings') is no act of sublimation, rather a contemplation of the state of the Divine. For the poet it is not how can I

247

make this satisfy and fend off suffering and pain, though writing or creating might incidentally provide that, as might many lesser activities, but rather, it is a reaching to such insight that receives the divine, the mystery plucked from universal time, and loses it again, but for the body or creation of that reception in the written word. If the sublime, which is the highest form of whatsoever might be in process were now our aim, as against sublimation, then we might again argue with Freud that when the artist gives his phantasies body, the intensity of that experience **does** transcend and transform, transfigure, metamorphose (all words that connote difference from the initial state of the phantasies to which a body never before so shaped has been found) the cruder primary instinctual impulses, thus giving eternal, universal, monumental satisfaction.

We might say then that a great creative and imaginative endeavour feeds eternally in ways that the hunger of and for everyday reality can never do. And we would have to challenge Freud's notion that this, the sublime (not sublimation) does more than convulse our being, the pleasure of creation, of giving forth and that fending off suffering here is not the aim, a short term activity unrelated to the sublime, but rather that the act of creation itself is a product of new, never before so shaped forces and challenges in some great or small way the monumental scale of death, equally and unequivocally as a representation of monumental Life. Thus a work of the imagination be it artistic or scientific in its use of this faculty will represent the sublime in so far as it approximates to the highest forms or planes of human capability. When that is so 'fate can do nothing against one' because one is One with the creation, not at odds, not striving, not an agent of its construction, but a bearer of its sublime truths, the conduit for its presence, one 'is' rather than 'does to'.

This state, however briefly recognised as attained between sessions and behind the couch, we might say at any point of the experience of life, and as an antidote perhaps to the strivings of psychoanalytic work and some of its shorter term aims and ambitions is a state that bears no equal, and can only be found in **the imaginative reconstruction of experience**, not in experience itself. This is open to us all, gifted or less gifted, it is a capacity within us and its pursuit and attainment potential, if not achieved by all of us in every aspect of its existence, whether by a piece of writing about it, such as this, or some other form of imaginative work.

To credit the imaginative powers in their apperception of the sublime seems not to be a trait of psychoanalytic understanding at this point in Freud's writing. It remains to be seen whether its due place in relation to the awareness of the sublime gains professional psychoanalytic credence and favour. If it does not, it nevertheless exists and psychoanalysis which owes so much to the imagination of its creator and those that followed

248

may suffer all that fate can do against it for its lack of acknowedgement. For it is the case that the word 'imagination', although a power used by Freud throughout his entry into psychoanalysis and its way of thinking, has no place in his index, no name for such a faculty, no acknowledgement for its part in breeding psychoanalysis. And we might say that to disregard this aspect of mentality whilst pursuing all others will, as psychoanalysts cost us dearly, from within our working lives and in the public arena. To imagine the sublime is a human trait of mind; we cannot, like Freud, excuse our unconscious for not yet knowing what it is metapsychologically and leaving it to the artists and the minority. Or should I say that if we do, fate can do anything against us.

Notes from my consulting room window

Valli Shaio Kohon*(London)*

Early Morning

I step out of the warm kitchen, smell the air. The big blue stoneware bowl glints with its disk of ice. Soft grey dawn, a pink tinge of cloud shows in the day. The overture, by the birds, had already started a couple of hours before. I unlock the consulting room door, my journey to work at an end.

One

As I wait, I notice the blackbirds waiting on the rim of the stoneware bowl for a turn to bathe. The tits watch from a low branch of the magnolia; when the blackbirds finish, they swoop down for a quick drink. One frozen day I put out a bowl of fresh water, thinking they all might be thirsty. To my surprise, many of them hopped in for a wash.

Two

The magpies are nest-building. One flies with a yard-long twig in its beak and plunges into the dense giant leylandii trees that loom over the houses at the end of my neighbour's garden. Nothing moves, I imagine the dark fragrance of their den. Then, spruce and elegant and pristine, the magpie stands nonchalant on a tiniest feather of tree-top, flies down to the old pear tree. There, underlined by the long branch of red sprouting rose leaves that trail through it, he quickly picks a few buds, cleans his beak. His toilette over, he flicks his tail importantly.

Three

A huge row in the garden and just as I am about to come out, in the five minute break, I stop in uncomprehending amazement. In the middle of the lawn stands a large dirty brown bustard astride a dead pigeon. Rocking to keep its balance, it pulls a strip of bloody flesh from the mess between its feet, surrounded by a fan of grey-white feathers.

Four

I put out some old grapes and plums on the lawn thinking, *they eat fruit, don't they?* But it's the squirrel who picks up each round green grape and eats it like a Granny Smith held between its paws, taking rapid bites. Later, it carries off a huge dark plum in its mouth, and, in an improbable feat, climbs up the fence and disappears.

Five

The wood pigeons are the biggest in my garden, balancing in their fat roundness on the thinnest twigs, or the edge of the fence, comical at mating-time. The tiniest bird came this week, perched with the blue-tits on the bare magnolia branches. Two inches long, brown, I wish I knew its name.

The late winter mornings are the best, black sharp stripes of venetian blind drawn on the wall by the early sunlight. The geometry of my day: wooden slats, lattice, fifty-minute spaces, holding the wildlife in and out.

On being an analyst / Judith Issroff c.1974 *(London)*

Unnerved, unarmed, or rather dislocated
in the having to listen and listening,
in the having to empathise leaking of me,
in the constant scrutiny
and waiting for my words,
by my awareness of their need for me,
by my essential inner withdrawal,
my polite distaste for,
my not really wanting to know
or placing a different significance
on their failed dreams, hopes, conflicts, plans -
I sit like Janus on so many thresholds
semi-indifferent in my scrutiny of their multiplicity of worlds
within, without, in, out, with,
interfacing
interpenetrating
non-penetrable
impervious
and vulnerable,
another functioning-structure relative
in the shifting space-time
of their-my worlds.

My undreamt dream eludes me.
Solitude evokes its own
admixed feelings,
calm, fears, longing.
Closeness also tantalises
with its unbearable distances.

Humans, improbably organised immensities,
macromolecules in inexplicable Brownian movements,
unique wave forms
bobbing, wobbling about, trying
to make sense
with inadequate symbols
of that which
they imagine they have lived, or might have, or might,
scrabbling about
clutching at ideas,
clutching at each other, 'letting go'
and not letting go:

symbols stimulate and the non-symbolic encounters compel
actions and reactions
all hustling back to
pristine quietude,
the eternal spectre sometimes glimpsed.

I represent something lost
       and not yet found,
       hinted at, a possibility
       of possession never claimed   all
       a love-affection constant   unviolated
       an indifference constant   and
       a respect constant   unviolable

You love and hate me
       for the intensity and depth of what we share.

Of course you must hate me
       for all the moments of intimacy and growth
       we might have shared and spurned

but haven't,
       for abrasiveness
       and for mutual failure -
       for our terrible awareness
       and withdrawal.

You hate me for the insincerity
       of the not-lived,
of the murdered mutilated boy/girl/mother/father presence

You hate me for finding someone else
       with the smile of the Buddha,
       the genuine thing,
equally inconstant.

M.M.R.Khan / Judith Issroff c. 1981

Once upon a memory
Mohammed Masud (self-styled) Rajah Khan:
(onetime one of my analysts)
patted my never adequately tamed curls
and graciously proclaimed:
'God bless you, my dear girl!'

'I never realised you were a believer.'

'It's a useful notion: relieves one of the burden
of so much omnipotence!'
came his swift retort.

When we started meeting, the first sally of this brilliant,
strangely insecure
(possibly bastard) Pakistani son of a dancer and local tyrant
was to inform me
that he came from a line of eight hundred years of princes
and that his father's suit of armour was on display
in the Imperial War Museum
while I was nothing but a commoner -
to which, with an inner chuckle,
thinking to myself that I am Judith, daughter of David-son of-Judah-son
of Israel, and my brother is named Saul,
our lineage perhaps almost two thousand years longer -
I replied merely that I had been reared
With a different set of prejudices.
And that night I dreamt him as 'John',
 Zulu servant of my South African childhood.

Once Masud said:
'Truth, who needs truth? That's for literature!'
and,
with a grand and accusing gesture:
              'You, with your damned Jewish sense
              of integrity and honesty,
              you're your own worst enemy!'
The day when Svetlana Beriosova,
haunted lovely haunting face peeping sometimes
when I passed,

his famous ballerina third wife, finally left him,
Masud stated firmly that he was
'not going to let four bad years ruin the memory of twelve good ones',
and wrote what he considered would be deemed 'the definitive paper'
about the *écriture* of the analyst to whom he'd sent her, Michael Balint,
'in order to be assured that his reputation will rest in my hands.'

Masud helped me to deal with Balint
(still then a supervisor of mine -
Michael Balint wanted me to work in Israel which
did not yet re-exist when he'd fled Nazified Hungary).
Balint took sadistic pleasure in reducing me to tears
by expecting me to do the impossible, 'better than best':
'Your first version was good enough for anyone else,
certainly quite good enough for the Training Committee,
but I expect you to do better,
'better than best' - like the *'prestissimo*, and yet still faster'
instruction for playing the finale of Schumann's Carnival!'
But Balint didn't pre-decease Masud by very many years,
and in whose hands or whose words or assessment
does whose reputation rest?

What's a 'reputation' in the chasing truths chasing literature?

Masud gave appreciative, full respect
to me and my 'matching headpiece' as Winnicott called it
when he insisted that I was enough myself and hale
to risk further analysis with his protégé
and enriching cultural alien shadow.

With my permission Winnicott was simultaneously
both my and Masud's supervisor:
he played with, quieted and 'held' me:
He held Masud in check till his death.
'A personal tragedy for you', said Masud,
hugging me after our post-funeral meditative hour
shared in communicative silence:
'D.W.W. said you gained more from him in five years
than everyone else in twenty five:
You needed one more year to become like me'

Did Masud never realize I never wanted to be anyone but myself?

Anyway, who can believe a self-confessed liar!?

255

I have been trying to rectify what Masud termed
my 'lack of a healthy sense of paranoia'
- living in Israel has helped -
I am not going to let his madness, his sadness, his seductive needs, target
practice in the living-room,
the let-downs, the messes, moodiness, and
despite all his 'very best friends',
the rabid anti-Semitic outbursts which ultimately led to his
ex-communication from the community of psychoanalysts
(to whom he contributed so very much)
spoil the muchness of the best of our meetings,
while I remain staunchly
my own worst enemy.

Cat's Tango* Gregorio Kohon *(Buenos Aires/London)*

I came back from El Tigre to our house in San Telmo
thinking that I'd still find you there
as usual
that we could again play together in the garden
I'd doze under the sun while you raced round my feet pawing my toes.
Before I departed
I spent some time with you in her room.
You were all atremble, wrapped in towels
on the blue carpet of her choice.
No one could stay with you for long
the stench of your breath invaded our clothes.
I didn't want to accept nor could I fully understand
that after your friend's death
after that tragic fall from the third floor window
you were the only thing left to us.

Nothing else could have kept us
to
  ge
    ther.

We took turns feeding you every four hours
we forced you to drink warm milk
and the syrupy medicine specially prescribed.
We fed you with a small plastic spoon
cleaned your whiskers and your weak paws
afraid of breaking any of your bones.
Sometimes you stood
-who knows where you're getting strength from?-
and paused in front of the door
waiting
begging us to let you go.
We knew what you wanted, Belmondo
to die in the garden, among the pampas-grass
hidden by the tall stalks with their silky racemes
closer to your friend's grave.

257

And I have to confess
that while travelling around
so far away from you
all those days I spent on the boat
going down the Paraná River
crossing from one bank to the other, stopping
in the small villages by the eternally brown waters
none of my thoughts
                    then
had been for you.
I couldn't believe that you'd ever die.

*(from *The Style of Desire*, unpublished)

After Dark, Before Dawn

Rosine Jozef Perelberg *(London)* & Bella Jozef *(Rio Dejaneiro)*

When Bella and I decided to write something together during one of my holidays in Brasil, we soon realised that we kept different hours. Bella is an early morning person, whereas I tend not to even start thinking about writing until the evening, when I am there. So we decided that we would each stick to our own individual pace and see where this would lead us. Each evening, as I switched on the computer, I saw what Bella had written during the day, and in turn each morning she approached what I had written the previous night. We embarked on thinking about Latin American novels. We chose the books we wanted to think about together; in many ways, the way we worked together seemed to match the multiplicity of structures and temporal dimensions of the books we examined. One that specifically comes to mind is *La Casa Verde (The Green House)*, by Mario Vargas Llosa.

What struck me most about the book is a feature which it shares with much Latin American literature, namely the construction of the narrative around many axes of temporality, a theme that is so familiar to psychoanalysts.

Although Freud did not attempt to write a systematic theory of time, such a theory can be constructed through reading his work. Freud's conceptualisation of the psychic apparatus postulates that distinct timings must be at work. Experiences are registered in the psychic apparatus, which is a system that exists in space and time, and these are re-experienced and externalised through the analytic process. Repetition, irreversibility and oscillation – are all present in the functioning of the mind and were discussed by Freud in his formulations about the psychic apparatus.

Freud suggested that the different timings of the id and the ego are inaugurated by repression. But when does repression occur? Here another aspect of time must be introduced. In 1926, Freud suggested that most of the repression which we deal with in our therapeutic work represents cases of repression by deferred action (*après-coup*). By this he meant that experiences, impressions and memory traces may be revised at a later date, when the individual reaches a new stage of maturity (Laplanche and Pontalis, 1985, p. lll). The notion of *après-coup* links up with the function of repetition. Freud stated that what is essentially new about his theory is the thesis that memory is present not once but several times over, that it is laid down many times.

259

The Green House (La Casa Verde) by Mario Vargas Llosa

There has been a great deal of debate about the number stories that can be identified in *The Green House,* which spans three generations and involves a total of thirty-four characters. It has been suggested that there are five stories, which constitute parallel worlds, each with their own rules, which give an imaginary dimension to characters and situations. The stories are constructed around two spatial axes, which correspond to the geographical reality of Peru: on the one hand the forest, in a little village in the Amazonian jungle, on the other the urban landscape of the city of Piura. *La Casa Verde* tells us stories of humiliations, of useless rebellions, and the progressive disintegration of human beings.

In the book, one learns about the effects of a fact before one is told many pages later, about the fact itself. This is true of the foundation of the green house itself, which takes place about a third of the way through the book when, after the journey that has taken the reader to that point, the author finally says:

'This is how the Green House was born. The building of it took several weeks; the boards, the beams and the adobe blocks had to be hauled from the other side of town, and the mules rented by Don Anselmo pulled painfully through the desert.' (p. 83)

The novel can be viewed as constructing a myth of foundation, a myth of origins. *La Casa Verde* is a whore house and the lack of historicity of one of the central characters, Don Anselmo, who appears from nowhere, allows him to represent the experience of profound alienation which is present with the lack of renunciation and the violation of social rules. *La Casa Verde* is the result of the kidnap and rape of an orphan, a blind girl called Tonita.

Tonita had grown into a beautiful pubescent adolescent and often, in order to avoid taking her to all her deliveries, Juana, who takes care of her, leaves Tonita sitting on a park bench. There Anselmo sees her for the first time and falls for her, infatuated by her silent beauty. He kidnaps Tonita, rapes her, and takes her to live with him in the tower of the Green House, where he plays the harp. Later Tonita dies while giving birth to a baby girl, La Chunga, and a large group of incensed women led by a priest burn down the Green House. Years later a second house, owned by La Chunga, rises in the desert.

In *La Casa Verde*, the multiple structure and the symmetrical arrangements of the narrative elements make it difficult for the reader to establish any reasonable or typical explanation of why things happen the way they do. Each character seems a mere asteroid travelling a capricious route through an exploding universe (p. 56). This is also so because the events that make up the story are constructed through the characters' memories, which are not, by definition, lineal.

The organisational technique of the stories, as well as the worldview they propose, is fragmented, complex, mobile and alienating. From the very beginning of the book the reader is bewildered and overwhelmed Yet the novel conforms to a strict organisational pattern that controls the dissemination of information and the multiplicity of points of view.

The images blur into one another, diluting events and effacing certainty. Vargas Llosa utilises internal monologues, shifts in the narrative focus, flashbacks, and temporal dissolutions to rupture the reader's sense of temporal continuity. It is an overwhelming illustration of primary process at work although, at the same time, its creation also expresses laborious effort on the part of the artist. The de-structuring of time allows the characters to be continuously re-born from the ashes.

The complex way in which dialogues are presented also serves to accelerate time: one conversation is set within the framing of another ongoing conversation. These techniques have been referred to by various critics as 'Chinese boxes', 'communicating vessels', and the juxtaposition of 'objective and subjective levels of reality'. Bella and I suggest that one could also conceptualise them as *co-conversations* in the sense that the story is actively constructed in the process, as one level of the conversation gives meaning to another level. They are not static forms, as Chinese boxes are, but a dynamic process that gives meaning to the process as it is taking place, in the same way as construction occurs in the analytic process.

The characters of *La Casa Verde* represent the new sisiphs in their struggle against the elements. They end up degraded or destroyed by themselves or by a mysterious fatality inherent to life. The imagery is linked to fish, reptiles, and other primitive forms of animal life.

In the myths created by these and other Latin American novels, one can discern the construction of a 'magic realism', where the writer faces the dramatic realities of Latin America. The characters are ambiguous, past and present become blurred, and life and death complement and are in a dialogue with each other. There is no escape from 'reality' to an imaginary world, where daily life is forgotten. In the process, the cartography of a continent, with its particular history and struggles, is delineated.

References

Jozef, B. (1993) *O espaco reconquistado* Petrópolis, Vozes, 1974; Rio de
    Janiero: Paz e Terra, 2nd ed., revista e ampliada, 1993.

Jozef, B. *Romance hispano-americano*. São Paulo, Atica, 1986.

Loayza, L (1968) *Los personajes de La Casa Verde*. In: *Loayza et alii.*
    Agresión a la realidad: Mario Vargas Llosa, Las Palmas, Letras
    a su imán, 1971.

Laplanche, J and Pontalis,J.-B (1985) *The Language of Psycho-Analysis*
    London: The Hogarth Press and The Institute of Psycho-Analysis

Oviedo, J.M. (1977) *Mario Vargas Llosa. La invención de una realidad.*
    Barcelona, Barral Editores

I Am the Very Model of a Modern Psycho-Analyst: Writing the lyrics for the Tavistock Clinic Pantomime

Brett Kahr *(London)*

One windswept autumn day, back in 1994, I boarded a British Airways flight from London to Edinburgh to meet Donald Winnicott's goddaughter, Dr. Elisabeth Swan, whom I had arranged to interview as part of my ongoing biographical research (Kahr, 1996). As the plane neared Scotland, we experienced horrific air turbulence, and some of the passengers began to look quite frightened. In order to manage my own anxiety, I found myself reaching for a note pad and a pen, and I then began to write a set of lyrics, a long-standing pastime, for the upcoming Tavistock Clinic Pantomime, for which I had agreed to provide a comical score. (As Marion Milner once told me, Winnicott as a young man, yearned to write musical comedy lyrics, so it seemed appropriate to engage in this Winnicottian pastime whilst on route to meeting his goddaughter).

In our madcap storyline for the pantomime, a popular annual event for staff and students at the Tavistock Clinic, the fictitious Chief Executive had absconded with all the clinic's funds, and both the Chairman and the Dean had to scramble to find a suitable replacement - someone who could take the blame. In our fanciful plot, the Chairman and the Dean decided to approach one Myron Goldberg, a long-suffering member of staff, and they offer him the plum post of Chief Executive. But sadly, Dr. Goldberg explains to his superiors that he must decline the exalted post as Chief Executive of the Tavistock Clinic because his own life cannot withstand any more responsibilities.

I would imagine that many of the references to local London mental health professionals will be familiar to most British readers of this edited book; however, those whom I have identified in the lyrics only by their first names deserve clarification. 'Estela' refers, of course, to Dr. Estela Welldon, Senior Consultant Psychiatrist in Psychotherapy at the Portman Clinic in London (now retired), who specialises in treating the forensic patient. 'Anne-Marie' will be well known as Mrs. Anne-Marie Sandler, former President of the British Psycho-Analytical Society. And 'Valerie' is, of course, Ms. Valerie Sinason, Director of the Clinic for Dissociative Studies, who has undertaken the pioneering work on survivors of ritual abuse and satanist abuse in Great Britain (Sinason, 1994).

Dr. Marcus Johns, a London-based psycho-analyst, and stalwart Tavistock Clinic Pantomime star, introduced 'I Am the Very Model of a Modern Psycho-Analyst', brilliantly rendered, to thunderous applause from appreciative colleagues and their families, who, I trust, enjoyed seeing our often masochistic tendencies towards workaholism being lampooned in this way. This song has become something of party piece for Dr. Johns, who has delivered *a cappella* renderings of it at a variety of other psycho-analytical conferences over the years.

In the next section are the lyrics which I penned for the character of 'Dr. Myron Goldberg', airborne somewhere above Scotland, en route to meeting with Winnicott's goddaughter, and sung to the melody of Sir Arthur Sullivan's jaunty tune, 'I Am the Very Model of a Modern Major General' from the Gilbert and Sullivan operetta *The Pirates of Penzance*:

References

Kahr, Brett (1996). *D.W. Winnicott: A Biographical Portrait.*, London: Karnac Books.

Sinason, Valerie (Ed.). (1994). *Treating Survivors of Satanist Abuse.* London: Routledge.

Part IV: <u>THE EMBODIED THERAPIST</u>

I Am the Very Model of a Modern Psycho-Aanalyst*

Dr. Myron Goldberg.
I am the very model of a modern psycho-analyst,
I'm pensive and expensive like a modern psycho-analyst.
I know libido theory and I quote the texts historically.
They said I once met Jung but I deny that categorically.
I am very well acquainted too with Abraham and Esther Bick,
And Bion helps me think about the patients who are very sick.
I've even read a page or two by Anna Freud and Winnicott.
I've done an infant observation of a baby in a cot.

> Dean, Chairman, and Chorus of Secretaries:
> He's done an infant observation of a baby in a cot.
> He's done an infant observation of a baby in a cot.
> He's done an infant observation of a little baby in a cot.

Dr. Myron Goldberg.
I am very good at working with the schizoid and the borderline.
At night I always say a prayer for Dr. Freud and Mrs. Klein.
I love to publish papers, and I'm thrilled to be a panellist.
I am the very model of a modern psycho-analyst.
                    ***
At six A.M., I rise and then I analyse my dreams a bit.
At seven, I read Rosenfeld and other texts of holy writ.
At eight, a private patient comes along to my consulting room.
By ten to nine, I'm filled with glum, projections of my patient's gloom.
And then a consultation with a social worker from RELATE.
At ten, some supervision with a cocky little candidate.
And then I take a swig of gin, oh yes indeed, I have a stock.
Then I hop onto my motorbike and ride into the Tavistock.

> Dean, Chairman, and Chorus of Secretaries:
> He hops onto his motorbike and rides into the Tavistock.
> He hops onto his motorbike and rides into the Tavistock.
> He hops onto his motorbike and rides into the Tavi-Tavistock.

Dr. Myron Goldberg:
A meeting, then a lecture, then patient, then another one.
Oh working at the Tavistock is riveting and lots of fun.
Then I pop into the Portman, Donald Campbell is the panellist.
It's Estela's latest paper 'bout her meeting with a cannib'list.
I am the very model of a modern psycho-analyst.
***

Then after work, I'm back at work, my room's on Fitzjohn's Avenue.
At six P.M., I analyse a teenage girl who's sniffing glue.
At seven, it's a fetishist who dresses in a leather suit.
At eight fifteen, a Scientific Meeting at The Institute.
I take some tea with Anne-Marie behind the bust of Ernest Jones.
We brace ourselves to hear about a patient who eats children's bones.
It's Valerie, of course, she always speaks with passion and with style.
Especially when she's talking 'bout a satanistic necrophile.

Dean, Chairman, and Chorus of Secretaries:
Especially when she's talking 'bout a satanistic necrophile.
Especially when she's talking 'bout a satanistic necrophile.
Especially when she's talking 'bout a satanistic necro- necrophile.

Dr. Myron Goldberg:
I jump onto my bike again and wend my way to Muswell Hill.
I'm feeling rather peevish now, if truth be known, I'm feeling ill.
I've had no time for supper, so I'm hungry as a cannib'list.
If only the Committee had asked <u>me</u> to be the panellist.
I'm tired and perspired, I'm a modern psycho-analyst.
***

By two A.M., I fall asleep, and then I have a nasty dream.
I'm in a leaky boat, without a paddle, hurtling down a stream.
When I awake I'm soaked in sweat and quivering with nameless dread.
I hug my trusted teddy bear and stumble bravely out of bed.
And then, to my dismay, I spy a note upon the counterpane.
A letter from my wife, in fact, which says, 'I've gone to live in Spain.
I never see you anymore, this marriage has become a joke.
Your children don't remember you, I'll have to wed another bloke.'

Dean, Chairman, and Chorus of Secretaries:
His children don't remember him, she'll have to wed another bloke.
His children don't remember him, she'll have to wed another bloke.
His children don't remember him, she'll have to wed another
'nother bloke.

Dr. Myron Goldberg:
I crumple up the letter then I climb back into bed again.
Ten milligrams of Prozac should alleviate this ghastly pain.
Then I stroke my favourite blanket and decide to be a flanellist.
Then I bite my little teddy for I'm vengeful as a cannib'list.
Why ever did I have to be a modern psycho-analyst?
***

My life is such a shambles that I wonder how I'll muddle through.
I should have done accountancy like any self-respecting Jew.
I call my Training Analyst for just a bit of sympathy.
She gleefully reminds me she retired in 1993.
I'm qualified in medicine, so I write up some Diazepam,
Chlorpromazine, Imipramime, Lorazepam, Temazepam.
And in a half an hour I'm feeling less depressed and less morose.
If truth be known, I'm feeling partly manic, partly comatose.

Dean, Chairman, and Chorus of Secretaries:
If truth be known, he's feeling partly manic, partly comatose.
If truth be known, he's feeling partly manic, partly comatose.
If truth be known, he's feeling partly manic, partly coma-
comatose.

Dr. Myron Goldberg:
I know my crises won't be solved by simple pharmacology.
Perhaps I'll try phrenology or even toxicology.
But then the phone starts ringing, it's a most distinguished analyst.
It's Kernberg from New York, inviting me to be the panellist
At a televised symposium `bout a most distinguished cannib'list,
To be followed by a conference on the treatment of a flanellist.
Thank God I took the trouble to become a psycho-analyst!
***

*Lyrics by Brett Kahr, psychotherapist
Copyright 1994, 1997, 2001, by Brett Kahr.

268

Presence of Mind and Body   Joan Raphael-Leff

"He that has eyes to see and ears to hear may convince himself that no mortal can keep a secret. If his lips are silent, he chatters with his finger-tips; betrayal oozes out of him at every pore. And thus the task of making conscious the most hidden recesses of the mind is one which it is quite possible to accomplish" (Freud, 1905 [1901], <u>Fragment of an Analysis of a Case of Hysteria</u>. SE 7).

We are embodied creatures – equipped with sensory organs to observe our patients, but also with bodies which 'ooze betrayal', not only of secrets but life-style. Luckily, not all of us lead Myron Goldberg's life. However, the way we do live **is** largely determined by practising an 'impossible profession'. As the contributions to this book illustrate, the interests and vicissitudes of therapists' experiences are many and various. Yet it seems that despite the theoretical schools of thought and modes of practice which divide us, we all bestow special significance on endeavours of work, love and play. Notwithstanding the inevitable tensions, we feel privileged, offered in profusion work satisfactions of both 'utility' and 'pleasure' mentioned by Freud, granting 'a secure place in a portion of reality' and attaching us to the wider 'human community' (not restricted to the narrower familial or collegial arena). Recognising that the diversity of desire counteracts formulating a 'golden rule' to pleasure-seeking, Freud stated that for each person choices depend on *'a question of how much real satisfaction he can expect to get from the external world, how far he is led to make himself independent of it, and finally, how much strength he feels he has for altering the world to suit his wishes. In this his psychical constitution will play a decisive part, irrespectively of the external circumstances'* (<u>Civilization and its Discontents</u>, *SE p.83).*

Possibly as a result of our personal analyses and continuing self-reflection, it seems that most of us strive to find a balance between solitary and socially derived satisfactions, between imaginative flair and sociopolitical realism. Whatever our individual lifestyles, in common, most 'depth' psychotherapists seem guided by qualities of thoughtfulness, tolerance of uncertainty and a belief in the existence of an unconscious domain which can enrich or sabotage rationality. Hopefully, the dispassionate rock of impartiality is tempered by compassion, and logic aided by preconscious fantasy when we come to analyse our ongoing experience.

For if many other professions rely on 'prosthetic' adjuncts to their skills, we therapists are our own tools, denuded in the consulting room of all but theoretical understanding, optimal receptivity and ethical self-reflexivity. Often, we tacitly assume that this means inhibiting the body, all the more to focus on the mind. But clearly, not only our patients are embodied; we ourselves are too, and within the therapeutic sphere, two or more corporeal beings utilise their sensory perceptions in varying degrees to process both their own and the other's emotional states.

Observation shows that babies gradually achieve body-boundedness through active discovery and negotiation of the carer's body alongside their own. It may be an uncomfortable thought, but our own corporeality is sensed, registered and explored in sessions by our patients. In fact, videoed studies of face-to-face therapy reveal the therapeutic dyad's unconscious mimicry of each other's resting postures and hand gestures. If parental disposition and unconscious disconnections are internalized, to manifest years later on our couches – our own bodily attitudes (tentative and guarded to full blooded, as they may be) are likewise absorbed by the patient. Conversely, like the metabolising mother described by Bion, as therapists we ourselves soak up wordlessly projected feelings and unthinkable anxieties in the form of somatically affective communications. We steep ourselves in the analytic process, like skin divers aware that the teeming underwater world becomes visible only to those who immerse themselves in the medium. But it is more than fascinated observation. Through free floating attention we encounter and convert raw sensory information into meaningful visual imagery, or auditory and olfactory impressions. Lending ourselves to the fluidity of intersubjective experience, swayed by undercurrents, we resonate to the unsaid within the said, and utilise our transformational capacities to fathom and transcribe the emotional somato-psychic reality of the other.

Freud's insistence on the 'erotogenicity' of all organs (1914:84) dnotes the transferability and plasticity of bodily fantasy, across corporeal sites, and even bodies. We often find ourselves on the receiving end of bodily projective identification, particularly with borderline patients who get under our own skins to promote actualisation of their relational representations, or those who express their erotic or aggressive transference by means of the body. As with all our clients we distinguish between psycho-physiological processessing of affect and psychosomatic bypassing of emotion. We register unwitting use of body as metaphor, subtle discrepancies between appearance and imaginary bodily schemata. We note demeanour, clothing, weight fluctuations, bodily sounds and odours (papers have been written about stomach rumbles and a Membership Seminar I attended years ago led by Hannah Segal discussed the particular smell of anxiety). We ourselves are often similarly scrutinised for telltale evidence of our feelings and lifestyle. Our awareness of patients' physicality is keenest in cases of conversion, perversion, dissociative and addictive bodily states with stymied enactments of rapacious desires and revelations of hidden incorporations. Knowing the regulatory power of prohibition and projections, in addition to symptomatic complaints we register various indications of excess, rupture and loss of control; autonomic reactions and nonhabituation; temperature fluctuations, goosebumps, trembling, floppiness or rigidity of posture – a whole range of manifestations of procedural memories, of unarticulated passions, pleasures and pain. These bodily signs are filtered through our own sensorimotor apparatus, which must be fine-tuned to perceive subtleties, receptive and vulnerable to exchange. But in our focus on the Other (or body subordination), we may tend to quell or bypass ongoing somatic reactions and kinesthetic happenings in ourselves during sessions. Unless caught unawares by autonomic fight-flight-freeze contertransferetial reactions or disturbing proprioceptive experiences, such as aches, hunger, nausea or drowsiness. Granted the close attention we pay to the psychophysiology of the patient's body, and given the visceral impact and stressful nature of our hourly engagements – are we sufficiently mindful of the materiality of our own bodies and backdrop?

Prevention:

I once heard a radio interview with the jazz pianist Earl Hines, then in his late 80's. 'Looking back' asked the astute interviewer 'is there anything you would have done differently?' 'Yes' came the drawled answer 'if I'd a'known I was goin' to live this long I'd've looked after my body'…

In our profession, given the number of people who depend on our continuing good health and conversely, given the dangers inherent in a sedentary lifestyle – we owe it to ourselves to look after our bodies. Health is partly a matter of *prevention*. Wishful thinking aside, none of us is granted eternal youth and, indeed, the late start and long training means that most therapists are getting on in age, and liable to develop some of the many ailments of creeping decrepitude. Without becoming hypochondriacs in the process, we all know it is wise to note and check out unusual symptoms (such as giddiness on standing up; bowel problems; extreme thirst, etc). But given our busy lives, tight schedules and difficulty in making time for extra appointments, it is not unusual for us therapists to neglect ourselves or postpone the necessary. In some countries annual medical checkups are built into the health system. In others, special provisions must be made for these. For instance, as we get older and visual accommodation changes more rapidly, eyes like teeth, need a regular examination to prevent strain, headache and fatigue. An occasional pedicure can help avoid problems related to poor circulation (from sitting still for long periods), and in our profession, any sign of encroaching deafness ought to be treated seriously and remedied rather

271

than dismissed. Age related conditions such as osteoporosis can be monitored with a simple bone density test. Regular self-checking of breasts, testicles and other squidgy bits can supplement, but not replace, regular screening tests such as mammograms (every 1-3 years), annual vaginal smears, etc. In some of these, time is of the essence. Foresight in *preventing accidents* is equally important. As we age and reflexes decelerate, it becomes increasingly necessary to re-examine work environments for hazardous irregularities and ourselves for obsolete bodily-confidence.

To end on a prosaic note, our ageing skins too, are affected by spending days sitting still in centrally heated or air conditioned atmospheres. Again, it is a matter of taking time to pamper ourselves. After all, skin is the largest organ in the body, site, surface and boundary between inner and outer. Luckily, apart from dietary imbalances, such dryness is extremely responsive to moisturising creams. (These needn't be expensive cosmetic super-cures – common old Vaseline or aqueous ointments, bathoil or emulsifiers work too, although a bit messier as less readily absorbed). Humidifying the atmosphere in the consulting room helps too – a discrete bowl of water or a pot plant near the central heating can do the trick (and setting the thermostat lower when possible). Some therapists install low-cost humidifiers, or even ionisers. Similarly, while eczema, psoriasis and scaly skin are common treatable skin conditions in us wrinklies, those who have spent hours on sunny beaches must treat reddened scaly patches or new phenomena such as lumps, small chronic sores and mole changes as suspect until proven otherwise.

Skin is also invigorated by enhanced blood flow. Aerobics which increase the heart rate do this. But for those of us who remain stuck in our consulting rooms for hours on end **deep breathing** is a good starter for improved circulation (and general relaxation). Sitting comfortably, count to 6 while inhaling slowly through your nose, making sure to fill lower lungs. Hold your breath for a second, then exhale completely through your mouth (3-4 seconds). Repeat 10 times, breathe normally for a few breaths and repeat the deep breathing.

Maintenance:

'*Body and Mind, two sides of the same join you said?*' [Marion Milner,
Mind the Gap]

While many of us deplore the consumer culture's commodification of the body, and its stylised images, responses to my surveys show that most therapists are well aware of their own need for exercise, although few feel they do enough. That said, some seem very vigorous, claiming to run daily, even making use of running tracks. Quite a few jog, walk, cycle or 'march' regularly. Others workout at home or go to a gym, use an exercise-bike or 'Nordic track' on a frequent basis while yet others engage in 'training' regimes such as weight lifting. Some swim or play tennis or squash couple of times a week or even daily. Such bouts of energetic activity are admirable and great for increasing fitness. But in our profession, whatever exertions you choose to do (or not), **'maintenance'** is a different issue. *On an hour by hour basis it is necessary to counteract the ills of sitting still by getting up, stretching and walking around between sessions and when possible, engaging in some movement behind the couch.* Below are a series of activities to choose from according to situation and the time at your disposal:

PAUSE– when you have a moment wherever you are:
- Sitting upright, lean back in your chair with your hands clasped behind your head, pulling your elbows backwards.
- With hands still behind your head, rock on pelvis back and forth (curving and straightening your spine)
- Make fists and release several times; touch each finger in turn to thumb, repeating sequence several times
- Rotate head 'drawing' the numbers 1 to 9 with your chin.
- Spread and clench toes inside shoes.
- Isometrically contract and release muscles in arms, thighs, buttocks, perineum and feet. *In time contractions can also be done behind the couch, entailing no visible movement and little conscious effort.*

WARM UP:
Standing with legs apart, stretch and lightly windmill both arms, starting in front of your face, then gradually raise them high above your head circling them together and separately; change direction. Loosening body, shake hands at wrists.

QUICKIES :
- Sitting, lean your head back, then forward, tucking in chin, then rotate head side to side.
- Sitting with legs outstretched, rotate ankles (in unison or opposite directions)
- Standing or sitting, raise both shoulders then drop them 5 times; circle both shoulders 5 times in each direction. Then do each separately.
- Drag fingertips from forehead to nape, pressing firmly and rotating hands above ears.
- Standing or sitting , cross your arms across chest and place hands on opposite shoulder. Rotate upper body to left, then right, several times.

- Hands linked, stretch arms forward, raise them above your head, then bend them right and then left.
- Standing, bend at waist and try to put hands flat on floor

CHAIR EXERCISES:

The advantage of the following exercises is that they can be done while sitting in your analytic chair between sessions. They appear deceptively easy but stretch many unused muscles. However, they are not overtaxing and I learned them by participating in the daily exercise group in a senior citizen's community, with my mother and her octo/nono-genarian friends. Try and build in a few more repetitions each day. Although they appear here in a particular order you can pick and choose.

For all exercises sit forward in your chair with your feet flat on the ground unless otherwise specified. Repeat as frequently as suits you. Kick shoes off if time permits.

1. Sitting centred, turn head to left, then right, up and down.
2. Feet on floor, 'walk' as far as you can go forward and back. Tuck feet under your chair and alternately tap heels and toes on floor.
3. Lean back in chair. Bring head down, chin resting on chest but tuck tummy in. Straighten up and sit upright without reclining. Slump and repeat 4 times.
4. Leaning back in your chair contract perineal muscles and relax them 10 times. [This contraction can be done standing too, and is so invisible that midwives recommend parturients practice it 'while waiting at bus-stops'].
5. Sitting comfortably, open knees, place feet pointing outward. Without moving feet, 'close' knees bringing head down. Then raise head while opening knees. Repeat several times.
6. Cup hands around knees. Press knees together while applying the pressure of both hands against closed knees to open them. [If you feel a slight pull in hips while doing this, it is merely muscles stretching].
7. Bring one knee up to forehead; down; then bring other knee up. (You can cheat a bit at first by reclining head but ultimately try to raise knee all the way).
8. Rock in chair keeping hands on stomach. Rock forward, then breathe out as you pull backward to reclining position. Repeat.
9. Sit upright on chair. Keeping your back straight, raise one leg, toes pointed upward. Rotate ankle. Repeat with other leg. Cross your legs. Stretch out both legs and point toes up and down.
10. Sitting upright on chair, bend right arm over head to left side; then left arm to right. Gradually stretch arm more; use other hand to pull arm a little further 2-3 times; alternate arms. Rotate body slightly to include hips, then shoulders while you bring arm over.

274

11. Stretch one arm straight ahead of you. Then the other. Alternate then bring both together outstretched and interlace fingers. Pull body back in chair, holding arms forward. Do the same overhead and slump while holding arms up.
12. Check if you have the space] Outstretch one arm behind you, the other forward; alternate arms; bring both forward; one to the side, rotate body from waist – alternate sides..
13. Sit forward. Raise your bottom off chair holding onto the chair arms.
14. Raise arms in an arc on either side of the chair. Bring down again. Bring arms round behind the chair and try to link hands. (Success obviously depend on the width of the chair). Bring arms back. Rotating wrists flick your fingers.
15. Swing one leg out then across other; shake legs and hands. Sit straight and breathe in and out fully several times.
16. Cross arms holding elbows. Bring them upwards as high as you can eventually bringing them up over and even back behind your head. Repeat
17. Still sitting spread legs. Raise knee out sideways from hip. Circle ankle. Other leg. Raise and then circle with ankle. Try and do both simultaneously. Bring legs down to floor and 'walk' feet.
18. Stretch one leg forward at 90 degrees and bend your back, both arms outstretched forward over leg. Try and touch toe. Alternate legs.
19. Rock forward/back contracting muscles in perineum and anus.
20. Press both hands along one thigh, palms and wrists down – massage back and forth along top and side of each thigh.
21. With fists draw circles along thighs; pinch thighs and under calves; continue with chopping/patting movements. Do same on each arm.

STANDING EXERCISES:
1. Stand with feet together, link fingers. Inhale while lifting your arms. Hold. Exhale and bring them down
2. Feet apart – stretch arms up high, then bend at the waist and let gravity pull you downwards (don't despair - in time you will find yourself putting your palm on the floor). Hang down there as long as you can. Eventually, try to 'walk' hands on floor.
3. Then holding your right ankle with your left hand, stretch right arm upwards, keeping eyes on outstretched fingers. Repeat with other arm.
4. Bring arms forward, palms outstretched upwards, back straight. Twist shoulders so that your lower arms 'hang' from your elbows. Repeat.
5. [Shoes off]. Facing your chair, put one foot on seat and lean forward as far as you can. Repeat with other leg
6. Stand up straight. Raise one leg outstretched as far as you can (aim at 90 degrees). Other leg. Holding back of chair, stand on one leg and stretch each leg backwards as high as possible.

275

7. Legs slightly apart, rise up on your toes and go down again 5 times. Keeping heels on the floor bend knees, then rise. Repeat 5 times

LYING DOWN:
1. Lie flat (no pillow); raise one arm straight up towards ceiling, lifting shoulder, then other arm in turn. Repeat 5 times each
2. Interlock fingers on outstretched arms then turn them inside out – palms towards ceiling. Stretch upwards.
3. Lie flat; raise legs in turn to 90° pointing toes at ceiling. Repeat 5 times each. Spread and clench toes.
4. Lie flat on your back. Keeping your hands under your hips raise them off the bed and bicycle in the air.
5. Fetal position. Roll from side to side.

In sum, keeping body in mind, ask yourself what will enhance wellbeing.

Self-Preservation
COMFORT: choosing the chair(s)
Much has been written about the couch – metaphorically as dream screen, holding arms, lap, bosom, container etc., and concretely as reflection-inducing recliner. Finding a good couch is of prime importance and may vary from sleek designer-recliner to comfy sofa, according to taste, space and pocket. However little consideration has been given to the chair in which the poor analyst sits hour after hour. (Freud's behind-the-couch chair was distinctly uncomfortable). In choosing the chair bear in mind that you will be stuck with it for years to come given how difficult it is to make changes in the consulting room. Clearly, it is essential to follow good seating principles (and to feel free to make a fool of yourself trying out as many chairs as possible before settling for The one):
- *Height adjustment* – feet should easily rest flat on the floor
- *Depth of seat* – should support thighs, ending just behind knees.
- *Props* – back of neck and arms need both firm support and freedom of movement. Ideally, the upright chair should extend to rest your head. Some chairs curve forwards to accommodate the hollow of the back, but if not, placing a cushion there helps avoid backache.
- *Angle* – the chair back should recline slightly following the spine's curvature. However, some back sufferers prefer an upright 90° with rigid support rather than soft upholstery. One innovative solution to avoid potential backache is a kneeling chair which shifts the weight forwards from spine to knees – however, you have to have the poise (social as well as physical) to carry it off. Others prefer a (retractable) footstool to secretly elevate feet to thigh level during the session – or less drastic, one which raises the knees above the coccyx

- *Extra comfort* – detachable cushions and slim neck-pillow enable frequent changes of position during sessions to avoid constant pressure points and potential trouble such as deep vein thrombosis.
- *Durability* – some materials, like leather, age gracefully if treated to an occasional waxing. Others fray, fade or become shabby and dilapidated or are unpleasant in hot weather. Choose both frame and upholstery with long-term use in mind
- *Versatility* – when activity includes several foci (i.e. patients on the couch and at other times patients, and/or supervisees on a chair elsewhere in the room), rotation might be an asset.
- *Appearance* – needless to say, your chair signifies relative status and some thought must be given as to the impression it creates in relation to the couch and other chairs in the room

Other chairs:

- Similarly, the chair used by patients and/or supervisees should have equal consideration given to support, comfort and appearance.
- Special thought should be given to a chair used for writing (albeit it can never match Freud's own). The desk should be at elbow level when seated. The seat should fully support small of the back, bottom and extended thighs with feet resting flat on floor.
- Finally, waiting room chairs are often seen as secondary, but they too can create an unconsciously absorbed atmosphere ranging from welcoming hospitality to a message about patients' inconsequentiality.

LAYOUT – a room with a view

Many work up to eight hours a day in the consulting room, whether institutional, a private office elsewhere or a room in one's own house. Aesthetics of the place in which we spend such long hours become a prime consideration. Clearly, each of us brings our own predilections to furnishing the space, on a spectrum from stark Minimalist to ornately Baroque. While some feel satisfied with the compulsory couch and two chairs, others may wish to include a writing desk, couch side table, book shelves, lamps, rugs, paintings and other ornaments. Some feel it is wiser to begin with less rather than more, as in terms of patient adjustment on the whole it seems easier to add things rather than remove existing ones.

Since the decor is assumed by the patient to reflect the analyst's personal taste, some care must be given to the impression and its effect, even in a rented consulting room. [Some years into my second analysis, after a few weeks in a newly rented consulting room, I boldly announced that either the wallpaper or I must go. My analyst candidly agreed that we were both investing too much energy in trying to ignore the overbearing pink and blue floral bouquets – and some time later he resumed working from home].

277

To my mind a window is a necessity, although we may not all be lucky enough to have a neutral view of trees or greenery. Placing a leafy plant on the inner windowsill can mask ugliness outside, while loosely woven light curtains provide concealment from a busy thoroughfare without obscuring the light. For the analyst if not for the patient, the window not only offers a visual focus but a link with the outside world, negating the consulting room as self-enclosed solipsistic cell. Where there is no window, a glass tank of tropical fish may offer a similar relaxing focal point and sense of world beyond the inner one(s). Cut flowers also provide a tranquil view, but as with pot-plants, their care or neglect is often noticed and interpreted by patients.

Working from home, whether in a bona fide office or one improvised from a garage or spare bedroom, it must be easily accessible without encroaching and revealing too much of one's private space. Ideally it should have wheelchair access, a toilet for patients' use, and a waiting room or shelter from the elements, especially for those who use public transport. Unavailability of these and parking facilities are essential information before an initial interview takes place.

In all new consulting rooms, it is always worth the therapist sitting in all the chairs and having a little lie down on the couch before finalising their location. Those of us who work in Victorian houses know the fascination of ceiling roses and plaster cornices. For most analysands (even more than dental patients) the most relevant view is that of the ceiling which they come to know far better than does the analyst. Indeed, one fastidious patient arrived for his final session equipped with a stool which he proceeded to place on the couch, then took from his pocket a large pair of scissors with which he snipped a small umbilical thread that had been dangling from the ceiling for years unbeknown to the analyst!

ANALYTIC SPACE:

Like clothes that feel comfortable and reflect one's own individual style and physique rather than fashion, the issue of furniture placement clearly varies with the shape and size of the room, the analyst's taste and the versatile requirements of that particular practice. [For instance, since I specialize in Reproductive issues, I have a chaise longue on which pregnant women feel more comfortable, and a large sofa-like analytic couch which can comfortably seat two or more when I see couples with or without babies]. However, whatever the specific needs there are several common issues which require careful consideration to meet the comfort of both analyst and patients:

- *Proximity* and *positioning* of chair and couch – these vary from almost touching to a considerable distance between (partly delimited by acuity of the analyst's hearing); Some prefer the chair to be tucked

278

way behind the couch; others sit at an angle or even beside the couch – again depending on practical restrictions and the analyst's theoretical viewpoint.

- *Discreteness* of entrance and exit from building, *security, safety* on stairs (hand-rails, adequate lighting, visibility) and *privacy* in waiting and consulting rooms. These seem self-evident but are likely to yield surprises if you yourself test it out with your more vulnerable and/or paranoid patients in mind.

- *Space, décor and comfort* – there are those who advocate special positioning of furniture relative to entrances, and others who, with a more mystical approach, emphasise compass directions to harness the forces of nature to beneficial effect and balance oppositional elements to enhance the 'flow of energy'. Yet others promote particular colour schemes to induce a sense of calm and 'harmony'. My own view is that whatever their philosophy, each therapist has their own taste and needs which will prevail for better or for worse. After all, it is we who have to spend most time in the room. Some patients will find it to their liking; others will be critical – and it is all grist to the analytic mill... But sitting there all day we may forget that patients' physical comforts vary and some may find the room crowded or chilly for reasons other than projection. Conversely, unnoticed by the resident therapist, the room often tends to become stuffy or overheated and it may be sensible to briefly open the windows between sessions. [This reminds me of a Japanese therapist's solution to the new 1980's phenomenon of teenage violence against parents. She called it 'Open the window therapy' with the instruction that the parents shame their errant kids by encouraging neighbours to hear the abuse. Apparently it worked]. Which brings us to the issue of –

- *Sound proofing* – especially between consulting room and common areas. Noise is an extremely tricky problem that ultimately can only be properly resolved by lead sheet insulation. However, a double door with foam-rubber or other sound absorbing material between the frames is an effective way of increasing privacy when the corridor is the source of the problem. Where there is a permeable common wall, a small fountain [relatively inexpensive and simple to operate] playing in the waiting room overrides any sounds emitted from the consulting room. Double glazing (especially with the optimal 9 inch gap between panes) eliminates most outside noises. Carpets, wall-hangings and curtains all mute emissions and muffle echoes within the room. Persistent noise through a common wall may sometimes be reduced by coating that area with large sheets of soft-board (the stuff commonly used for notice-boards) or bookcases – but that said, it is amazing how little attention most patients pay to meaningless intrusive sounds which might set the analyst's teeth on edge.

279

- Finally a useful piece of advice the late psychoanalyst Nina Coltart gave to new practitioners – get a metal waste bin and keep it handy in case of uncontainable patient upchucks.

Sustenance:

I won't attempt here to reproduce those items from *'Freud's Own Cookbook'* [a spoof edited some 15 years ago, by James Hillman (the Jungian analyst) and Charles Boer] – which included such delicacies as *Banana O., Bernay's sauce* (made in double-Bleuler, natch), *Totem & Tapioca, Moses and Matzoballism, Little Hansburgers, Kraeplin Suzettes* followed by an *Interpretation of Creams* (especially Viennese schlag) which, needless to say all resulted in *Civilization and its Indigestion*...

Most of us have neither inclination nor time to produce elaborate midday meals. So I shall focus here instead on the achievable – simple, quick and nutritious dishes which can be rustled up in that jiffy between sessions, or during the longer breaks – contributed by therapists I polled around the world.

REFRESHMENTS:

Given our busy life-styles, many therapists try to pack an awful lot into their brief 10 minute breaks between patients. The essential note-keeping, phone calls, administrative necessities, not to mention responding to urgent letters and email. Even given longer breaks this leaves little time for nutrition. Some people restrict themselves to two or three meals a day; others feel the need for more frequent fressing. For those who get peckish, a varied *fruit bowl* is a great companion during an intensive working day, and *nuts* (brazils, pistachios, cashews, walnuts, etc.) or *dried fruits* (dates, apples, pears or especially figs and apricots which are also good sources of iron and calcium) provide easy and filling snacks.

Kitchen aids may increase efficient use of your short break. An essential (unless you have a café round the corner) is an electric kettle or some other means of boiling water rapidly. Similarly, for those who need to feed themselves, a microwave or small toaster oven can expedite quick gastronomic treats in colder climates, and a small refrigerator is essential in warm ones. Kitchen utensils vary according to geography, fuel and diet. Apparently, the majority of Americans posses a coffee makingmachine, and 80% of Australian kitchens boast a wok. For those with flair and a kitchenette or sunny window sill, a pot of *fresh herbs*, such as basil enhances everything. If you can rise to a few plants, fresh mint can double up as a tea, or transform lemonade to 'lemonana'. Parsley or dill (more difficult to grow) are great additions to most dishes. But...don't forget to water them before the weekend away.

Clearly, appetites are modulated by daily schedules, body rhythms, food availability, local tastes and cultural patterns, i.e. whether the midday

280

or evening meals are regarded as mainstays. Differences occur both between individuals, and between the sexes. Of note to members of our profession, research shows that women have a lower sedentary metabolic rate and tend not to lose weight from exercising without dieting. Conversely, the resting male's expenditure of energy is 5-10% greater. Men also turn over protein faster, need more calories weight for weight than women and require about 45% more zinc (as in red meat, which some claim increases 'good' high density lipoprotein cholesterol without affecting the 'bad'). Just mentioning red meat is anathema these days of vegetarianism, mad-cow, and dietetics, with health considerations influenced by cultural beliefs and temporal trends. One prevalent assumption sets the ideal diet in an 80:20 ratio of alkaline-producing to acid-producing foods, ie. Fruit & veg vs. meat, sugar, coffee, processed foods, white flour and preservatives. However, these dietary facts are not always clear cut. For instance, statistically the Japanese eat very little fat and suffer fewer heart attacks than the British or Americans. On the other hand, the French eat a lot of fat and also suffer fewer heart attacks than the British or Americans. One logical conclusion might be that the danger stems not from eating fat but speaking English!

Nevertheless, several universal truths do apply:
- If you intend to see patients soon after lunch, keep your midday meal light (high carbohydrates tend to induce drowsiness while digesting).
- Similarly liquid intake necessitates peeing. Gauge quantities with a view to the next opportunity to empty your bladder.

Two other ubiquitous proposals:
Rule one:
Flip the kettle switch as you enter the kitchen area, while you're deciding what to have. Chances are it will need boiling water.
Rule two:
Estimate before starting to cook how long your food will take to prepare and eat, as one tends to curse patients who innocently come on time just as the appetising snack materialises.

Readiness is all...

As one of my aunts once said – the freezer was invented to await the microwave. Most refrigerators have a small freezer compartment. The secret is fine slicing and parboiling. For quick (h)eating between sessions, small individually frozen portions of food in double-function containers, can be easily transferred from freezer to microwave or oven without thawing. Ready breaded frozen or fresh thinly sliced chicken, turkey schnitzels, beef or fish 'goujons' or similarly small morsels of vegetarian foods can usually be grilled or stir-fried in under ten minutes, and in 30-60 microwave seconds. For the latter, ready chopped vegetables are added in

281

decreasing order of density (have the oil in wok or pan smoking hot; fry for less than a minute, adding soy sauce or wine last). A good supply of corn, broccoli and petit pois are great frozen standbys (not to mention ice cream). A good wholesome staple is soup in individual portions. Cooked rice frozen in sealed plastic bag can be rapidly thawed by dipping in boiling water. Small rolls, pittas, nans or pancakes may be frozen, and individually thawed in toaster when needed, then filled or dipped. Similarly, frozen sliced bread can be separated with a strong (or heated) knife and defrosted quickly in the toaster or grilled. Refrigerated pre-grated cheddar or similar hard cheese is a useful addition or basis for many dishes. A stock of cans of tuna, chopped tomatoes, baked beans, sweet corn, rice pudding, etc. are useful standbys. Herewith some survey suggestions:

QUICK MUNCH FOR SHORT BREAKS:
Sesame or granola bars
Yoghurt, *Halva*, chocolate
Apples, raw carrot or celery sticks
Mange Tous, sugar snaps, cherry tomatoes
Bread with honey or preserves

Or when you fancy something savory -
Toast and paté or olive paste
Pickled herrings, smoked mackerel or other fishy delicacies
Salamis, sausages, smoked or salted dried meats
such as beef-jerk or (South African) *biltong*
Popcorn, sunflower or pumpkin seeds, various nuts
Prepared nibbles such as mini-pretzels or Japanese rice crackers.

OTHER SNACKS:
From my international polling it seems that the most common between-session snack for therapists is the faithful **banana**. Quite apart from any symbolic connotations, it is a high-energy, low 92 calorie, quick fix with the added feature of neat zippability. **Chocolate** comes second as a satisfying fast treat. Small fruits such as cherries and grapes come close third for minimal but healthy nibbles. Fruit availability and choice varies geographically. Americans, tend to be more health conscious, snacking on apples, citrus segments, berries or melon slices. New Zealanders swear their high-potassium kiwi contribute to a sense of wellbeing. Therapists in the Mediterranean basin go for fresh dates and figs.

Many 'continental' analysts enjoy pastries and coffee in their morning breaks while the Brits, à la Wallace & Gromit, love cheese and crackers. In the Middle East olives, pitta-bread with *houmous*, smoked-roe salad

282

(*tarama* or *ikre*), aubergine dips or *te'china* are nutritious mainstays. Filled tacos or tortillas are Latin American standbys.

Interestingly, some child analysts and therapists mention joining their clients during sessions for 'cookies, candies or soda' (in USA) or a (sweet) biscuit and milk in the UK. But between patients all over the world, it seems that **bread** (in any form) takes the biscuit, so to speak.

SANDWICHES:

Invented by the Earl of Sandwich to avoid leaving the gaming table, sandwiches have become the mainstay of all busy people. The great chef Clement Freud (Sigmund's grandson) quotes the *Larousse Gastronomique* definition of a sandwich: 'Foodstuff composed of two slices of buttered bread with some edible substance in between'. He feels it deserves to be elevated and offers tasteful fillings, such as fresh salmon with grated (and squeezed) cucumber and stiff lemon based mayonnaise (home-made, natch). Sardines, Dijon mustard and Worcester sauce; crab and mayo – not to mention omelette sandwich!

In general **fillings** are a test of ingenuity – almost any free association will do. Chopped hardboiled egg (enhanced by mayonnaise, anchovy, eggs, capers, dill or cress); cheddar cheese and non-vegetarian staples such as tuna, thinly sliced turkey, chicken or pastrami provide an easy base, accessorized by lettuce, cole slaw, pickled cuke, olives, raisins, chutney or any number of moistening helpmeets.

In my experience, whatever they consist of, the ultimate aim of fillings is to be flavorsome, evenly spread and at least as thick as the bread. Butter or margarine are only necessary to protect the bread from getting soggy, so can be dispensed with in sandwiches intended for immediate consumption.

Psychoanalytically speaking, it seems many of us were introduced to sandwiches in our school lunch boxes and have nostalgic cravings in that direction. Finding ourselves harking back to delicious moments from the past, favourite fillings often reflect this, albeit suitably disguised in adult form. Some clear cut nursery throwbacks are chocolate spread; mashed bananas and 'hundreds and thousands'; cream cheese, crushed canned pineapple and nuts; and…that all American favourite – peanut butter and jelly (jam to Anglo Saxons).

However, sandwiches are not necessarily dyadic symbols of successful merger, but can be one-slice events, open and esthetically pleasing. Scandinavian kids tend to carry cleverly constructed lunchboxes to safeguard their innovative *Smorgasbord*, which may include various cheeses, intricately arranged vegetable decorations and such delicacies as shrimps, or little meatballs. In some countries packed lunches involve no bread at all, but like *Sushi*, rely on density of compaction or a seaweed 'skin' to keep the filling in place. Chinese and Japanese lunchboxes also

283

have elaborate cubbyholes to separate various wet and dry, hot and cold constituents, while Indian tiffin boxes are constructed in multilayered vertical compartments for the same reason. Needless to say, western takeaway containers employ equal ingenuity, and some deli's or sandwich firms excel in creative combinations. Whatever its source and however transported, the hedonistic hint is – *ENJOY!*

A great winter snack (albeit one which leaves a tangy cooking smell, if your consulting room is close by) - **grilled sandwiches**. Many electric stores offer small double sided sandwich-makers which fuse two (or four) pieces of bread around a variety of possible filling – ham & pineapple; sardines or tuna; cheese (grated cheddar or mozzarella) & pickle, or tomato – but beware, some grilled ingredients get surprisingly hot! Grills needn't be savoury. The art of culinary combinations is imaginative experimentation: cottage or cream cheese makes a good base with celery, grapes, mandarin & honey... Banana is luscious grilled, and thinly sliced apple will cook through and is tasty with raisins, jam or chutney. For more substantial meals - some suggest grilled minute steak & mushrooms; egg & something or beefburger & tomato. In the absence of a toaster, closed sandwiches can also be fried. Single-slice under-the-grill variations are melted goat's cheese with ginger jam (beware, the burned palate!), pre-marinated sliced mushroom, cheddar and tomato and of course - the classic *Welsh Rarebit:* Toast bread. Combine butter, grated cheese, a teaspoon each of ale (can be omitted) and ready mustard. Pour onto toast and pop under grill. The equally delicious *French Toast* is another matter entirely — bread which has been left to soak over the course of a session in beaten egg, then fried and eaten savoury sprinkled with salt and pepper, or sweetened with honey, or cinnamon and sugar.

Light meals:

Another common analytic favourite around the world is the faithful **avocado pear** which has the advantage of amazing versatility – on its own with a dash of lemon, drizzle of olive oil and a dusting of salt & pepper it is a great starter or sandwich filler. Liquidised with consommé and lemon juice it makes a good cold soup or less pulverised and mixed with a spoonful of crème fraiche, it forms a rich dip. Avos are often combined with garlic, techina, humous or cream cheese in the Middle East, or with tomatoes, garlic, chillies and/or Tabasco in a Mexican avocado-guacamole. Filled with flaked tuna and chopped bell peppers or shrimps (and thousand-isle dressing) it is a dish fit for a swanky restaurant. An avocado mousse prepared in advance will keep for days in the fridge [processed avocado flesh with finely chopped onion and lemon juice and/or mayonnaise set in gelatine]. Italians make a neat salad of spinach leaves, avocado slices and walnuts (or chopped grilled bacon) with lemon juice and olive oil dressing. Similarly, chopped avocados (a little messy, this) with tomatoes, hard boiled egg and anchovies makes a delightful salad, particularly when capers are added. **Eggs** can be slow - they take about 14 minutes to hard-boil (peeling easily if plunged immediately into cold water). So when time is of the essence, boil several in one go, and they'll keep in the fridge for 3-4 days (marked with an X to avoid confusion with raw ones). However, omelettes, scrambled and even poached eggs are quick and nourishing (and the latter have the advantage of being relatively odourless). In a very short break, eggs can even be scrambled in the microwave. Eaten with smoked salmon pieces (on bagel?) they make a one course feast.

Another world-wide staple is the **potato,** adaptable, satisfying, heart warming stuff...from humble mash to potato-salad, potato gratin to baked potatoes (time consuming but the process can be speeded up by first microwaving for 7-8 minutes, and then leaving in the oven to bake over one session). Colleagues from Spain inform us that added to omelette pre-boiled potatoes transform a snack into a meal - *Spanish Omelette:* Fry onion, garlic, chopped red (and/or green) pepper and frozen peas. Add cubed boiled potato and pour in eggs beaten with milk, salt and pepper and grated cheese. Cook over low heat for 10 minutes, or five on stove and 5 beneath the grill. Can be eaten hot or cold. By the way, a *Nicoise* variation keeps the omelette but substitutes tuna, anchovy fillets, olives and French beans for the Spanish ingredients, withholding the cheese. In all other respects, it is identical!

Cold cuts and salad make a tasty summer lunch for omnivores. For vegetarians, a substantial salad, cold quiche or cheese plate is filling and lasts over several meals. Similarly, Prosciutto ham and melon (and some mint leaves?) is a great combination, as is thinly sliced smoked turkey or leftover cold chicken, mayo and grapes (and basil?). **Pasta** is many people's favourite throughout the world, especially when the sauce can be prepared (or bought) in advance. **Stir-fries** are quick. Apart from thinly sliced vegetables and broccoli florets, chicken pieces or tiger prawns with mange tout and spring onions are delicious additions! Quick-cook noodles or **farinaceous grains** such as rice, bulgur, couscous or other presoaked cracked wheat add substantiality to any dish. For a more ample meal, unbreadeded breast of **chicken or turkey** can be cooked rapidly in the microwave (in a few tablespoons of white wine or stock) for fahitas or in the oven wrapped around spinach and feta and/or mozarella, adding spices such as cumin and sweet paprika for an exotic touch. Finally, if you have chopping facilities, a refreshing cold treat is **sour cream** or smetana with diced cucumber (and red bell-pepper) fresh mint or dill if available. For desert - ruby **grapefruit** segments (cut in half, grapefruit can also be grilled for special effect, enhanced by rosewater).

Liquids –
COLD DRINKS:

No need to extol the virtues of **milk** to analysts; but in addition to the straight stuff, those with electric blenders or processors swear by milkshakes (simply add milk to icecream) and that remarkable treat – **smoothies**: to a container of plain yoghurt and half as much of milk, add any soft fruit – such as bananas and peaches, or mango and berries or kiwi, experimenting with different combinations. Add sugar if necessary. Keeps refrigerated for 3-4 days. A delicious variation is the Indian Lassi plain and salted or sweet, which can be made with buttermilk or yoghurt and pulped mango. For variation, use orange juice as a base instead of yogurt and/or milk, adding fruits for substance. Those who don't have the time to fiddle with these, fresh fruit juices are now available in many countries and can be kept refrigerated for a few days. However, it seems many therapists believe that simple water is best. In fact some swear by several (up to 8!) pints daily of water for healthy hydration, and tend to drink a glass of tap or bottled water between each session.

HOT BEVERAGES:

In addition to the standard coffees and teas (a surfeit of which do us no favours) there are caffeine-free herbal teas. But hot lemon or apple juice with honey and a dusting of ginger warm the cockles wonderfully as do hot blackberry cordials, and of course, that old favourite — hot chocolate. (If you like it frothy, a tiny battery operated milk-aerator is now available). Heating milk in the microwave speeds up the process (but never a full cup). For a special treat — miniature marshmallows can be added to the cocoa powder in the mug before stirring in hot milk. Another delicious treat is hot frothed milk with almond or hazelnut essence.

Above all - therapists wax lyrical about that nutritious meal in a cup – **hot** or **cold soup**. Good soups are often time consuming to prepare as prolonged simmering is necessary to enable ingredients to blend. However it is always possible to reheat soups previously prepared or to thaw frozen portions, and in some countries fresh soups can now be bought and easily microwaved. Concentrated canned creamed soups can be enhanced by using milk instead of water, and supplementing with fresh titbits of mushroom, asparagus or celery respectively, or adding grated cheddar or mozarella cheese to canned tomato soup

Here are some national soup recipes: A quick delicious cold Lithuanian *Borscht:* grind, grate or blend ready pickled beets and adjust the sweet-and-sour taste with a combination of sugar and salt (dissolved in a little boiling water), adding lemon juice to taste. Great with chopped hard-boiled egg or a hot boiled potato. Can also be heated. Russian Borscht tends to have tomatoes, cabbage and sometimes meat in it. Cold *gaspacho* may be rapidly (if unorthodoxally) rustled up from a base of whizzed canned tomatoes, olive oil and vinegar (raspberry is great!) with anything you have in the fridge as garnishes. But, if you just happen to have the time and ingredients, Spanish colleagues advocate a light yet substantial hot meal - *Mediterranean Fish Soup:* Sweat a large chopped onion and one garlic clove in butter for 5 minutes. Add a cup of dry white wine and an equal amount of fish stock. After boiling for two minutes add about half a cup of passata (sieved tomatoes) and juice of half an orange (and bouquet garni if you have one). Simmer covered for 15 minutes before adding one and a half cups of cubed white fish. When cooked (about 5 minutes), add the same amount of grams each of cooked peeled prawns and ready mussels then stir in 4 tablespoons of double cream. *Scandinavian fish soup*: As above but substitute salmon for white fish and eliminate the passata. *Hungarian Goulash* is a meal in itself, even without dumplings but beware the post-prandial (my spell-check suggests 'parricidal') stupor. French onion soup starts off with caramelized onions later stewed in salted water, to which white wine and a touch of flour may be added. Once done, top the bowl with a slice of french bread or rounded toast covered in grated cheese and grill for a few minutes. Time consuming in the making and very hot results – so allow time to eat. Good old chicken soup (sometimes referred to as the 'Jewish penicillin) is a great restorative but really needs a long simmer of wings and other unmentionable bits along with onion, carrots, celery, parsley and sometimes leeks to get the full flavour. However once made it can be stored hot in a vacuum flask for a quick between sessions 'schluk'. A more substantial chicken soup can be made, Greek-style as in *Avgolemono* with added lemon and cornflour, or Chinese-style with beaten egg, chicken pieces and corn (equally tasty without adding monosodium glutamate).

To end this section, *two recipes from named analysts*:
Low fat, curried tomato-buttermilk summer soup (courtesy of **Judith Issroff**): Mix one cup packet or heaped table spoon of powdered tomato soup with equal quantity of curry powder and sherry (dry or medium). Any curry powder can be used. Add half a pint of buttermilk. Garnish with chopped chives, parsley or basil, and/or a dash of thicker yogurt. Keep chilled and refrigerated. Provides two servings. Can be diluted to taste. If one wants a gaspacho-like consistency add finely chopped tomatoes, Spanish or spring onions, shallots, cucumbers, nasturtium leaves, croutons, etc., but the 'pure' almost instant soup has quite an elegant, far from peasant consistency and flavour because of the sherry. **Dilys Daws**, child psychotherapist and psychoanalytic psychotherapist with adults sent in a recipe from the late British psychoanalyst **Lois Munro**. "In the early 60's Lois Munro supervised my adolescent training case. She spent weekends and holidays at her cottage in the village of Duddenhoe End in Essex, UK Her vegetable and fruit garden were

legendary. On one occasion she gave me some pears and in her usual forthright manner told me how to cook them. For me it's a reminder of her encouraging though tough style of supervising. It's a very simple recipe, and delicious. Cook the pears in red wine, with brown sugar and cinnamon. An alternative I've come up with is to cook the pears in ginger wine, with additional ginger and other spices".

Supervisions can be good places for gastronomic exchange. I recall that in my own supervision with Paula Heimann we reached a reciprocal arrangement that I supplied the homemade chopped herring and she the words of wisdom…

THE PLEASURE PRINCIPLE

Although the ego is first and foremost a bodily one, apart from Freud's response to Lou Andreas Salome's overzealous schedule of analytic work as a 'badly concealed attempt at suicide', the physical effects of our sedentary and emotionally taxing profession on our bodies are infrequently discussed. In principle we all agree that driving ourselves is daft but in our commitment to professional obligations and attendant organizational involvement, not unlike the proverbial 'modern psycho-analyst' above, we sometimes may feel stretched to the limit.

There are ways of combating burnout. One good idea is to vary our surroundings and activities during the course of the working day. During a short break away from the consulting room or a stroll out of doors, even half an hour can feel like a mini holiday. Many therapists report spending their intervals making phone calls, catching up on headlines, or watching/listening to the news. Eating is often done on the trot. This is partly to counteract prolonged sitting - however, a mini-meal at a table, on a bench in the garden, or in the sunshine on the fire-escape varies the posture and is said to aid digestion. Some colleagues report instituting a longer break at least once a week, to go to a local café, alone or with friends (but warn against 'offloading' over lunch, as tables tend to be eaves-droppingly close). Other therapists grab a sandwich and dedicate the lunch break to sociable activities such as jazz-aerobics (or even water-aerobics) with friends. One analyst proposes treating one's own city as if it was a new place, occasionally visiting tourist attractions.

Some extol the soothing properties of watering a garden in the break or the displaced revenge of deadheading a few flowers. Wandering around the back yard or a local park, allows time for reflection. Even in the absence of nearby open fields, tending a pot plant or topping and tailing cut flowers may have the same relaxing effect. [This brings to mind a story about Miriam de Rothschild, the famous British horticulturalist who advocated preservation of wild flowers, saying: 'However small your garden, I do suggest you set aside an acre (a massive 4840 square yards) or two to foster natural growth'].

288

Analytic abstinence and blank-screen anonymity notwithstanding, in many locations therapists do not wait to go elsewhere to let their hair down but find ways of discretely enjoying themselves between sessions. In some large cities where one is unlikely to bump into patients at midday, swimming, ice-skating, miniature golf, indoor climbing, scootering, horse-riding, tennis or even tap-dancing, are but some more active between-session pursuits reported. I have also been informed by therapists of more exclusive activities such as creative writing classes, jewellery-making, choir-singing or African drumming (vetted for patient-attendance), among indulgences they have set aside time for during their working week. Psychoanalytic understanding elucidates the imaginary body inscribed on the corporeal one as coded text of danger and desire. Given contemporary 'secularisation' of the body (no longer the vessel of either Satan or God), and self-knowledge, if there's a message to be had from this survey, it seems to be (to mix dialects) – *discover your 'druthers'* (cockney for what you'd rather have) and *'dinna stint yerself'* (as the Scots say).

Finally, while we know carnivals can be an annual abreactive event enabling people to engage in their wilder fantasies, we also know that regular access to imaginative hedonism is healthier than a strict Apollonian/Dionysian division. This applies to daily patterns of fasting/feasting, as well as weekend bingeing – whether on food, alcohol or sleep. Incidentally, regarding the latter, it appears that after middle-age the optimal sleep is *seven hours* a night, with longer or shorter sleep bouts actually associated with <u>shorter</u> life-spans! Interestingly, studies claim that because cortisol is released some hours before rising and peaks about four hours after waking, sleeping-in on a weekend 'confuses' the internal diurnal clock and suppresses this surge, thereby <u>adding</u> to fatigue rather than relieving it. Some early rising therapists (especially in hot climates) prefer to take a siesta in the middle of the day, every day, and research shows that 15 minutes nap mid-day is worth an hour and a half of night sleep! Other therapists tend to schedule earlier bedtimes to compensate for those crack-of-dawn patients.

Similarly, although most weekends and summer vacations may be designated as time for leisure, many therapists don't wait for their holidays to have fun, but allocate space throughout the week. The list of pleasurable activities sent in includes evening cooking, reading, listening to jazz or classical music, going to concerts/the opera or playing an instrument. Daytime activities include gardening, painting or drawing and/or visiting art galleries. Crafts, including embroidery and crocheting are popular (but none admitted to 'doing an Anna Freud' and knitting behind the couch). Others find engaging in a variety of hobbies like weaving, collecting unusual objects or running model electric-trains rewarding after a hard day's work. Activities such as skiing, boating or skin-diving clearly necessitate a particular season or place, but may be supplemented out of season by ongoing forays to the local boating lake or dry-ski centre. Some British therapists have a country cottage (or better still, friends with one). Some visit parks or botanical gardens. Many North and Latin Americans are fortunate enough to live close enough to mountains or beaches to spend weekends walking, swimming or fishing.

The important point seems that even in the busiest of lives it is possible to make space for enjoyment. In our concern for others, we in the caring professions may overlook self-care we so readily cultivate in our clients. For instance, reading poetry or perusing literature outside the psychoanalytic sphere. Some therapists are so swamped by keeping up with journals and professional literature they have to wait until they are on a beach before relaxing with a book. Others say they always have a novel by their bedside even if they only read a page or two after midnight. One time-twisting trick is listening to 'talking books'. In a fraught metropolitan atmosphere headphones on public transport or the tape-player in a car offer opportunities to listen to those classics one never has time to read until retirement. [Having myself relished recordings of *'The Odyssey'*, *'Remembrance of Things Past'*, an unabridged *'Ulysses'* and even *'War and Peace'* on a series of regular long journeys, I've even been known to sit in car parks on arrival to complete an exciting chapter].

Spending leisure time is a matter of personal modalities and discriminatory decisions. At the end of the day, some therapists crave casual human companionship after the long and intense span of concentrated listening. Others desire intimacy. Some seek depth of engagement, feeling that any form of idle chit-chat and trivial social pursuits pale by comparison to the privilege of having had hourly access to heartfelt instalments from each protagonist on the couch. Others feel drained and like those analysts Ernest Jones compared to fish, at the end of the day may just want to escape from the depths. Many analysts go to lectures, write papers or read in the evenings. Others, abhorring more words, prefer concerts, or playing duets with partners or in chamber groups. Some prefer visual input – TV, movies, dance or art. Live theatre is a prime choice for some, but a 'busman's holiday' for others – perhaps because by definition plays deal with scenarios of dramatic intensity. Foodwise - some gravitate to restaurants; others to home-cooked meals and family gatherings, or alternate according to whim and circumstance. Some prefer to avoid colleagues and fraternise outside analytic circles. Others, or at other times, feel it is only fellow analysts who have the true measure of life's complexities. Yet other therapists seek sunset musings, solitude and silence. Clearly, discerning tastes vary individually and at different times, and experimentation may extend the range. The many contributions to this book demonstrate that the basis of health is finding your own rich, caring and fulfilling lifestyle by cultivating non-disjunctive body-mind, self-other, intake-output Reality **and** Pleasure Principles.

And as the concluding poem attests – we who are journeying learn to savour the process as much as partaking of life's abundance…

290

EPILOGUE:

Ithaca   Constantine P. Cavafy (1911)

When you set out on your journey to Ithaca,
pray that the road is long,
full of adventure, full of knowledge.
The Lestrygonians and the Cyclops,
the angry Poseidon – do not fear them:
You will never find such as these on your path,
if your thoughts remain lofty, if a fine
emotion touches your spirit and your body.
The Lestrygonians and the Cyclops,
the fierce Poseidon you will never encounter,
if you do not carry them within your soul,
if your soul does not set them up before you.

Pray that the road is long.
That the summer mornings are many, when,
with such pleasure, with such joy
you will enter ports seen for the first time;
stop at Phoenician markets,
and purchase fine merchandise,
mother-of-pearl and coral, amber and ebony,
and sensual perfumes of all kinds,
as many sensual perfumes as you can;
visit many Egyptian cities,
to learn and learn from scholars.

Always keep Ithaca in your mind.
To arrive there is your ultimate goal.
But do not hurry the voyage at all.
It is better to let it last for many years;
and to anchor at the island when you are old,
rich with all you have gained on the way,
not expecting that Ithaca will offer you riches.

Ithaca has given you the beautiful voyage.
Without her you would have never set out on the road.
She has nothing more to give you.

And if you find her poor, Ithaca has not deceived you.
Wise as you have become, with so much experience,
you must already have understood what Ithacas mean.

[Thanks to George Barbanis a talented amateur,
for use of his fine translation] (see http://www.penelopesithaca.com)

Ithaka*

As you set out for Ithaka
hope your road is a long one,
full of adventure, full of discovery.
Laistrygonians, Cyclops,
angry Poseidon-don't be afraid of them:
you'll never find things like that on your way
as long as you keep your thoughts raised high,
as long as a rare excitement
stirs your spirit and your body.
Laistrygonians, Cyclops,
wild Poseidon-you won't encounter them
unless you bring them along inside your soul,
unless your soul sets them up in front of you.

Hope your road is a long one.
May there be many summer mornings when,
with what pleasure, what joy,
you enter harbors you're seeing for the first time;
may you stop at Phoenician trading stations
to buy fine things,
mother of pearl and coral, amber and ebony,
sensual perfume of every kind-
as many sensual perfumes as you can;
and may you visit many Egyptian cities
to learn and go on learning from their scholars.

Keep Ithaka always in your mind.
Arriving there is what you're destined for.
But don't hurry the journey at all.
Better if it lasts for years,
so you're old by the time you reach the island,
wealthy with all you've gained on the way,
not expecting Ithaka to make you rich.
Ithaka gave you the marvelous journey.
Without her you wouldn't have set out.
She has nothing left to give you now.

And if you find her poor, Ithaka won't have fooled you.
Wise as you will have become, so full of experience,
you'll have understood by then what these Ithakas mean.

[*With thanks to Random House for use of this version
translated by Edmund Keeley & Philip Sherrard
Complete Poems of C.P.Cavafy, Chattos & Windus, 1998]